FAITH IN ACTION
Vol II

Pastoral Renewal, Public Health and the
Prophetic Mission of the Church in Africa
Since the Two African Synods

FAITH IN ACTION
Vol II

Pastoral Renewal, Public Health and the Prophetic Mission of the Church in Africa Since the Two African Synods

Editors

Stan Chu Ilo
Justin Clemency Nabushawo
Ikenna U. Okafor

☙PICKWICK *Publications* • Eugene, Oregon

FAITH IN ACTION, VOLUME 2
Pastoral Renewal, Public Health and the Prophetic Mission of the Church in Africa Since the Two African Synods

Copyright © 2020 Paulines Publications Nigeria. All rights reserved. Except for brief quotations in critical publications or reviews, no part of this book may be reproduced in any manner without prior written permission from the publisher. Write: Permissions, Wipf and Stock Publishers, 199 W. 8th Ave., Suite 3, Eugene, OR 97401.

Pickwick Publications
An Imprint of Wipf and Stock Publishers
199 W. 8th Ave., Suite 3
Eugene, OR 97401

www.wipfandstock.com

PAPERBACK ISBN: 978-1-7252-9387-8
HARDCOVER ISBN: 978-1-7252-9386-1
EBOOK ISBN: 978-1-7252-9388-5

Cataloguing-in-Publication data:

Names: Ilo, Stan Chu.

Title: Faith in action, volume 2: Pastoral renewal, public health and the prophetic mission of the church in African since the two African synods/ Stan Chu Ilo.

Description: Eugene, OR: Pickwick Publications, 2020 | Includes bibliographical references.

Identifiers: ISBN 978-1-7252-9387-8 (paperback) | ISBN 978-1-7252-9386-1 (hardcover) | ISBN 978-1-7252-9388-5 (ebook)

Subjects: LCSH: Christianity in Africa | Catholicism in Africa | Missions in Africa | Catholic Missions

Classification: BL2462.5 I462020 (print) | BL2462 (ebook)

Manufactured in the U.S.A.

Contents

Foreword
    Sr Rosemary Nyirumbe 9
Introduction
    Stan Chu Ilo, Justin Clemency Nabushawo & Ikenna U. Okafor ... 13

I
Dialogue and Inculturation
in the Christian Mission in Africa

1. An Inculturated Church in Africa:
   Lessons and Failings since *Ecclesia in Africa*
       Charles A. Ebelebe, CSSp 27

2. Dialogue and Conflict Resolution in Our Churches:
   Lessons and Failings since Ecclesia in Africa
       Justin Clemency Nabushawo 53

3. Fraternal Solidarity and the Ethics of Care
   and Compassion in Church and State in Africa:
   A Theological Re-reading of *Things Fall Apart*
       Ikenna U. Okafor 89

II
Dialogue and Reconciliation
in the Christian Mission in Africa

4. Engaging the Catholic and the Pentecostal-Charismatic
   Forms of Christianity in a Conversation:
   Towards An Authentic African Christianity
       Lawrence Nchekwube Nwankwo 117

5. Dialogue in Cultural Conflicts between the Church
   and African Traditions: Lessons from Biblical Traditions
       Cosmas Uzowulu OFMCap 145

6. The Role of Religion in Africa's Twentieth Century
   Wars and Genocides: Lessons for African Churches
   SimonMary Asese Aihiokhai 168

III
Communicating the Truths of Faith:
Marriage, Family Life, Health and Wellbeing

7. The Challenges of Poverty in African Families:
   Ecclesial Action Since African Synods I & II
   Raymond Olusesan Aina, MSP 191

8. Serving the Vulnerable Among us with Integrity:
   Best Practices of Accompaniment
   Annah Nyadoma 225

9. From Silos to System: Assessing Conditions
   for Integration of Faith-based
   Health Service Organisations
   Barry C. Eneh and Theresa Abah 248

10. The Role of International Catholic Charities
    in Promoting Global Health
    Susan Nedza 271

IV
Reflections on Doing the Works of God

11. "Igniting Theologies from Below in Africa"
    Kairos Methodology as a Resource: a Case Study
    of Violence Against Women and Sexual Minorities
    Nontando Hadebe 299

12. Afterword:
    Celebrating and Assessing the Blessings of
    the Church in Africa: *Allocutio*
    Bonaventure Ikenna Ugwu, CSSp. 321

CONTRIBUTORS 331

Dedication

This volume is dedicated to:
Sr Maryjina Ihisa (1954-2020), Educator, Spiritual Guide,
and Congregational leader of the Sacred Heart Sisters.
AND
Fr Jean Sinsin Bayo (1950-2020), Great Catholic theologian
from Cote d'Ivoire, preacher, professor and champion of
African inculturation theologies.

Foreword

I would like to begin this short foreword with a reflection on the life of my best friend. The Covid-19 pandemic is really hitting many of our people so badly as we see a good number of our friends, family members, colleagues, and entire humanity impacted in one way or another by deaths, sickness, loss of jobs, and uncertainties. In this time of the pandemic, we must be united together in solidarity as one human family and share in the pains and sorrows of one another. My dear friend, Sr Maryjina Ihisa went to be with the Lord on the eve of the Feast of the Sacred Heart of Jesus.

Sr Maryjina Ihisa served the congregation of the Sisters of the Sacred Heart of Jesus in many capacities, as a leader and formator. She worked as a Provincial Superior of South Sudan and later became the Superior General for the whole congregation. Maryjina was the first of the Sisters to join the University of Makerere in Uganda for her Science Education where she studied Biology, Chemistry, Mathematics and Physics. She later on went to the Catholic University of East Africa (CUEA) for her Maters degree in religious Studies.

She was a very highly intellectual person, who always remained humble and faithful to her calling to religious life. She was a great educator and a formator with a broad vision about the role of women in the Church, especially in Africa. Sister spent all her life serving the most vulnerable people, particularly children in South Sudan, even during the most difficult time of the long civil war in Sudan. She was not afraid to share in the suffering of others. She served the vulnerable people with a lot of dedication, and lived a life of faith in action.

The death of Sr Maryjina reminds me of how many people live simple lives of faith, as seen in their daily actions. We see them everywhere in our churches, schools, offices, market places, highways and alleys. They are like the salt and light spoken of in scripture. The path she walked was marked by faith and action which could be seen by the fruits of her labour in our religious order, and in the dioceses where she served with so much dedication and heroism.

The wave of shock at her untimely death shook me and many people who knew her. Is this not the same shock and pain we all feel seeing so many of our brothers and sisters in Africa and the rest of the world die from preventable diseases, caused by hunger and lack of access to healthcare facilities, poverty and civil wars? We have witnessed the death of so many children and women during the war waged by the Lord's Resistance Army in Northern Uganda. A good number of those that survived the war are still living with the traumatic experience of abduction by the rebels. This is what has made me see how faith in action can inspire hope.

It was faith that inspired the work of the Sisters of the Sacred Heart of Jesus in St Monica, Uganda, to get involved in mending the broken lives of many vulnerable women during and after the war. It is a ministry to which I have dedicated my entire life and I see how simple but courageous acts of love, carried out in total trust in God, can sew back broken lives, restore hope, and bring about a new creation.

In the uncertain times that we face in Africa and the world today, we need courageous faith, not empty words, or anger that things are not right. We must turn our anger, like St Thomas of Aquinas recommends, in works of love to change the world. We must go out with faith to the streets, bushes, hospitals, highways, prisons, market places and our parliaments to make a difference in the world, by our authentic and credible Christian witnessing. These were the principles for which Sr Maryjina stood. She worked for the Lord with so much faith even in the fragility of her health. She trusted the Lord totally in everything that she did and was not afraid to go out even with an empty hand, knowing that God would fill her with love, light and grace.

Faith and action demand courage and sacrifice. My friend Sr Maryjina was motivated by faith and filled with courage in selflessly serving people, like a true shepherd who does not run away from the flock. When people from South Sudan took refuge in Uganda during the climax of the civil war, Sr Maryijina courageously continued to lead one of the best Primary schools in Juba, Usratuna Basic School, which has more than 1000 children. She encouraged the Sisters to work with the vulnerable and to have the smell of the sheep.

Inspired by her words and courageous witnessing, the Sisters have continued to serve the least of the brethren, through education and health care to people who could not run away from the site of suffering and pain. This was the choice she made without thinking of her safety and health. A woman of faith and courage indeed! The simple motto she lived by and always reminded me to follow is "Government of Action." The presence of the Sisters of the Sacred Heart, under the dynamic leadership of Sr Maryjina, encouraged the Sisters to remain with the vulnerable and not flee to safety, but to be prepared to die for the poor. Her witness is truly a reflection of how to serve the people of God. She is a symbol of faith in action. She was described as the 'Mother of Education and Human Resource Development' by some of her old students who are working in different parts of the world.

I want to encourage anybody who comes across this book, to go deeper into what it means to be a Christian. These African scholars teach us the meaning of faith in action and how this looks like in the Africa of today. You will come to learn about so many people who are, perhaps, least known but are very inspirational in our broken world, where faith gets easily shaken by all the bad things we witness and get from social media as well. We hear more bad news than good news everyday especially about so many people dying from the Covid-19 pandemic. All these should increase our faith and push us to render more selfless services to our brothers and sisters.

This is the moment to put our faith in some tangible action by becoming "salt and light" in the life of our brothers and sisters at such a time as this. Be one of those practicing Faith in Action, and get this volume as a special gift for your friends and families.

Sr Rosemary Nyirumbe,
Founder of Sewing Hope Foundation,
Winner of CNN Hero Award,
Winner of Pope John Paul II Veritatis Splendor Award
and Time 100 most influential people in the World.

Introduction

Faith in Action in Africa

Stan Chu Ilo, Justin Clemency Nabushawo & Ikenna U. Okafor

The essays contained in this volume address how the Church in Africa can meet some of the challenges facing African societies today. These essays are practical in nature, but at the same time they deal with conceptual and theoretical issues in interpreting and understanding Africa's social context from the perspectives of faith and life. The essays do not stop at the analysis of problems, but each chapter offers concrete solutions to these challenges. Contributors to this volume explore the limitations in current theological and pastoral approaches to some of these challenges, and make concrete proposals on how to deepen and strengthen the social mission of the Church through critical and creative social, historical, biblical and theological analysis.

The volume has been structured in such a way to pay attention to the three Bs of religious faith and life which social scientists identify—belonging, behaving and believing.[1] Theology must answer the questions about belief, behaviour or belonging. The validity of any theology depends on the extent to which its answers to these three Bs, captures the cultural, spiritual and moral imagination of adherents and connects them to the founding narratives and ideals of their traditions in its historicity. The credibility of any theology will depend on the extent to which it answers to these three Bs and speaks to the deepest needs, fears, expectations and hopes of the adherents, that is, the extent to

---

[1] Robert Putnam and David Campbell, *American Grace: How Religion Divides and Unites Us*. NY: Simon & Schuster Paperbacks, 2010, 7.

which it helps them to be at home with themselves, their brothers and sisters, and with their God and their cosmos.

The Church in Africa can be an instrument for justice, healing and peace through her teaching about God, human dignity, the cosmos and how all things are related (*belief*), through creating a community of the beloved where everyone feels like a first born child (*a sense of belonging*), and through the actions and choices of her members and her institutional priorities and practices; her advocacy and witnessing in the world (*behaviour/ practices/ecclesial models of a new world*).

The polarisation in the Church today, which has become loudest in the post-Vatican II era, and has come to its head in the papacy of Francis, is rooted in the contested identities within the Church and how progressives and traditionalists understand social change and the movement of history. Interestingly, this polarity is also present in the divisive ideological battles among different camps in the Church which we saw in the divergent responses to the anti-racism protests, and the Black Lives Matter movement in the U.S and elsewhere.

However, the Church has the inner capacity to hold these polarities in a healthy balance and can overcome these historical contradictions if she returns to her trinitarian identity. Indeed, we are convinced that the Catholic Church can offer a capacious and inclusive tent where the great multitude spoken of at Pentecost (Acts 2:8-12) and in the Book of Revelation (Rv 7:9) — every tribe, language, and people and nations — can find a home. The essays in this volume attempt to project the Church as a depolarising space not only for discourse, but also for belonging and for transformation through dialogue. They help us see how the Church in Africa can be a family of God and a salt and light. The essays also offer some new insights on methods for doing interdisciplinary ecclesiastical studies. They also offer us solutions and best practices in three of the most pressing needs facing all Christians in Africa today — wealth, health and hope.

The three main concerns for our people today are *wealth (land)* that is how can every person in this continent have access to food security, human security, social security and peace in their homes, on the streets, and in their neighbourhoods and countries? In other words, what does it mean to be human in today's Africa and how can everyone's dignity, human fulfilment, and social and economic progress be promoted through equal access to social mobility, eco-system's health, and access to the three 'L's' which Pope Francis spoke about in his speech to slum dwellers in Nairobi—Land, lodging and labour?

The *second is health* (life in abundance), how can our people in Africa have access to quality healthcare so that our people are not dying in our continent from treatable and preventable diseases. How many lives are being lost in our continent and how many times have we legitimized the suffering and deaths of our people through religious narratives. Covid-19 has exposed the growing health inequities in Africa and in our world. Indeed, the need for holistic health and human wellbeing will continue to face us as a people and a Church. This is because many of our people are dying today from preventable and treatable diseases and the lack of food security, climate change and pollution which continue to affect the quality of life and life outcomes for most of our people.

The third quest of our people today *is for hope*, how and where can our people find hope? The Church exists as a space of belonging where all God's people can find a home. The Church serves as the site of learning where people unlearn false realities and embrace the truth of God which can help them for example to discover the beauty of diversity through the Trinitarian model. In this kind of space, people are inspired to embrace those ethical choices which are driven by gospel values and which help to bring about in history the fruits of the reign of God. The hope which the Church can help give to the world is a reversal of history and strengthening the capacity and agency of our people so that they can become artisans of their own destiny.

The Church is a space for reimagining a better possible world where people are moved to embrace life-giving choices which make concrete in people's lives and cultures, the saving and transforming grace of the Risen Lord. This saving hope is particularly needed in those places where people feel deep wounds and suffer injustice and the painful consequences of oppression and suffering.

Hope is a movement which shows people in their lived realities that their history is not contaminated, but that there is a reversal which is real in an experience of redemptive history today. Christian hope is not an idea or an ideal, it is a concrete emergence of a new agency and a new experience of triumph and release from the chokehold of history for those who have been battered by racism and other social evils. In the essays that follow, one would notice that these three dreams—wealth, health and hope—are the three quests through which our authors attempt to engage the themes which they discuss in the chapters.

Summary of Chapters

The volume is broadly divided into two sections. The first broad section includes essays that address the issues of dialogue in African society and in the churches in Africa and the ethics of solidarity and belonging. Authors in this section develop some practical approaches to how the Church in Africa can help bring about a more prosperous, and peaceful society in Africa and how theologies in Africa can contribute in strengthening the foundations of African ecclesiology where African Christians are at home with themselves, their churches, societies and the world. The second section contains essays which address the social issues in Africa and the witness of churches and Christians in the areas of healthcare, poverty eradication, international development, and advocacy for human rights and human dignity especially for minorities and the poor.

Charles Ebelebe opens the first section with chapter one, on dialogue and inculturation by helping us to think of a more expansive and concrete inculturation of the Gospel in Africa. Inculturation is one of the most discussed subjects in *Ecclesia in Africa*. **Ebelebe** discusses the (im)possibility of inculturation in the Church in Africa. He points to some successes in inculturation endeavours, while stating that progress has been slow due to some obstacles. Colonial mentality, Rome's influence, and lack of purposeful leadership demand a process of de-colonisation and re-evangelisation if inculturation is to be possible in Africa. A well-thought out catechetical programme, in his view, is relevant to a conscious re-education that will make African Catholicism truly African.

Clemency Justin Nabushawo in chapter two takes us into the painful world of conflicts in Africa. This chapter explores causes of conflict in Africa through a study of some selected cases. The author critically examines some of the approaches to conflict resolution and transformation. Some of these approaches include dialogue and traditional means of peace building and justice. She shows the strengths and weaknesses of these approaches, while proposing that dialogue, peace-making and giving, among God's people is the best gift which the Church can give to Africans in different parts of the continent, where people are still living in conflict situations. The author stresses that the Church should be the icon of peace; a sanctuary for the victims of violence, the poor and strangers at all times thus the African approaches to peace-building and peace-making should be inculcated in the Church's mission.

Ikenna U. Okafor in chapter three engages with the centrality and significance of the ethics of compassion, care, and fraternal solidarity. The chapter sheds light on how the marginalisation of the ethic of care from the polity has weakened and ultimately led to the collapse of pre-colonial traditional African society. Using a theological interpretation of the postcolonial narrative of

Chinua Achebe in *Things Fall Apart*, the author argues that the realisation of most of the visions of the First African Synod, to salvage Africa from the brink of collapse, would require a renewed appreciation of the values of the ethics of care. Africa must reject the dominance of the ethics of power and aggressive 'manliness' which leads to uncritical fundamentalism and violent exclusions. The chapter concludes with the recommendation of a four Ps matrix-approach to ministry in addressing the challenges of modern African society.

Lawrence Nwankwo explores the nature and features of Pentecostalism in Africa in chapter four. He puts this important movement in conversation with African Catholicism and African Traditional Religion. He argues that this movement is part of the challenging context of modernity in Africa and the cultural, religious, and economic factors which are important drivers in this movement. His work is an excellent demonstration of how to develop and apply tools of theology and socio-cultural studies in doing a dialogue within the different religious traditions in Christianity. He concludes with an emphasis on the power of love as a key to Christian discipleship. He also shows that some aspects of the Pentecostal-Charismatic dimensions should be appropriated rather than dismissed, particularly with regard to what it means to be a child of God, to have a personal relationship with God, the kinetic dimension of faith, and the performative aspects of faith which are often lost in an all too familiar, repetitive and ritualistic normative Catholicism.

Conflict is a part of human relations which could either be destructive or constructive to the well-being of the feuding parties and their ideologies/positions. In chapter five, **Cosmas Uzowulu** points to the Catholic Church, as an institution with its own traditions. Thus, an encounter of the Church with African cultures is a meeting of two institutions rich in traditions and values. The two traditions have to mutually work together in respectful and reciprocal mutual self-mediation in the service of humanity. The chapter concludes with a call for contextualization of African cultures.

Simon Mary Aihiokhai, in chapter six studies the complex scenario of conflict, war and violence in Africa and the role religions play in legitimising and sustaining wars. His essay answers two questions: How can Africa break away from these vicious cycles of exploitation and negative hyper-religiosity that define the contours of violence shaping the history of the continent? What is a new vision of religious harmony amongst the religiously and culturally diverse communities in Africa that takes seriously Africa's religious and cultural focus on the sacredness of life as well as the preservation of communal peace? Notable in this chapter is his analysis of religious fundamentalism, and his proposals for a reimagination of a new way of dwelling in common through a new ethics of inclusion and fraternity.

Raymond Aina in chapter seven highlights the African synods' understanding of the proclamation of the Gospel and evangelisation as an embrace of a struggle in defence of personal dignity, justice, social peace, liberation and integral human development of all people and of every individual. The author argues that the Church needs to be full of 'fire in the belly' in her commitment and readiness to move out of her comfort zones to contribute towards human flourishing. The Church should do this by going back to the synods' propositions which encourage among other things an empowerment of the poor and the vulnerable through the establishment of micro-finance and agrarian programmes that constitute what is understood as ecclesial incarnation of solidarity.

Annah Nyadombo in chapter eight explores how the Church in Africa could serve the most vulnerable through accountability and transparency, while preserving their dignity and integrity. In examining aspects of vulnerability in the African context, she proposes pastoral practices for the care of the vulnerable in Africa, including advocacy, human investment and promotion of social justice, equality, and equity.

Barry Eneh and Theresa Abah, in chapter nine develop an important pattern for integrated healthcare systems in Africa especially in faith-based settings. Through a scoping review of extant articles, they examine how faith-based organisations might successfully adopt the complex adaptive system framework to bolster their operational efficiency, strengthen organisational capacity, and improve access to affordable, quality care for individuals and populations. They also show that faith-based entities have an important role to play in the face of new infectious diseases like Covid-19. They offer some recommendations on how the faith-based agencies can help to provide effective healthcare to people in Africa.

Susan Nedza in chapter ten develops what one might call a field note for how to move away from a defunct model of short-term medical mission (STMM) from the Global North to the Global South. The old model was based on need and intervention, but the new model which she proposes is based on accompaniment, partnership, and strengthening local capacities. The old method is a neo-colonial, asymmetric model of charity that does not address the root causes of global health inequities; the new model she proposes builds collaborative partnerships with International Catholic Non-Governmental Organisations (CNGOs) committed to a model of accompaniment for those being served. She draws from her ministry as the President of an American-based CNGO, Olancho Aid Foundation, to develop some best practices in sustainable medical partnership between Western CNGOs and countries in the Global South.

Nontando Hadebe, re-reads the Kairos document in the light of the new contexts, sites of pain and struggles in Africa and the world. Her chapter is a prophetic clarion call to the Church in Africa and the world to fully embrace the movement of the Spirit in history, which was articulated in the Kairos document—one of the most powerful and transformative document on how to liberate the oppressed and create a world of justice ever produced in the continent. She argues for a Church that looks more like what she preaches in how the voices of women and their gifts are welcomed in the church, and a Church which stands with and for the poor. She shows how intersectional hermeneutics ties the struggles of race, sexuality, gender, social status, ethnicity and all the exclusionary hierarchies of power in the same garment and develops a pathway for the Church in Africa on how she can be on the side of those who are forgotten.

The volume concludes with an afterword by **Bonaventure Ugwu** presented as an *allocutio* to the Congress delegates. His is a celebration of the work of God that has been carried out in Africa since the Second Vatican Council. His message is a clarion call for a hopeful Africa and a movement away from bemoaning our past or an over-emphasis on lamentation of the present. He proposes that the Church in Africa shares in the hope given by the Lord about his coming in glory at the fullness of time. It also lives in hope that despite all the challenges of dependency, poverty, misery, corruption, diseases, and bad leadership, it will gradually rediscover itself as a major player in the World Church. He invites the Church and all God's people into this space of hope and reimagination through commitment, cooperation, reflective practices and individual and collective actions to bring this hope about in our times.

Then Came the Anti-Racist Protests

When we gathered in Enugu, Nigeria for the Congress in December, 2019, none of us knew that Covid-19 pandemic would ever come to Africa. Not many in the world outside China at that time even knew about this disease which started to afflict people in Wuhan China around November/December, 2019. However, as at the time of writing this introduction, the whole world has been affected by this terrible pandemic in a very devastating way. Even though Africa has been spared the worst form of this, no one knows how the future will look like with the vulnerabilities which our continent already faces. In the midst of this pandemic, most people of African descent and all men and women of goodwill were moved by another and more virulent pandemic which continues to afflict humanity since the first African slaves were taken from the African Motherland — racism and white supremacy.

Racism is a problem which we all experience more so in our interactions as blacks with white people and non-blacks. It is also a problem which we need to address as Africans by first understanding the nature of racism, developing the historical consciousness to read modern history in an objective, critical and creative way. It is important to understand the asymmetries of power in the world and the unequal power relations which the epistemological hegemony of the North has foisted even in our ecclesiological studies. This is what Emmanuel Katongole means when he writes that 'history matters' in developing the craft of theology as an African; it is the same power dynamics that Nontando Hadebe points to when she calls for an intersectional liberation hermeneutic to help us be the voice of all those who are oppressed and those condemned to die.

It is so easy for us to condemn the evils of racism, but we also need to see the logs in our eyes especially how we have created exclusionary practices based on ethnicity, religion, class, politics, gender and other social hierarchies in our continent and sometimes in our churches. We must pay attention to the cries of the poor (Raymond Aina), and the pains of the vulnerable (Sr Nyadoma) in Africa and address ethnocentric biases, the kind that led to the Rwandan genocide and the xenophobia in Africa which we saw in South Africa and in Darfur, Sudan.

Most of the authors in this volume challenge the Church in Africa and African theologians to commit to transforming the many conflicts and violence which confront us in Africa by understanding the roots of these conflicts and wars, and questioning the kinds of identity and cheap politics of exclusion which define the nation-states in Africa. Our hope is that the essays in this volume can challenge you to see how to do the works of God not simply as a theoretical or theological reflective exercise, but as a prophetic commitment that moves from claims of faith to acts of love through which we mirror a new world which is always in the making in history.

Dialogue and Inculturation
in the Christian Mission in Africa

Chapter One

An Inculturated Church in Africa: Lessons and Failings since *Ecclesia in Africa*

Charles A. Ebelebe CSSp

Introduction

Elochukwu Uzukwu is right in identifying inculturation as "*the* burning issue in the African Church."[2] At least, it was in the lead-up to the First Special Assembly for Africa of the Synod of Bishops, which celebrates its twenty-fifth anniversary this year, and the memorial of which is partially the reason for this Congress. Although Francis Oborji identifies two other major trends in African theology today as those of liberation and reconstruction,[3] neither of these two is as important nor as dominant as inculturation. These categorizations must, however, not be overstretched as they are interconnected. Uzukwu, for instance, is against an inculturation theology that is "content with liturgical sedation," ignoring "the oppressive heavy hand laid on the people …."[4]

The literature on inculturation is extensive, such that attempting a literature review of the relevant material would be a her-

---

[2] Elochukwu E. Uzukwu, *A Listening Church: Autonomy and Communion in African Churches* (New York: Orbis Books, 1996), 64. Emphasis is his.

[3] Francis Anekwe Oborji, "Inculturation in the Changing Face of African Theology," in *Inculturation: God's Presence in Cultures*, eds. Klaus Krämer and Klaus Vellguth (Queson City, Philippines: Claretian Communications Foundation, Inc., 2019), 89.

[4] Elochukwu E. uzukwu, *God, Spirit, and Human Wholeness: Appropriating Faith and Culture in West African Style* (Eugene, Oregon: Pickwick Publications, 2012), 33.

culean task. The volume of writing on inculturation is, however, not matched by the practice of inculturation in Africa. It is now 25 years since the First Special Assembly for Africa of the Synod of Bishops, which was held in Rome from April 10 to May 8, 1994.

This synod was a major ecclesial event in Africa and the universal church in the years preceding the Jubilee Year 2000. One of the achievements of this synod was a ringing endorsement of inculturation. But how much has this unequivocal support for inculturation translated into a more inculturated African church?[5] There have definitely been some successes, some achievements to celebrate. But the promise of the synod on inculturation, it must be said, has yet to be realised. This chapter highlights some of the successes recorded so far as well as the failures. It discusses the reasons for the failures and proposes possible ways of overcoming them. To begin, let us first define our key term.

What Is Inculturation?

Inculturation is the incarnation of Christian life and of the Christian message in a particular cultural context, in such a way that this experience not only finds expressions through elements proper to the culture in question, but becomes a principle that animates, directs and unifies the culture, transforming and remaking it so as to bring about a new creation.[6] This definition, provided by one-time Superior General of the Jesuits, Pedro Arrupe, captures the essence of inculturation and shows in what ways it goes beyond the previous terms that were in use, such as adaptation, indigenisation and Africanisation.

---

[5] In this essay, the expression "African church" refers to Catholic churches in Africa, especially those in sub-Saharan Africa.

[6] Quoted by Peter Schineller in *A Handbook on Inculturation* (Mahwah, NJ: Paulist Press, 1990), 6.

Peter K. Sarpong agrees with Arrupe. According to him, "When we talk about inculturation, we are always thinking about dancing and singing and drumming. That is liturgical inculturation. It is important but not the end of the affair. Inculturation has to deal with the entire Christian experience; it has to deal with the Christian message as a whole."[7]

Since my reference point in this chapter is the First Synod of Bishops for Africa, it is necessary to learn what *Ecclesia in Africa* says about inculturation. The Synod Fathers considered inculturation an urgent priority as well as a challenge in the life of the particular churches in Africa.[8] John Paul II, who issued *Ecclesia in Africa*, locates the basis of inculturation in the Incarnation, for just as the "the word became flesh and dwelt among us," (Jn 1:14) "so too the Good News, the Word of Jesus Christ proclaimed to the nations must take root in the life-situation of the hearers of the Word."[9] For the pope, inculturation is the "insertion of the Gospel message into cultures. For the Incarnation of the Son of God, precisely because it is complete and concrete, was also an incarnation in a particular culture."[10]

The pope recognises therefore that "inculturation includes the whole life of the Church and the whole process of evangelisation. It includes theology, liturgy, the Church's life and structures."[11] Archbishop D. S. Lourdusamy[12] underscores the importance of this statement from the Synod Fathers. "Every

---

[7] Peter K. Sarpong, *Peoples Differ: An Approach to Inculturation in Evangelization* (Legon, Accra-Ghana: Sub-Saharan Publishers, 2002), 34.

[8] John Paul II, *Ecclesia in Africa: The Church in Africa and its Evangelizing Mission Towards the Year 2000* (Washington, D.C.: United States Catholic Bishops Conference, 1995), 59.

[9] John Paul II, *Ecclesia in Africa*, 59.

[10] John Paul II, *Ecclesia in Africa*, 60.

[11] John Paul II, *Ecclesia in Africa*, 62.

[12] Lourdusamy was Prefect of the Congregation for Oriental Churches. He passed away in 2014.

aspect of the life and activity of the Church," he says, "should be inculturated or indigenous: indigenous life-style, indigenous arts, spirituality, indigenous forms of religious life, indigenous organisations and institutions."[13]

These emphases are noteworthy, for often times because liturgy has so dominated the conversation as well as the scholarship on inculturation, there has been a general tendency for people to immediately think liturgy once the topic of conversation is inculturation. The statements above remind us that inculturation is much wider than liturgy and that liturgical adaptations are only a small aspect, albeit a very important aspect, of the inculturation project. If, by a stroke of good fortune, we were to achieve all the key proposals that have been put forward so far by way of African adaptations of the Roman liturgy and no more, the African church will still be a long way in the journey to an inculturated African church.[14] This is because, as important as liturgy is, it does not represent "the whole life of the Church" that John Paull II and *Ecclesia in Africa* envision for the inculturation project.

If I may use the Igbo Church to which I belong and with which I am most familiar as an example, one aspect of the life of this church that is scarcely touched by inculturation is the ministry of leadership. The Igbo is traditionally republican. In the pre-colonial era, a few Igbo communities, such as Nri and Onitsha, had kings, but such kings were nothing like the Oba of Bini, the Ooni of Ife, or the Sultan of Sokoto, powerful monarchs

---

[13] As quoted by Schineller in *Handbook*, 24.

[14] For a good summary of some of these liturgical proposals, see Austin Echema, "African Eucharistic Liturgy in a Postmodern Church," in *Theology and Liturgy in the Life of the Church: Proceedings of the 26th Annual Conference of the Catholic Theological Association of Nigeria*, eds. Luke E. Ijezie, Stephen Audu and Agnes I. Acha (Portharcourt, Nigeria: CATHAN Publications, 2012), 34-45.

from some of the more established kingdoms in Nigeria. Even in those few Igbo communities that had kings, leadership was exercised collegially.

The king always had a cabinet and a council of elders who help him in the governance of the community. For the generality of Igbo communities, decisions are taken at the village square after a long 'palaver,' in which every adult male who wants his voice heard is heard. Some decisions also require the input of the women. The exercise of leadership and authority at the village and township levels is still characterised by this practice of extensive consultation and discussion.[15] This is in spite of the fact that practically every Igbo community now has a traditional ruler who exercises some measure of authority over its inhabitants. The powers of these traditional rulers are limited. They exercise their powers through a cabinet or council of elders. There is hardly any traditional ruler that has the kind of powers or authority over his town or community that a bishop has over his diocese.

The bishop has a kind of power over his diocese that is foreign in Igbo traditional culture. Even though there are all kinds of councils through which the bishop administers the diocese, they are all advisory; he could very well ignore their counsel as often as he pleases. Any meaningful inculturation of faith and church life in Igboland must affect the exercise of power and authority in the church. While not advocating a wholesale adoption of traditional Igbo democracy in the exercise of the ministry of leadership in the church, any inculturation of the Igbo church that does not include the lay people in some real way in the decision-making apparatus of the church would certainly be deficient.

---

[15] For a good summary treatment of the concept of power and authority in traditional Igbo society, see Charles A. Ebelebe, *Africa and the New Face of Mission: A Critical Assessment of the Legacy of the Irish Spiritans among the Igbo of Southeastern Nigeria* (Lanham: University Press of America, 2009), 16-22.

Culture is dynamic and ever-evolving,[16] and this means that inculturation will always be an ongoing process. This being the case, there will never be a time when we can say that the African Church has completed this process; that it is now fully inculturated. Inculturation will always be a work-in-progress. The Synod Fathers took this on board when they observed that, "Considering the rapid changes in the cultural, social, economic and political domains, our local Churches must be involved in the process of inculturation in an ongoing manner, respecting the two following criteria: compatibility with the Christian message and communion with the universal Church ... In all cases, care must be taken to avoid syncretism."[17]

Cultures are also human creations, which means that they can be flawed. This is why the synod proposes the Mystery of the Incarnation and of the Redemption as the grounds for discerning the values and counter-values of cultures. "Just as the Word of God became like us in everything but sin, so too the inculturation of the Good News takes on all authentic human values, purifying them from sin and restoring to them their full meaning."[18]

This being the case, John Paul II reminds us that "Inculturation is a difficult and delicate task, since it raises the question of the Church's fidelity to the Gospel and the Apostolic Tradition amidst the constant evolution of cultures."[19] These notes of warning are a common theme in many magisterial statements on inculturation. The African church must not be scared away from inculturation by such warnings. Where would orthodoxy

---

[16] The classicist would likely qualify this statement, but more about this in the next section.

[17] John Paul II, *Ecclesia in Africa*, 62.

[18] John Paul II, *Ecclesia in Africa*, 61.

[19] John Paul II, *Ecclesia in Africa*, 62.

be today without the heresies of the past? There are bound to be mistakes in the course of inculturation and this is okay.[20]

Faith and Culture: History of a Relationship

Inculturation involves the interplay of faith and culture. Faith, in the context of our discussion, refers to the Good News of salvation as revealed in the life, death, and resurrection of Jesus Christ. Culture, on the other hand, can be described as the totality of a people's way of life, involving three important aspects or dimensions: ideational, performance, and material.[21] Bernard Lonergan identifies two approaches to culture in history: the classicist and the empiricist.[22]

For the classicist, culture is normative, universal, and unchanging while the empiricist holds the opposite view, seeing culture as non-normative, particular, and changing. When the classicist speaks of culture, what he or she has in mind is the Western culture. This is the culture that is normative, universal, and unchanging, unchanging not in the sense that it does not develop but that it has in Western culture reached the height of its development.[23] This was the mindset of both the European colonisers of Africa and their missionary compatriots. Both the

---

[20] At the Fourth Synod of Bishops on Evangelization (1974), the Archbishop of Zoa demanded this for Africa: "Allow us to err. You yourselves have had 2000 years to err" (Quoted by Uzukwu, *A Listening Church*, 62.

[21] Stephen B. Bevans and Roger P. Schroeder credit Jens Loenhoff by way of Robert Schreiter with this view of culture. See their *Constants in Context: A Theology of Mission for Today* (Maryknoll, New York: Orbis Books, 2004), 47.

[22] See Bernard Lonergan, *Method in Theology* (London: Dartman, Longman and Todd, 1972), xi.

[23] Bevans and Schroeder, *Constants in Context*, 47. Bevans and Schroeder provide, in this book, an overview of the attitudes or relationship to culture of the three dominant types of theology in history that they identify (pp. 47-49, 60-61, 70-72).

colonisers and the evangelizers were on a "civilising" mission. Ogbu Kalu speaks of the "alliance of GOLD, GOD AND GLORY or commerce, Christianity and civilisation ...."[24]

The European missionaries who brought the faith to Africa considered their own cultures far superior to the culture of the Africans. That is, if they had any culture to speak of. They carried out their evangelizing mission in Africa in the context of colonialism, which provided a powerful reinforcement of this view. The picture is not uniform across Africa, but in general, European missionaries had a dim view of African cultures and made little or no effort to integrate them into the Gospel message. On the contrary, they transmitted to their African converts elements of European culture as part of the deposit of faith. One might attempt to excuse the European missionaries' failure to integrate the faith and the cultures of the peoples of Africa on the ground that they did not understand the cultures in question and so could do no better.

This is a weak defense because it was not just that they failed to integrate the faith and the African cultures, they, in general, denigrated and devalued these cultures. If they did not understand the cultures that they sought to evangelize, the least one would expect from a culture-sensitive evangelisation was to do no harm. European missionaries to Africa, however, had official documents from Rome urging them not just to do no harm to the cultures they sought to evangelize but to try to understand and to integrate these cultures into the gospel message where possible. An example of such a document is a 1659 instruction from Propaganda fide to missionaries in China. It says in part:

> Do not regard it as your task, and do not bring any pressure to bear on the peoples, to change their manners, customs, and uses, unless they are evidently contrary to religion and sound morals. What

---

[24] Ogbu U. Kalu, *The Embattled Gods: Christianization of Igboland, 1841-1991* (Trenton, NJ; Asmara, Eritrea: Africa World Press, Inc., 2003), 59.

could be more absurd than to transport France, Spain, Italy, or some other European country to China? Do not introduce all that to them, but only the faith, which does not despise or destroy the manners and customs of any people, always supposing that they are not evil, but rather to see them preserved unharmed. ... Do not draw invidious contrasts between the customs of the peoples and those of Europe; do your utmost to adapt yourselves to them.[25]

The emphasis on inculturation in the African Church is best understood against the background of the failure of European missionaries in Africa to heed such wise counsel from Rome in their evangelisation of Africa. With the dawn of independence for many African countries and the growth in self-awareness and consciousness of their identity as a people, Africans began to question what they received from the European missionaries as the good news of salvation. African intellectuals and especially theologians criticized the kind of faith that Africans received from European missionaries. Many were convinced that the European missionaries passed on to Africans a Europeanised version of the Gospel as the authentic Gospel.

Philip Igbo identifies this "Graeco-Roman cultural grip on Christianity" as one obstacle to inculturating the faith in other cultures.[26] The whole emphasis on inculturation in the African church has been a reaction against the harm done to the African peoples and their cultures by the Europeans in an effort to undo the damage. I agree with Peter Schineller that this may be more difficult than preaching the Gospel to a new people for the first time. According to Schineller,

> The fact is that lack of adequate inculturation in previous missionary efforts has often resulted in the need to focus on inculturation. In Nigeria today, for example, one is not usually sharing the gospel

---

[25] See Bevans and Schroeder, *Constants in Context*, 192.

[26] Philip Igbo, "Christian Faith and the Challenge of Inculturation," *African Journal of Contextual Theology* 4 (June 2013), 67.

for the first time with those who have never heard of Jesus Christ. Rather, one encounters a western European form or model of Christianity that is widespread and growing, but a form that is not indigenous to Nigeria. In other words, one has to in some ways de-westernize Christianity, strip it down to the essentials, in order to creatively inculturate gospel values into Nigeria. And this, I suggest, may be much more difficult than inculturation into a society or village that has never heard of Jesus Christ.[27]

It has indeed proven much more difficult to de-Westernise Christianity in Nigeria, especially in Igboland, in order to inculturate faith and church life. In the case of Igboland, for instance, the decades of negative portrayal of Igbo culture by the Irish Spiritans who evangelized Igboland seem to have done a lasting harm to the psyche of many an Igbo man and woman and to the Igbo church. Thus, even after Rome has ceased being an obstacle to inculturation, inculturating the faith in Igboland has remained an uphill task.

To be sure, it is not entirely true that Rome has ceased to be an obstacle to inculturation. We can find several examples of the Vatican or Rome, as they say, 'talking the talk' about inculturation, but examples of Rome 'walking the walk' are few and far between. Besides the instructions of Propaganda fide cited above, other examples of Rome 'talking the talk' on inculturation[28] include: Pope Gregory the Great's instructions to Augustine of Canterbury through the Abbot Mellitus on how to go about missionary work among the Anglo-Saxons (601); Pope John VIII's defence of Cyril and Methodius' use of the vernacular in the evangelisation of the Slavs (880); Pope Benedict XV's apostolic exhortation *Maximum Illud* (1919); Pope Pius XII's encyclical letters *Summit Pontificatus* (1939) and *Evangelii Praecones*

---

[27] Schineller, *Handbook*, 11.

[28] That is not to say that this word appeared in any of these documents. The earliest that the word inculturation appeared in a Vatican document was in Pope John Paull II's encyclical letter *Catechesi tradendae*, no. 53 (1979).

(1951); Vatican II's *Gaudium et Spes* (no. 44); and Pope Paul VI's 1969 address to African bishops at Kampala.[29]

This list is by no means exhaustive. What is more difficult to identify or come by are concrete steps that the Roman magisterium has taken to advance inculturation—that is, to match its words with action.[30]

Obstacles to Inculturation

A Colonial Mindset

Besides Roman obstructionism, there are a few more obstacles to inculturation. Changing the African mindset after the Europeans have finished working on it has proven more difficult than one would expect. In many African countries, many people who saw and experienced the European missions are still alive. These individuals were catechized to view their own culture in a negative light, as something to be discarded. Not only did they seem to have taken in this message deeply; it appears that they have inculcated this into their children, who have likewise inculcated the same to their own children.

The result is generations of Africans who view their traditional cultures negatively and who see them as fundamentally opposed to the good news of salvation. Getting these people to think differently of their culture, to value and cherish their traditions, has proven to be very difficult, and this has hampered the task of inculturation. This is the kind of mindset that produced

---

[29] Nathaniel Ndiokwere has a good summary presentation of these magisterial statements. See his *African Church Today and Tomorrow, vol. II: Inculturation in Practice* (Enugu: SNAAP Press, 1992), 18-24. I have deliberately kept the list to pre-1970, when many European missionaries were still very active in many parts of Africa, including in Igboland.

[30] Uzukwu criticized this practice of the Popes not matching their words with action on the subject of inculturation. See his *A Listening Church*, 62-65.

the following reactions from some African students in Rome after viewing a film recording of the Zairean Mass, as captured by Nathaniel Ndiokwere:

> This is a caricature of the Roman Rite;
> It can't be a Mass that has been celebrated;
> Africa is exposing herself to ridicule;
> The experiment should not continue;
> Africa is not mature to produce her own rite of the Mass;
> Please, no adulteration of the Mass;
> Africa has a long way to go.[31]

Interestingly, Ndiokwere reported that non-Africans in the audience, including Europeans and Asians, appreciated the liturgy. Luke Ijezie has a slightly different take on this obstacle to inculturation. He sees it not so much as a problem of colonised minds, as a lack of enthusiasm for inculturation, especially among Africa's younger generation who "see inculturation as a retrogressive movement championed by people who are perceived to be either anti-progressive or suffering from nostalgia for the past."[32]

This problem is caused by a wrong understanding of both culture and inculturation as dealing with things of the past. As has been noted above, culture is dynamic and it changes. It is this today culture that inculturation must deal with not a culture that is dead and forgotten. Whether the 'progressive' young Africans are aware of it or not, they are products of their culture and environment. Authentic evangelisation requires that the faith be inculturated in every culture, including in advanced post-modern first world countries.

---

[31] Ndiokwere, *African Church*, 155.

[32] Luke Emehiele Ijezie, "The Second Vatican Council on Culture and Faith," *African Journal of Contextual Theology* 4 (June 2013), 43.

Lack of Leadership

According to Pope John Paul II, it is the responsibility of bishops to guide the implementation of inculturation.[33] For better or for worse, the Catholic Church is very much a clerical church, by which I mean that very little happens in the church without the active interest and leadership of the ordained men of God. One could say that the level of inculturation in a diocese is directly proportional to the interest of the local bishop in the subject. Anywhere in Africa where there is some progress being made on inculturation, you will always find a local bishop driving the progress. It is difficult to imagine the Zairean Rite without the leadership of Cardinal Joseph Malula.[34] The same could be said of the Archdiocese of Kumasi under the leadership of Archbishop Peter K. Sarpong. Conversely, wherever one sees one of these bishops, whom one could describe as "more Roman than the Romans," very little advance will be made on inculturation.

I once attended a priestly ordination in one of the rural dioceses in Igboland where the bishop conducted the ordination Mass entirely in Latin. Meanwhile, there were hardly any foreigners in the congregation. The overwhelming majority of those taking part in the Mass were Igbo people: priests, consecrated men and women, seminarians, and the common folk. When I asked one of the diocesan priests why the bishop would prefer to use Latin in such a Mass, he told me that the bishop loves Latin and that everyone in the diocese knows it. The bishop is definitely handing down his love for Latin to his priests and seminarians because when a day later I attended the Thanksgiving Mass of

---

[33] John Paul II, *Redemptoris missio: On the Permanent Validity of the Church's Missionary Mandate.* In Acta Apostolicae Sedis, 83 (1991), 249-340. English translation published by the Office for Publishing and Promotion Services, United States Catholic Bishops Conference, Washington, D. C., 1990, 52.

[34] Archbishop of Kinshasa from 1964 to 1989.

one of the newly ordained priests, he used Latin for his common of the mass, and this was in an Igbo village church.

Contrast this with the opposite situation, which someone narrated to me some time ago, of a celebration in one of the dioceses in Tanzania where the bishop conducted the Mass entirely in Kiswahili, even though there were Europeans and other foreigners in the congregation. The latter example might be seen as a little insensitive and inconsiderate to the non-Kiswahili speakers in the congregation, but it does highlight the importance that the bishop places on the local language and culture. There is no doubt that if we had more Malulas and more Sarpongs among the Episcopal class in Africa, we would be at a different place than where we are today on the subject of inculturation. If Rome wants to encourage inculturation of faith and church life in Africa, it would appoint bishops that are more theologically progressive and courageous than those that are said to be 'more Roman than the Romans.'

A Multiplicity of Languages and Cultures

There is no doubt that one of the greatest strengths of the Latin Mass is its universality. It is definitely a plus when one can travel from Enugu to Manila to Cologne to wherever else and participate in the Mass without any help from anyone. But what is gained in this universality is lost in the dryness and foreignness of the liturgy and in the lack of diversity.

Language is the vehicle of inculturation. Pope John Paul II understands this when he enjoins foreign missionaries to contribute to the process of inculturation by mastering the people's culture, starting by mastering their language.[35] Inculturation is also driven by the local church, which ordinarily translates to a

---

[35] John Paul II, *Redemptoris Missio*, 53.

diocese or to a regional grouping of local dioceses. Inculturation becomes a difficult task when there are ten or more languages used in a diocese or region. The problem of the multiplicity of languages and cultures in Africa also speaks to the age-long debate as to what is more accurate – to speak of African culture or cultures and of African Traditional Religion (ATR) or African Traditional Religions (ATRs)?

It would seem that this debate is more or less settled in favour of a "both/and" position, where there are enough commonalities among the multiplicity of cultures in Africa that would permit one to speak of African culture and African Traditional Religion while allowing for differences at the micro level that would justify the use of the plural form for these realities. Accordingly, the inculturation of the African church might follow a two-tier approach where there are pan-African elements at the macro level, for example, dance and culture-specific elements at the micro level, for example, kola nut ritual for the Igbo.

Besides the multiplicity of languages, there is the situation, such as we have in the church in Igboland, where the local language is in decline.[36] I have attended many weddings and funerals in Igboland's village churches where the readings for Mass are read in English because the readers, who are usually drawn from among the couples for weddings and from members of the bereaved family in the case of a funeral, are unable to read in Igbo.[37] The question then becomes: how does one inculturate

---

[36] A discussion of the factors responsible for this situation is beyond the scope of this chapter but suffice it to say that the Irish Spiritan missionary praxis in Igboland is implicated in the current travails of the Igbo language. For more on this, see Ebelebe, *Africa and the New Face of Mission*, 100-102.

[37] This problem is related to the problem of a colonial mindset discussed above. Many young people have grown up and are growing up in families, and have attended and are attending schools, where little value is placed on the Igbo language in favour of English. The church can help to change this colonial mindset through its many schools and parishes. The ideal should be for the Igbo to be fluent in both Igbo and

the Igbo church for an Igbo people who are not literate in Igbo language, and in many cases not even fluent in it?

The solution to this problem is not to abandon the Igbo language in favour of English. To do this would be to hasten the demise of the local language, which the church is implicated in its decline. In fact, insisting on the Igbo language as the language for inculturating the Igbo church could be the Catholic Church's way of atoning for the sins of its missionary forebears, the Irish Spiritans.[38] The needs of the Igbo faithful who lack fluency in the Igbo language would be accommodated through English translations, even as they are encouraged to gain this fluency in any way possible.

These are but a few of the obstacles militating against the inculturation of faith and church life in Africa. Despite these obstacles, one can find some examples of successful inculturation in the African Church. I will now highlight a few of these successes, which were shared by my Spiritan brothers on mission in these various places in Africa. They have been edited by me as needed.

Examples of Successful Inculturation of the Church in Africa

Uganda[39]: *The Ugandan Martyrs as Ancestors*

All the traditional religions in Uganda have a special place of honour for ancestors, with a belief that they influence the living in one way or another. It is, therefore, not surprising that in the first century of the advent of the faith in Uganda, the massacre of

---

English. This should be perfectly possible, and the church can help to bring it about.

[38] Ebelebe, *Africa and the New Face of Mission*, 101.

[39] Courtesy of Fr. Chibuzor Ifeanyi, CSSp, St Daniel Comboni Polytechnic, Naoi Moroto, Uganda.

the Ugandan martyrs was massively embraced as the inadvertent enthronement of powerful and influential Christian ancestors.

The annual Uganda Martyrs celebration on June 3 is the single biggest religious event in Uganda. The celebrations show that this is one day when the Ugandan Catholics feel that Christianity is theirs and not just a foreign religion. The martyrs' images decorate churches and shrines across the country. They are reliable intermediaries, protectors and role models, and to assign them these functions, most do not need specific Catholic catechesis.

Hilltop Worship Sites

The Ugandan terrain is generally hilly, with a few scattered mountains. Traditionally, shrines were built atop these hills and on mountainsides. A cursory look at most worship sites since the advent of the faith here shows that the traditional pattern of locating worship sites on hills and mountains has largely been replicated, thus reinforcing the idea that God is the "Most High" who watches over his people and their situations, as is the case of the traditional religion here.

This subsequently means that many people, including old people and children, have to struggle uphill for worship programmes, a fact that many do not seem to mind or even consider because it takes them to the roots of traditional African spirituality. Rubaga Hill, which hosts the cathedral in Kampala, Uganda's capital city, is a case in point. The very shapes and makes of these sites also speak to inculturation. Most churches take the hut shape that is very African and are usually made with brown clayey bricks, reflecting their deep connection to the African earth/soil.

This commendable architectural inculturation in Uganda contrasts with the situation in Angola, where one could see churches constructed as in Europe with no fans or air conditioners, never minding how hot it can get in Angola. My priest informant[40] reports having been in a cathedral in Angola where, after being at the altar for a two-hour Mass, he was almost passing out. It gets so hot that water is sometimes served to those on the altar. Yet, in spite of this unhealthy situation, some people insist that the Portuguese architecture should not be changed.

Congo-Brazzaville[41] *Le Moment d'Action de Grace*

One positive impact of inculturation in the Congo church is the culture of thanksgiving known as "Le moment d'Action de Grace." This is a moment during the Eucharistic celebration when after the communion, the commentator, through his/her short words of exhortation, invites the worshipping community to thank the Lord for all the graces and blessings received during the Eucharistic celebration (such as lessons from the readings and homily, forgiveness of sins, the reception of the body and blood of Christ through the Holy Communion, etc.).

At this moment, the choir sings a song of thanksgiving (action de grace) and the worshipping community manifests their gratitude to God for all these enumerated favours received, through their gestures of clapping of hands and dancing to the rhythm of the choir. This is so exciting and brings out the real meaning of the Eucharist as "Thanksgiving." This extended and "loud" Thanksgiving after Communion is also obtainable in DRC as well as in Angola, where it is called *Acção de Graça* in Portuguese.

---

[40] Fr Kenechukwu Uzor, CSSp, São Tiago Maior de Lándana, Province de Cabinda, Angola.

[41] Courtesy of Fr Daniel Echetebih, CSSp, Paroisse Saint Michel, Madingou Poste, Nkayi, Congo Brazzaville.

Zimbabwe[42] Respect for Elders and for God in the Context of the Mass

Zimbabweans believe in communitarian life and thus every human being is seen as attached to a community and is recognised through his family and community. An individual elder is addressed and recognised through a plural pronoun. The elder who ordinarily should be addressed as "he" is addressed as "they;" this is because an elder takes a higher responsibility of promoting community life by sharing his life with others through security and provision of food. He is therefore recognised through the plural pronoun since he cannot live alone.

Whenever an elder is greeted, he is greeted with a plural connotation. In like manner, God, who is the universal Father, is addressed with a plural pronoun in the Zimbabwean liturgy. The Shona liturgy shows great reverence for God, who is the universal father and sustainer of life. God is referred to as *Mwari* and recognised as "our father" (Baba vedu). Whenever God is being addressed, he is being addressed with a plural connotation all through the liturgy.

The word of an elder is not separated from the elder himself. Hence, an important message coming from an elder has to be accorded respect, whether based on delegation or physical presence. Bible procession in the solemn Shona liturgy becomes the best way of showing respect to the King of kings who manifests himself through his word. The liturgical dancers present the book of the word of God in a dignified way and the minister receives the book of the Gospel in corresponding dignified manner, placing it on the lectern. In this manner, the congregation welcomes the word of God that would carry the congregation along throughout the sacred liturgy.

---

42 Courtesy of Fr Sylvester Oyeka, CSSp, Immaculate Heart of Mary's Catholic Church, Snake Park, Harare, Zimbabwe.

The Shona people of Zimbabwe are very respectful; hence, when an elder is speaking, everybody has to sit down to listen to him. Communal speeches are often made with its congregants sitting as a sign of respect and recognition of anyone vested with the power to address the community. Standing while formal speeches are being made is seen as disrespectful and uncalled for. In Shona liturgy, therefore, the Gospel is read while the congregation remains seated.

Solemn blessings are done while the congregants are kneeling down. Standing while solemn blessings are given is abhorred. Whenever prayer of the faithful is being said, the congregation is obliged to kneel down since this is considered an important appeal to the King of kings. The penitential rite of the Mass is done while the congregation is kneeling down. Sitting and kneeling are therefore gestures that connote respect and submissiveness to an authority.

Dance

Dance is an important part of the life of the Shona, and this has been integrated into the liturgy. Thus, the Zimbabwean church could be described as a dancing church. This is because almost every member of the congregation is involved in active dancing during the liturgy. Culturally, dancing is always the best way of receiving a king and acknowledging his greatness; the traditional chief, heads of state and important dignitaries among the Shona people are often received with dance. It is therefore pertinent that in Shona liturgy, there should be liturgical dancers, especially at a solemn Mass. The liturgical dancers remain close to the sanctuary throughout the Mass in a solemn Shona liturgy. The presence of the liturgical dancers connotes the importance of the liturgy and the royal character of the sacred liturgy since Christ, who is the invisible minister, is the King of kings.

Democratic Republic of the Congo[43] The Zairean Rite

The Zairean rite is an African (especially Congolese) adaptation of the Roman liturgical rite of the Mass. It was approved by the Holy See in 1988. The establishment of the "Zairean rite" corresponds to the practice of the idea of inculturation, seeking to involve the faithful in liturgical life by recognising and taking into account the local culture. It is celebrated in the parishes of the DRC once a month.

Briefly, in the Zairean Rite, which does not have the same structure with the universal Roman Rite except for the Readings and the Words of Consecration, the Mass begins with a traditional procession, with the priest dancing to the altar accompanied by the ministers, including two acolytes carrying spears. Reaching the sanctuary, raising his two hands, he kisses the altar traditionally four times (the four edges of the altar), with the invocation of the Ancestors like we find in the traditional African setting. With this kissing, the Gloria is intoned.

Thus, he, accompanied by the concelebrants and the deacon(s), if any, and the servers and the readers, incenses and dances round the altar as long as the Gloria lasts while the acolytes dance their traditional dance steps round about the sanctuary. The people sing, dance and shout as is customary to them. The sprinkling of holy water, penitential preparation and the rite of peace take place in the middle of the Mass, before the offertory. The dialogue between the celebrant and the assembly is very developed.

Another peculiarity is the invocation of ancestors and saints, which holds an important place in the Zairean liturgy. Prayers are pronounced according to the ancestral tradition: the litany of ancestors, the particular preface and the penitential rite

---

[43] Courtesy of Fr. Francis Offia, CSSp, Maison Provincial, Quartiers Bel-air, Kampemba, Lubumbashi, DRC.

are placed after the "I believe in God." It is an eschatological affirmation of the Christian assembly and an essential evocation that is part of Congo's culture.

One thing is common in these examples of successful inculturation in these various local churches in Africa: they are all centred around the liturgy, and in this case, the Mass. From this, one could conclude that whatever successes the African Church has recorded in inculturation is mostly in and around the holy Mass. But the Mass or liturgy in general is only one area of faith life in Africa that requires inculturation. Every area of life of faith of the African Christian needs to be inculturated.

Towards a More Inculturated African Church

Leadership

It would be difficult for the African church to make any headway on inculturation without purposeful leadership. In the Catholic Church, as far as inculturation is concerned, this leadership is usually provided by bishops. If Rome is sincere about encouraging and promoting inculturation in the African Church, it needs to do better on the quality of the priests it appoints as bishops in Africa. For this to become a reality, the whole process of the appointment of bishops needs to be reviewed. The current process is shrouded in secrecy.

At present, a small club of senior clerics, including the incumbent bishop, decides who gets appointed bishop. We need to return to the practice in the early church where the lay faithful had more say in who becomes their bishop. Inculturation is both a subject of the heart as well as the head. Many bishops in Africa lack the intellectual capacity to drive the project of inculturation. Africa needs more intellectually capable bishops, especially those that lean more progressive, to drive forward the project of inculturation in the African Church.

Training of the Agents of Evangelisation

The importance of leadership for the task of inculturation has already been highlighted. This leadership is not limited to bishops. It includes other agents of evangelisation, especially priests. There is no doubt that seminary training has seen some improvements since Vatican II, especially regarding the curriculum of study. But still more improvement is called for. Africans have lamented the assault on their culture by foreign missionaries, who brought the faith to Africa. How pitiable is it then that in our days, it is indigenous priests who are leading the assault against African culture! Seminarians need to be trained to understand, value, and have a greater appreciation of their various cultures. Courses like African philosophy, anthropology, African traditional religion and such need to be taught in the seminary and by competent experts in these fields.

Catechesis

Catechesis is the process of handing on the faith. This is an indispensable part of the life of the Church. Just as new members of the society are socialised into the life of the community, so it is in the church. In connection with inculturation, catechesis will have to do more than hand on the faith; it will be broadened to include decolonising the African mind. African children must be schooled from very early on to understand and value both their faith and their culture. They must be schooled to love themselves for who they are. This self-appreciation must include appreciation of their local language. The importance of a well-thought out program of catechesis cannot be over-emphasized in relation to the project of inculturation.

Conclusion

Among the Two-Third World, if Asia is identified with mission as dialogue and South America with mission as liberation, Africa is identified with mission as inculturation. This is an over-simplification, of course. In reality every region of the church is involved in all these aspects of mission. Inculturation received a boost 25 years ago at the First Extraordinary Assembly for Africa of the Synod of Bishops, when the Synod Fathers came out strongly in support of it. One had hoped for more rapid progress in inculturation with this official support. Progress, unfortunately, has been rather slow, with a few exceptions here and there, especially in the area of liturgy.

The lack of purposeful leadership from the ranks of the African clergy, especially the bishops, is one of the reasons for this. Another is Rome's history of saying the right things but doing little to encourage inculturation. And yet another is a colonial mentality on the part of many Africans who have been socialised to despise their own culture in favour of the Euro-American. The mentality of this class of Africans needs to be de-colonised and then re-evangelised before they can embrace, as well as become, agents of inculturation.

Such a re-education is what a well-thought out catechetical programme can achieve, something that is lacking in many African Catholic dioceses today. Many have said that the future of the Church is in Africa. This statement is empty unless African Catholicism becomes truly African and truly Christian.

Bibliography

Bevans, Stephen B. and Roger P. Schroeder. *Constants in Context: A Theology of Mission for Today*. Maryknoll, New York: Orbis Books, 2004.

Ebelebe, Charles A. *Africa and the New Face of Mission: A Critical Assessment of the Legacy of the Irish Spiritans among the Igbo of Southeastern Nigeria*. Lanham, Maryland: University Press of America, 2009.

Echema, Austin. "African Eucharistic Liturgy in a Postmodern Church." In *Theology and Liturgy in the Life of the Church: Proceedings of the 26th Annual Conference of the Catholic Theological Association of Nigeria*, edited by Luke E. Ijezie, Stephen Audu and Agnes I. Acha, 26-48. Portharcourt, Nigeria: CATHAN Publications, 2012.

Igbo, Philip. "Christian Faith and the Challenge of Inculturation." *African Journal of Contextual Theology* 4 (June 2013): 49-71.

Ijezie, Luke Emehiele. "The Second Vatican Council on Culture and Faith." *African Journal of Contextual Theology* 4 (June 2013): 31-47.

John Paul II. *Redemptoris mission: On the Permanent Validity of the Church's Missionary Mandate*. In Acta Apostolicae Sedis, 83 (1991), 249-340. English translation published by the Office for Publishing and Promotion Services, United States Catholic Bishops Conference, Washington, D. C., 1990.

_____. *Ecclesia in Africa: The Church in Africa and its Evangelizing Mission Towards the Year 2000*. Washington, D.C.: United States Catholic Bishops Conference, 1995.

Kalu, Ogbu U. *The Embattled Gods: Christianization of Igboland, 1841-1991*. Trenton, NJ; Asmara, Eritrea: Africa World Press, Inc., 2003.

Lonergan, Bernard. *Method in Theology*. London: Dartman, Longman and Todd, 1972.

Ndiokwere, Nathaniel. *African Church Today and Tomorrow, vol. II: Inculturation in Practice*. Enugu: SNAAP Press, 1992

Oborji, Francis Anekwe. "Inculturation in the Changing Face of African Theology." In *Inculturation: God's Presence in Cultures*, Klaus Krämer and Klaus Vellguth, eds. Queson City, Philippines: Claretian Communications Foundation, Inc., 2019.

Sarpong, Peter K. *Peoples Differ: An Approach to Inculturation in Evangelization*. Legon, Accra-Ghana: Sub-Saharan Publishers, 2002.

Schineller, Peter. *A Handbook on Inculturation*, Mahwah, NJ: Paulist Press, 1990.

Uzukwu, Elochukwu E. *A Listening Church: Autonomy and Communion in African Churches*. New York: Orbis Books, 1996.

_____. *God, Spirit, and Human Wholeness: Appropriating Faith and Culture in West African Style*. Eugene, Oregon: Pickwick Publications, 2012.

CHAPTER татTwo

Dialogue and Conflict Resolution in Our Churches: Lessons and Failings since *Ecclesia in Africa*

Justin Clemency Nabushawo

Introduction

Africa still grapples with the same problems about the continent that perturbed the First African Synod's Fathers twenty-five years ago. From Rome, the bishops lamented:

> One common situation, without any doubt, is that Africa is full of problems. In almost all our nations, there is abject poverty, tragic mismanagement of available scarce resources, political instability and social disorientation. The results stare us in the face: misery, wars, despair. In a world controlled by rich and powerful nations, Africa has practically become an irrelevant appendix, often forgotten and neglected. For many Synod Fathers, Africa is a continent where countless human beings — men and women, children and young people — are lying, as it were, on the edge of the road, sick, injured, disabled, marginalised and abandoned. They are in dire need of Good Samaritans who will come to their aid.[44]

This essay 1) explores causes of violent conflicts in Africa; 2) shares and evaluates some commonly used methods of conflict resolution in Africa; 3) makes a comparative analysis

---

[44] John Paul II, *Post-synodal Apostolic Exhortation Ecclesia in Africa of the Holy Father John Paul II to the bishops, priests and deacons, men and women religious and all the lay faithful on the Church in Africa and its evangelizing mission towards the year 2000* (Nairobi: Paulines Publications Africa, 1995), no. 40–41.

of the Catholic Church's teaching on dialogue as a means of conflict resolution; and 4) proposes models aimed at mitigating conflicts in Africa.

Peace is a key mission of the Church. In his farewell discourse, Jesus Christ bestowed peace to the world through his disciples, saying, "Peace I leave with you; my peace I give to you" (Jn 14:27). This is the same peace that his Church gives to the world. Jesus further prayed for the unity of his Church, "...that they be one just as we are" (Jn 17:11). The Church not only gives peace, but fosters unity, forgiveness, reconciliation, and justice. These gifts are heavily dependent on dialogue, as stated in Isaiah, "Come now, let us set things right, says the LORD" (Is 1:18).

Invested in dialogue and conflict resolution, is language and the power of the word: "Lord, I am not worthy to have you under my roof; only say the word and my servant will be healed" (Lk 7:6-10; Mt 8:5-11). Consequently, amidst all gloom, the Church is "...to bring glad tidings to the poor...liberty to captives and recovery of sight to blind, to let the oppressed go free..." (Lk 4:18-19; Mt 12:18-21).

The causes of the conflicts experienced in Africa are about the resources of the earth, mostly natural resources. The Church's leadership — bishops, clergy, religious — and all the baptised in Africa should be the Salt and Light (Mt 5:13-16) of the continent. The Church has authority to teach and condemn evil in society (2 Tm 4:1-5). The founding father of the republic of Kenya, Mzee Jomo Kenyatta, reiterated the Church's authority while addressing AMECEA (Association of Member Episcopal Conferences in Eastern Africa) bishops, saying:

> we need the Church in our midst to tell us when we are making a mistake. The Church is the conscience of society, and today society

needs a conscience, do not be afraid to speak. If we go wrong and you keep quiet, one day you may have to answer for our mistakes.[45]

This trust and authority, invested in the Church's pastoral agents, is valid only if they de-link themselves from whatever compromises their ability to dialogically transform situations of conflict within and among people. Many of our people are crying out to the church from refugee camps, as internally displaced people, as wandering migrants to help bring an end to conflict in Africa and fight for justice and good order in our continent. Their cry is in our times the only weapon the weak in our continent use to lament their plight and to pray to God as they struggle to cope with the unbearable oppressive structures of governance and management in Africa.

Conflict and the African Experience

"Where do these wars and battles between you first start? Isn't it precisely in the desires fighting inside your own selves? You want something and haven't got it; so you are prepared to kill. You have an ambition that you cannot satisfy; so you fight to get your way by force" (Jas 4:1–3). Unfulfilled needs are the major conflict triggers. This is the scenario experienced in Africa, and perhaps elsewhere. Africa's conflicts are socio-economic, cultural and political in nature. Most of their causes are intertwined, sharing in each of the above dimensions.

---

[45] Jomo Kenyatta, "Building Christian Communities," opening address to AMECEA Bishops' Plenary, *African Ecclesia Review (AFER)* 18, no. 5 (1976): 1.

Biswanath Ghosh suggests three views of conflict, the traditional, the behavioural, and the interactionist.[46] The traditional view perceives conflict as harmful—the conflict perpetrator should be rooted out. For the behavioural view conflict is normal and so cannot be avoided. The interactionist view encourages minimal conflict in the pursuit of change, improvement, and avoidance of complacency.

The conflict situations in Africa can also be interpreted from the interactionist view, a view that seeks change and improvement of systems that have unsettled societies. For example, the effects of attempts to escape poverty are considered by Antoine Berilengar, "Looking around the world and in Africa, it may be seen that oil and minerals dependence is significantly correlated with corruption, authoritarian government, government ineffectiveness, high levels of military spending, and a heightened risk of civil war (oil fueling civil war)."[47]

Africa's resources are a double-edged sword, rather than benefit the people, they are often "fueling civil war," as per the following experiences.

Selected Cases

Elias Omondi Opongo analyses the causes of conflicts from the socio-political, economic and religious perspectives of the AMECEA countries: Uganda, Kenya, Tanzania, South Sudan, Ethiopia, Eritrea, Malawi and Zambia. These causes include unemployment and skewed resource distribution; corruption, poverty, lack of accountability, nepotism, political suppression and dictatorial leaderships, rebel wars (such as Northern Ugan-

---

[46] Biswanath Ghosh, *Human Resource Development and Management* (New Delhi: Vikas Publishing House, 2000), 245.

[47] Antoine Berilengar, "Advocacy for Just Distribution of Oil Revenues: The Case of Chad," in *Peace Weavers: Methodologies of Peace Building in Africa*, ed. Elias Omondi Opongo (Nairobi: Paulines Publications Africa, 2008), 87.

da and South Sudan), perennial post-election violence (Kenya, 1997 and 2007-8) and inter-religious tensions (South Sudan, Ethiopia, Eritrea, Tanzania, Malawi).[48]

a) Corruption and Mismanagement

Development in these countries is skewed toward ethnocentrism and nepotism, as noted by Berilengar: "Hence experience shows that incomes from natural resources are often distributed to friends, family within the ethnic or religious group of the leaders."[49] These observations show that nepotism and ethnocentrism can cause conflict. Churches in Africa should persistently challenge those in power to ensure that distributive justice is achieved.

Many African leaders have the audacity of appointing their own wives, children, friends, and close family members to government positions. Further, the same people are given a luxurious living at the expense of the poor tax payers. This means that when national resources are plundered, the common person bears the brunt. The Church should stand in defense of the vulnerable. Among nations where nepotism is practiced with impunity are Uganda and Burundi, countries where the first ladies hold ministerial posts. In Uganda, the president's son, General Muhoonzi Kainerugaba, is the head of the army. In Zimbabwe, the late president Robert Mugabe's wife, Grace Mugabe, wielded much political power, which unsettled the locals.

Leaders of countries who stay in power while disregarding the national constitution also cause hostility, disparity and marginalisation, leading to violent conflict. This has been witnessed in Libya, Zimbabwe, the Democratic Republic of Congo, Burun-

---

[48] Elias Omondi Opongo, "The Church on the Road to Emmaus: Situational Analysis of Conflicts, Wars and Instability in AMECEA Countries," *African Ecclesial Review (AFER)* 51, no. 3 (2009): 193–215.

[49] Berilengar, "Advocacy for Just Distribution of Oil Revenues," 87.

di, Rwanda, and Egypt, among many others. In recent times, leaders from some of these countries were removed from power after so much violence.

Such experiences are widespread in Africa. People continually groan under the burden of dictatorship and marginalisation, coupled with unbearable livelihoods. These conditions are not because their countries are poor, but because wealth is concentrated in a few hands, leaving the majority wallowing in abject poverty. These insufferable conditions suck the marginalised into strife, unrest, and conflict, as observed by Opongo:

> Inequality of household incomes, ownership of land as well as poor economic performance of a country, can also lead to conflict. These conditions breed general discontent…leading to civil strife and protests…armed guerrilla groups which lure the unemployed youth…hence creating an alternative source of income through extortions and criminal activities.[50]

Unemployed, energetic youth need at least a livelihood. When this is elusive, they feel hopeless, and some turn to lawlessness as a basis of survival. In some cases, some of the challenges are exacerbated by natural calamities. These include unpredictable effects of climate change such as drought, floods, mudslides, destruction of crops by locusts, and pandemics such as COVID-19. These force people to search for a livelihood, which sometimes leads to conflict.

Other conflicts are man-made crises, such as the high cost of living, and heavy taxation on foods. These can be blamed on the corruption and other vices mentioned earlier. Food scarcity and its high cost have often prompted scenes of riots in many countries in Africa. Population increases and political instability contribute to inadequate food production. Food insecurity in countries like

---

[50] Opongo, "The Church on the Road to Emmaus," 203.

Cameroon, Senegal, Burkina Faso, Kenya, and Malawi can to a major extent be attributed to mismanagement and depletion of land by the people themselves, and their governments.

These problems heighten internal and cross-border immigration, putting strain on the limited available resources. For example, predictable post-election violence in Kenya (1992, 1997, and 2007–8) forced people to relocate to other countries and continents, due to internal political and religious tensions. These changes cause conflict between the 'guests' and the 'hosts.' So too has the political instability in places like South Sudan, Sudan, Mali, Chad, and Somalia.

b) Natural Resources: Major Contributors to Conflict in the Continent

Natural resources are meant to be a blessing. Unfortunately, Africa's natural resources collectively have been more of a curse than a blessing, given the levels of destructive conflicts witnessed on the continent. Violent conflicts have been rampant in countries with abundant natural resources, as attested by Berilengar: "Rich natural resources can also have negative effects on the government, leading in particular to unequal distribution, corruption, and authoritarianism. It is worth noting that almost all the oil–exporting countries of the Gulf are non-democratic, and other countries with oil have dictatorships or are ravaged by war."[51] Such are the sad testimonies about resources in Africa.

c) Land as a Source of Conflict in Africa

Land is a precious major natural resource continually sparking violent conflicts among people in Africa, from family to na-

---

[51] Berilengar, "Advocacy for Just Distribution of Oil Revenues," 87.

tional levels. Land, houses, and natural resources are involved, but in many instances, land is also depleted through extraction of minerals, logging, and misuse through farming. The landslides destroying lives and properties on the slopes of Mount Elgon in both Uganda and Kenya is nature's response to human abuse.

Persons in government often own massive parcels of land. In most cases, these are unused, yet there are many cases of land squatters mercilessly evicted from such parcels, out into the cold with their families! These people are oftentimes clobbered by police and hired goons sponsored by the rich and powerful. Land squatters are left destitute in their own home countries due to selfishness and corruption, where wealth is hoarded by the few.

Demolition of African people's houses and property by governments, to make way for 'developments,' are common. These have mostly targeted the 'poor,' who are left bitter and are sometimes not adequately compensated. With the recent wave of oil and mineral discoveries in some parts of the continent, initial occupants of such places are asked to give way for the extraction of oils and minerals, but, again, compensation takes forever. These discriminative acts cause resentment, leading to perennial conflicts on the continent.

Land has further been degraded at the expense of the environment, on which all lives depend. The depletion of the Mau Forest in Kenya and the Mabira Forest in Uganda are but examples. The former is a key determinant of a balanced climate in the entire nearby Great Lake region, and beyond. The issue of logging and human settlement in these forests and wetlands is normally politicised, at the expense of millions of lives that depend on it environmentally. This leads to conflict between nature and human beings, including wildlife. No wonder nature is raging, in landslides, drought, floods, and unexplained invasion of pests. These conditions prompt internal and external migrations, which eventually strain limited resources, resulting in conflict as people scramble for them.

d) Scarcity and Over-pricing of Resources

Xenophobic hostilities are occasionally meted on foreigners in South Africa by the locals, in a scramble for limited resources. Foreigners can be resented when they are perceived to have taken over jobs and privileges meant for the locals. Natural resources are God-given for his people. The Church should take a lead in guiding individual governments on how to sustain and equitably share resources for posterity. Furthermore, the Church should teach humanity how to care for the environment (Gn 9:1–4) so that the environment may care for humanity. Opongo notes:

> Sudan, Tanzania and Zambia experience the challenge of poor use and distribution of national and natural resources, particularly given the large amounts of mineral resources. The governments of these countries have signed mining contracts with multinational companies that reap the respective countries of the maximum profits…leaving them very poor. Working conditions in the mines are inhumane and the mining activities on the environment have serious impacts.[52]

African states invest heavily in the training of their citizens, locally and internationally, in all professions. These include engineering and technology. This is why one is forced to wonder if Africa cannot trust and invest in her own personnel, and maintain her industries and factories to do the job, instead of entrusting her wealth to foreign expertise? By so doing, African governments are not only dodging accountability, but are sadly denying their own people employment. African leaders are accomplices in the stealing of Africa's wealth.

Mineral and oil discoveries in Africa should provide employment, development, and revenue for the entire continent. Sadly, most of the oil refineries in places like Nigeria, and Angola and

---

[52] Opongo. "The Church on the Road to Emmaus," 203.

mines in South Africa, Sierra Leone, and Botswana to give a few examples are controlled by foreign companies and interests. (Granted, there can be a pressing need for expertise, but this should not deny the locals their livelihood.)

Africans have a culture of hard work. All they need are opportunities to work, and to earn an honest living. Unemployment is an underlying cause of conflict, as 'an idle mind is the devil's workshop.' Churches can engage individual home governments through dialogue on modalities of distributive justice.[53] Tinyiko Sam Maluleke accuses the churches in South Africa of silence amidst a people's suffering:

> The second illustration of a wrong theological choice is the churches' choice for silence when it might be better to speak and to act. There are different types of silence: the interested silence of the powerful and the fearful silence of the powerless; the empty silence of the hopeless and the calculated silence of the vulnerable; loud silence and soft silence; eloquent silence and coherent silence; active silence and passive silence. There are many occasions in which the churches appear to have chosen a certain type of silence in relation to the arms deal saga, the xenophobic violence, the worrying conduct of the ruling party, the apparent strife within the judiciary, the crisis in Zimbabwe, and the growing culture of violence in our country.[54]

The Church must heighten her prophetic voice to defend vulnerable humanity. Helpless people, who look up to the Church for protection, get disillusioned and lose faith when their expectations are not met by their spiritual and moral guide, the Church. Philomena Njeri Mwaura decries the 1994 Rwanda genocide, and compares the events to what nearly befell Kenya

---

[53] AMECEA, *The African Synod Comes Home: A Simplified Text* (Nairobi: Paulines Publications Africa, 1995), 20.

[54] Tinyiko Sam Maluleke, "A Postcolonial South African Church: Problems and Promises," in *African Theology on the Way: Current Conversations*, ed. Diane B. Stinton (London, UK: Society for Promoting Christian Knowledge, 2010), 157.

in 2005, during a referendum on the draft constitution and the 2007-8, post-election violence: the "Church in Kenya, faces the challenge of credibility after failing to provide moral leadership throughout this period, church leadership in Kenya was deeply polarized along party and ethnic lines."[55]

The Church in Kenya had for decades been respected for her firebrand voice in fighting injustice, especially during the times of bishops Elexander Muge, Raphael Ndingi Mwana a'Nzeki, Timothy Njoya, and Cardinal Morris Otunga, to name but a few. The churches should reclaim their credibility. It is worrisome when evil is at work and the prophet [Church] is tight-lipped. The Church, as prophet, is God's mouthpiece. Has God ceased to communicate through his prophets, or is it the prophets who have refused to talk? In the second book of Timothy, St Paul encourages church leaders to, "...proclaim the word; be persistent whether it is convenient or inconvenient; convince, reprimand, encourage through all patience and teaching...be self-possessed in all circumstances; put up with hardship; perform the work of an evangelist; fulfill your ministry" (2 Tm 4:2–5).

Other conflict experiences in Africa include intercultural and clan conflicts over water, pasture, and perennial cattle marauding between pastoral communities. Examples include the Turkan and Karimonjong in Kenya and Uganda, and banditry conflicts between Somalia and Kenya.

Models of Conflict Resolution for the Church in Africa

"Come now; let us set things right says the LORD" (Is 1:18). Africans value communal relations, and thus peace. Whenever issues threatening the unity of the community or family arise,

---

[55] Philomena Njeri Mwaura, "Christian Identity and Ethnicity in Africa: Reflections on the Gospel of Reconciliation," in *African Theology on the Way: Current Conversations*, ed. Diane B. Stinton (London, UK: Society for Promoting Christian Knowledge, 2010) 132–33.

people are invited to dialogue, with the aim of restoring disrupted unity. In traditional Africa, family issues are first handled within the family, involving only close family members. Under the guidance of the elders, most explain themselves, own up, and ask for forgiveness. Shaking hands and an embrace, as well as sharing of a meal by eating from the same plate, would seal reconciliation. A conflict that threatens the peace of the larger community involves the community and even Church leaders.

Differences in traditional Africa are settled through dialogue, as exemplified in the verse from Isaiah above. Even the most difficult situation of conflict is melted into submission through right, timely words, and restitution through the African palaver. "Indeed, the word of God is living and effective, sharper than any two-edged sword, penetrating even between soul and spirit, joints and marrow, and able to discern reflections and thoughts of the heart" (Heb 4:12). The AMECEA bishops, in their Sixteenth Plenary, after acknowledging the existence of conflict in their region, recommended a return to traditional cultural means of resolving conflicts.[56]

The Church's silence when people are afflicted might legitimize vengeance, as observed by Pope John Paul II: "People excluded from the fair distribution of the goods originally destined for all could ask themselves: why not respond with violence to those who first treat us with violence?"[57] Just as governments look up to the churches for guidance, ordinary people too look up to the same churches for guidance in the time of crisis. Jesus exemplifies this when he speaks with his depressed disciples on the road to Emmaus, leaving them relieved (Lk 24:13–35).

---

[56] Justin Clemency Nabushawo, "Editorial," *African Ecclesial Review* 51, no. 3 (2009): 162.

[57] John Paul II, *Sollicitudo rei Socialis*, papal encyclical, Vatican web site, December 30, 1987, www.vatican.va/content/john-paul-ii/en/encyclicals/documents/hf_jp-ii_enc_30121987_sollicitudo-rei-socialis.html, (accessed June 24, 2020), no. 10.

Jesus uses dialogue to restore life to the centurion's servant, thus dispelling stress from the army commander (Mt 8:5-11). Examples of Jesus relieving people of conflict dominate his ministry, showing that freeing humanity of any baggage and giving them full life is Jesus' mission through his Church. This then is the mission of the Church, to use dialogue to restore life and joy and dispel stress among people.

In an address given in Brazil in 2013, Pope Francis states, "When leaders in various fields ask me for advice, my response is always the same: dialogue, dialogue, dialogue."[58] Dialogue is a prerequisite for collaboration, development, and restoration of broken relationships. Dialogue helps people to articulate their needs, and that is how differences are understood and resolved.

Laurenti Magesa affirms, "If you are not addressing the needs of the people for whom you are preaching the Gospel, you are not dialoguing and you are not properly evangelizing at any deep level either. The conflicts going on in Africa are a challenge to the whole Church in Africa and, in particular, to the way we evangelize. This challenge was made obvious by the genocide in Rwanda in 1994."[59] This statement, by one of Africa's finest theologians, urges pastoral agents in Africa to audaciously re-evaluate current methods of evangelisation, their personal witness style, their attitude toward those to whom they proclaim the Gospel, and their perception of dialogue.

As a pastoral agent, how has the Gospel you proclaim to others transformed your life, so that you may serve as teaching aid to others? Do you talk with, or to, people? Are you patient with those who question, seek clarification, and even express their

---

[58] Francis, *Address of Pope Francis, Meeting with the Brazil's Leaders of Society, Municipal Theatre, Rio De Janeiro*, Vatican web site, July 27, 2013, http://w2.vatican.va /content/francesco/en/speeches/ 2013/july/ documents/papa-francesco_20130727_gmg-classe-dirigente-rio.html (accessed June 24, 2020), no. 3.

[59] Laurenti Magesa, *Rethinking Mission: Evangelization in Africa in a New Era* (Eldoret, Kenya: AMECEA Gaba Publications, 2006), 66.

uncertainties and doubts about God? Do you listen and amicably agree to disagree? Do you have foresight, and can you read the signs of the times? What drives your evangelizing agenda? Answers to these questions will determine the spiritual fruits of your evangelizing ministry.

Eduard Achermann echoes these sentiments in stating that evangelisation demands "harmonious coexistence, generosity, mutuality, and responsibility for one another...respecting the other's culture, totally being there for each other, and even gaining salvation together."[60] Exemplary pastoral leadership is a profound evangelisation, and one that is most sought-after today. Some conflicts in the mission of evangelisation manifest via incompetency and inconsistency of pastoral agents. This can be in terms of resource mismanagement, poor or improper relationships, and poor communication, among others. Dialogic evangelisation can lessen violent conflict in Africa by enhancing peace and love (Jn 15:10–12). Hence, we sing: "How many times must his people be told, before they know they are one? The answer my friend is deep in your heart, the answer is deep in your heart."[61]

In the words of Pope Francis, Church shepherds should "take on the smell of the sheep."[62] This was exemplified by Bishop Cornelius Korir of the diocese of Eldoret, during Kenya's 2007-8 post-election violence:

> When we arrived, riotous Kalenjin youth were forcibly evicting people and threatening to burn down the town...police were

---

[60] Eduard Achermann, *Cry Beloved Africa! A Continent Needs Help* (Munich: Kinshasa African University Studies, 1996).

[61] Joseph Bragotti et al., *We Pray and Sing to the Lord* (Nairobi: Paulines Publications Africa, 1990), 422.

[62] Francis, *Evangelii Gaudium*, apostolic exhortation, Vatican web site, November 24, 2013, www.vatican.va/content/francesco/en/apost_exhortations/documents/papa-francesco_esortazione-ap_20131124_evangelii-gaudium.html, sec. 24.

trying to contain the violence but were overwhelmed and asked me to talk to the hundreds of the youth armed with bows and arrows. I stepped between them and the police putting my hands above my head and shouting 'Don't shoot! Don't shoot!'...the youth agreed to retreat if I could agree to escort them so that they would not be shot in the back by the police. We clergy could use our moral authority and the symbolic impact of the Cassock and collar to persuade people to put down their arms.[63]

The clergy, as Jesus' apostles, have authority to calm storms (conflicts) in people's lives, because all creation is subject to Jesus' authority (Lk 8:22-25; Mk 4:35-41). This authority is enshrined in those anointed and set apart to proclaim his good news. Thus, Saint Irenaeus said in the second century, "The glory of God is a human being who is fully alive."

A booklet from AMECEA on the First African Synod acknowledges, "Dialogue is the way of having a voice, a role to play and a contribution to make in the decisions of the community."[64] Dialogue to some leaders in the Church, is a sign of defeatism. This is a misconception because failure to engage people in dialogue is but courting conflict. As John Mbiti puts it, "I am because we are, and since we are therefore I am."[65] Unity is realised through consistent pursuit of peace and justice. Unity is attained through dialogue.

We need to acknowledge that injustices the world over are conduits of conflict. The Church anywhere is both an emblem of peace and is itself a peacemaker (Mt 5:3-10). That is why victims of violence always take refuge in churches, and run to pastors for protection. As Bishop Korir affirms, "Today, the Church is

---

[63] Cornelius Korir, *Amani Mashinani (Peace at the Grassroots): Experiences of Community Peacebuilding in the North Rift Region of Kenya* (Eldoret, Kenya: Catholic Diocese of Eldoret, 2009), hereafter cited in the text as *AM*, 10.

[64] AMECEA, *The African Synod Comes Home*, 22.

[65] John S. Mbiti, *African Religions and Philosophy* (London: Heinemann, 1969), 113.

still called to be a protector of the displaced, a minister to the victims of violence, a provider of relief to those threatened with harm" (*AM*, 11). Churches can only be true to this mandate if they stop forming ethnic cohorts within, for personal enhancement at the expense of their holy calling, and of the flock entrusted to them.

Writing of Zimbabwe, Hamilton Mvumelwano Dandala reflects, "The Church must accept the challenge to be an advocate of those who are suffering. The nature of prophetic responsibility requires the Church to speak powerfully to those who wield power, be it political and/or economic."[66] He goes on, "It has to be acknowledged then, that the prophetic witness of the Church in the Zimbabwean situation is questionable. The Church has left itself open to the accusation that it is not actually being prophetic, in the sense of standing up for justices and responding in the name of God to all the suffering of the people in Zimbabwe."[67] This scenario is widely replicated in Africa, and can be largely blamed on some Church leaders' alliance with political leaderships for personal gain. Maluleke responds:

> The strategy of critical solidarity has made it possible for us to stand by and watch the abuse of power and resources. It has enabled us to let the poor die. Critical solidarity with government means that we have ceased being in solidarity with the poor. Like Zacchaeus...the Church needs to climb down the tree of elitism, speak against violence, defend the poor and strangers in our midst and speak truth to 'Pilate,' despite the cost.[68]

---

[66] Hamilton Mvumelwano Dandala, "The Challenges of Ecumenism in African Christianity Today," in *African Theology on the Way. Current Conversations*, ed. Diane B. Stinton (London, UK: Society for Promoting Christian Knowledge, 2010), 104.

[67] Dandala, "The Challenges of Ecumenism," 105.

[68] Maluleke, "A Postcolonial South African Church," 159.

Jesus never condoned injustice. He rebuked the Pharisees for their hypocrisy, (Lk 12:1-2; Mt 23:1-36); he whipped money-changers out of his father's house (Mt 21:12-13); he reprimanded Peter, saying, "Get behind me, Satan! You are an obstacle to me. You are not thinking as God does, but as human beings do" (Mt 16:21-23). Conflicts in Africa could be nipped in the bud if Church leaders — who wield moral power and respect — boldly seized their prophetic role.

But as Magesa observes, "Like all institutions, the Church tends to be static, sometimes slow or unwilling to move even in the face of compelling evidence to do so."[69] The silence of churches while humanity groans under the socio-economic and political baggage of injustices is a great betrayal of all who look up to the churches as their sanctuary.

Silence is not always golden. A timely word saves, while a good word too late is a waste. The AMECEA booklet states: "When we struggle for justice we want to bring Gospel values into Society. Work for justice is part of evangelisation because politics and economics are not outside God's rule."[70] This declaration bequeaths pastoral agents to resolve conflicts in word and action (cf. Jas 2:14).

Peace is humanity's common need. Stan Chu Ilo asserts, "... the civilization of love opens religious groups to dialogue...We dialogue to restore our broken love relationships."[71] Thus, we sing: "We are one in the Spirit, we are one in the Lord. And we pray that all unity may one day be restored. And they will know we are Christians by our love, yes, they'll know we are Christians by our love..."[72]

---

[69] Magesa, *Rethinking Mission*, 87.

[70] AMECEA, *The African Synod Comes Home*, 34.

[71] Stan Chu Ilo, *The Face of Africa: Looking Beyond the Shadows* (Bloomington, IN: AuthorHouse, 2006), 291.

[72] Bragotti et al., *We Pray and Sing to the Lord*, 430.

Four African models for resolution of conflict are described in the following sub-sections.

a) Kenya's 2007–8 Post-election Violence

The late Bishop Korir was a national peace icon in Kenya. He mediated political-ethnic conflict in the North Rift Region in 2007–8 saying afterward, "Without their [locals] hard work and commitment to dialogue, our efforts would have been meaningless. They were the real peace actors" (AM, ii). He sees conflict resolution directly engaging affected parties in many ways, for which he offers twelve steps.

1. "*Analyze, intervene and interrupt*" (AM, 9). Since conflict at this stage is palpable, the mediator should use reason, and persuade and plead with disputants to think about being "productive rather than destructive" (AM, 9–10).

2. *Provide all disputants* with basic needs — security, food, clothing, and sanctuary/shelter. Korir suggests: "If someone is running for their life, you must never turn them away. The church must step in the breach to aid the suffering" (AM, 11–13).

3. "*Help them talk to each other*" (AM, 9–27).

4. The power of the tongue (words) to resolve any misunderstanding is unrivalled. Violence only begets violence.

5. *During the initial meetings, disputants may be encouraged* but not forced to share a meal, tea, or some soft drinks, as a gesture of willingness to reconcile. Korir argues that in traditional Africa, the sharing of a meal is a sign of friendship and trust, since people who are enemies do not share meals.

6. *The conflict mediator should meet with and listen to intra-ethnic groups separately,* and over and over, while maintaining impartiality and confidentiality.

7. *Encourage and facilitate conflicting groups to meet in a neutral place with neutral facilitators,* and to express their grievanc-

es in a controlled manner, devoid of provocation of raw emotions. Korir advises that each group could write down their grievances, and allow a facilitator to read them out loudly in a combined group, with no emotions attached.

8. *Prepare an agenda for inter-ethnic meetings with peace-loving representatives* from each side, and then launch a dialogue for peace.

9. *Let group representatives report to their individual caucuses the outcome* of combined small groups discussions.

10. *Suggest and implement peace-connector projects,* such as sports, and involve all as peace talks continue.

11. *Let the two disputing groups sign a social contract of participation,* and share responsibilities and accountability for the initiated social connector projects, and,

12. *Assign mediators to monitor developments* and agendas of the two groups (*AM*, 27).

Dialogue and conflict resolution are parts of an on-going process. It is neither easy nor straightforward, but through patience and goodwill, it bears fruits of peace. Also, approaches can differ, depending on the nature and level of a conflict. This particular method was successful for Korir in resolving conflicts in the North Rift Region of Kenya.

Churches and their pastoral agents are sanctuaries and intermediaries for victims of violence. Regrettably, in the past some churches in Africa have chosen partisanship and allegiance to denominational ethnicity. Such was the case in the 1994 Rwanda genocide, and with the Kiambaa Kenya Assemblies of God Church in Eldoret, Kenya in 2007–8 post-election violence. These sanctuaries became human slaughterhouses.[73]

---

[73] Government of Kenya, "Report of the Commission of Inquiry into the Post-Election Violence" (Nairobi: Government Printer, 2008), 44–52.

b) Peacebuilding and Reconciliation in Northern Uganda

Bishop John Baptist Odama has written of his experience of conflict resolution of a religious-political nature. This involved the Holy Spirit Movement of Alice Auma ('Lakwena'), and the Lord's Resistance Army (LRA), led by Joseph Kony, in Northern Uganda. The conflict was resolved through the formation of the Acholi Religious Leaders' Peace Initiative (ARLPI), a body composed of different faith groups, for peace in Northern Uganda. The group encouraged forgiveness, reconciliation, and peacebuilding through dialogue. Traditional intervention included the drinking of juice by disputants, made from the bitter roots of *mato oput*.[74] Participation in the ritual involved all, including family members of disputants who confessed publicly and sought communal forgiveness and restitution. The drinking of bitter *oput* demonstrated a willingness to reconcile and seal the agreement for peace.[75]

c) Conflict Resolution in the Great Lakes region

Martha Okumu writes of a conflict transformation group in the Great Lakes region of East Africa, the Peace Tree Network (PTN). It was founded in the year 2000, and is similar to one in Northern Uganda. PTN uses a regional integration approach in resolving conflicts in the area. Okumu writes, "But most importantly, PTN encourages dialogue between parties in conflict as this is one of the ways that root causes of conflict can be highlighted, and both parties can come to a compromise regarding a situation affecting them."[76] The Church, as a community of com-

---

[74] Perpetrators of conflict, together with victims and their families, drink *mato oput* as a sign of owning up to that which was wrong, and seeking forgiveness and reconciliation.

[75] John Baptist Odama, "Conflict Resolution, Peacebuilding and Reconciliation in Northern Uganda," *African Ecclesial Review* 51, no. 3 (2009): 297–303.

[76] Martha Okumu, "The Impact of Regional Networking in the Great Lakes Region: The PTN Experience," in *Peace Weavers: Methodologies of Peace Building in Africa*, ed.

munions, is best placed to broker peace in and among peoples, through dialogue as a non-violent and sustainable means.

d) *Gacaca* for Peace Restoration in Rwanda

Agbonkhianmeghe Orobator explains a traditional African peace strategy used in Rwanda, known as *gacaca*. This strategy aims at knowing the truth, handling conflict perpetrators, banishing impunity, and encouraging reconciliation and unity between conflicting parties.[77] With this peace methodology, wrongdoers are "offered a forum to own up to their misdeeds, offer reparation and ask for pardon from the community."[78]

The Church's Teachings on Dialogue

Holy Scripture is replete with inexhaustible acts of dialogue between God and humanity, and within the Godhead. In Genesis, through the power of the Word, God orders creation into being (Gn 1:1-25). But when making man, God says, "Let us make man in our image, after our likeness" (Gn 1:26). The "us" is a reference to the Godhead, the Triune God: God the Father, God the Son, and God the Holy Spirit, participate in the making of man. This involvement is the essence of dialogue.

When humanity disobeys God and sins, there is dialogue between the woman Eve and the serpent, and later dialogue between God and the couple, Adam and Eve (Gn 3). God uses dialogue to redeem humanity (Jn 1:1-15). In the Old Testament,

---

Elias Omondi Opongo (Nairobi: Paulines Publications Africa, 2008), 103–4.

[77] Euthalie Nyirabega, "Transitional Justice in Rwanda: The courts and challenges of reconciliation," in *Peace Weavers: Methodologies of Peace Building in Africa*, ed. Elias Omondi Opongo (Nairobi: Paulines Publications Africa, 2008), 225.

[78] Agbonkhianmeghe E. Orobator, "Catholic Teaching and Peacemaking in Africa: A Tale of Two Traditions" in *Peace Weavers: Methodologies of Peace Building in Africa*, ed. Elias Omondi Opongo (Nairobi: Paulines Publications Africa, 2008), 39.

God reaches out to the prophets he wants to send to his people, through dialogue. In the New Testament, God again reaches out to the Blessed Virgin Mary, Mother-to-be of the Redeemer, through dialogue (Lk 1:26–38).

In the letter to the Hebrews, God speaks with his people: "In times past, God spoke in partial and various ways to our ancestors through the prophets; in these days, he spoke to us through a son, whom he made heir of all things and through whom he created the universe...who sustains all things by his mighty word" (Heb 1:1–4). The Church, as the advocate of God's mission on earth, is the product of dialogue. She teaches, converts, and saves through dialogue.

The Christian community of Antioch used "two-way communication principles and practices, the professional use of dialogic method."[79] Similarly, the Gospel is dialogically proclaimed through involvement, questioning, interpreting, explaining, and conviction. The Holy Sacraments (all seven of them) are not administered passively, but actively. Dialogue is a series of mutual, ongoing conversations between or among persons, seeking a common understanding. Dialogue is a means to an end, not an end in itself. The Church is made up of communities of communions. She cannot develop and sustain her communities and relationships without dialogue.

Dialogue, as such, is at the core of the Church's mandate to proclaim the Gospel to the ends of the world and to make disciples for Christ (Mt 28:19–20). Carl Rogers opines: "Communication is the experience of self and others through dialogue. Dialogue creates the inter-human or commonness."[80] Dialogue,

---

[79] Paolo Mefalopulos, *Development Communication Source Book: Broadening the Boundaries of Communication* (Washington, DC: World Bank Publications, 2008), 7.

[80] E. M. Griffin, *A First Look at Communication Theory* (New York: McGraw-Hill, 2000), 45.

therefore, is an effective tool of conflict resolution because it is interactional, collaborative, reassuring, informational, and resulting in understanding.

C. S. Rayudu writes: "Communication, like birth and death, is part of individual life as well as organisational existence...communication is the process of understanding people."[81] Dialogic communication enables coordination, cooperation, instruction, decision-making, information-giving, and guidance.[82] Drawing from her own incarnation and the Paschal Mystery demonstrated through the Triune God, the Church is both leader and manager. She can help the continent overcome violent conflicts by engaging the citizenry in dialogue. According to Rayudu, "The yardstick for managerial and leadership efficiency is communication."[83] Church leaders have to enhance dialogue among themselves and with God's people to fully accomplish Jesus' mission.

Dialogue envisions openness, honesty, flexibility, patience, and respect. It avoids imposition of one's views on others. John McKenzie observes: "Jesus does not dominate men, but invites them to a free decision. If they refuse to make the decision, they must accept the consequences: but he exercises no coercion upon them. He has power from the Father, but it is presented as power to serve and save."[84]

Church leadership the world over is respected, even by non-believers, as long as it is exemplary and impartial. Such leadership is best suited for conflict mediation and resolution because

---

[81] C. S. Rayudu, *Media and Communication Management* (Mumbai: Himalaya Publishing House, 1998), 30.

[82] John White, *IC's Role in Competitiveness and Innovation* (New Delhi: Maya Publishers, 2003), 3–5, 10–11.

[83] Rayudu, *Media and Communication Management*, 32.

[84] John L. McKenzie, *Authority in the Church* (New York: Sheed and Ward, 1966), 28.

of the people's trust in it. Today, and as expressed earlier, trust in some church leadership in Africa is diminishing, due to the churches' perceived alliance with political powers, neglect of the poor, counter witness, scandals, and unexplained silence, at a time when churches are expected to give guidance as the 'conscience' of society.

Trust is a prerequisite of dialogue and conflict resolution. If the Church is to succeed in conflict resolution, it must win peoples' trust. Nevertheless, churches in Africa have used dialogue to enhance ecumenism with non-Christian religions and traditionalists. Johnson A. Mbillah attests that inter-faith initiatives between Muslim and Christian religious leaders in Sierra Leone and Liberia achieved peaceful co-existence through collaboration. He adds that peace on the continent is possible if religious leaders and communities are at peace with each other. He further argues that Islam and Christianity can take advantage of their popularity and following to broker peace in and beyond the continent.[85] Mbillah is seeking dialogue and conflict resolution for a peaceful Africa.

Wounded Healer? Conflict Within the Internal Structures of the Church

John Mary Waliggo observes the context of the First African Synod:

> It took courage for the bishops to fully recognise publicly that the African Church needs to make a critical examination of conscience. Justice and respect for human rights have sometimes been lacking within its internal structures and decisions. If the Church gives witness to justice, she recognises that whoever dares to speak to

---

[85] Johnson A. Mbillah, "Interfaith Relations in Africa," in *African Theology on the Way. Current Conversations*, ed. Diane B. Stinton (London, UK: Society for Promoting Christian Knowledge, 2010), 113.

others about justice should also strive to be just in their eyes. It is therefore necessary to examine with care the procedures, the possessions, and the lifestyle of the church.[86]

Socio-economic, spiritual, and cultural imbalances exist among Church leadership. Development, equitable sharing of resources, and fair and just treatment of collaborators — especially those from minority groups — are generally skewed amid the internal structures of churches in Africa. Tribalism, nepotism, and marginalisation of minority groups are open issues sadly associated with the Body of Christ, the Church in Africa today. These squabbles scandalize the faithful and give counter-witness. For credible evangelisation, the churches have to own this delinquency, and courageously face and rectify the situation internally.

Mwaura echoes Waliggo: "In February 2008 the member churches of the National Christian Council of Kenya (NCCK) publicly confessed their complicity in fueling ethnic hatred and sought forgiveness. This is a commendable act and the NCCK has continued to reclaim her prophetic role by speaking out against injustice and proposing a way forward in healing and reconciliation."[87] As much as NCCK was remorseful and sought pardon, many people were already scandalised, and felt duped by the churches' counter-witness.

Don Page says the actions of a leader include coordinating through communication and responses; representing the interests of followers; and indiscriminately mentoring, protecting, inspiring, and gathering those entrusted to his/her care.[88]

---

[86] John Mary Waliggo, "The Synod of Hope at a Time of Crisis in Africa," in *African Theology on the Way: Current Conversations*, ed. Diane B. Stinton (London, UK: Society for Promoting Christian Knowledge, 2010), 44–45.

[87] Mwaura, "Christian Identity and Ethnicity in Africa," 135.

[88] Don Page, *Effective Team Leadership: Learning to Lead Through Relationships* (Nairobi: Evangel Publishing House, 2008).

Emerging, yet hushed conflicts in local churches in Africa are encrusted with the unfulfilled needs of both leaders and collaborators. Surprisingly, some of the conflicts that afflict society, such as tribalism and nepotism, are deeply entrenched in churches in Africa!

The churches' silence over certain social injustices might be telling in themselves. An unfulfilled pastoral agent is unhappy, and is a danger to self, to others, and to the mission of evangelisation. A captive cannot proclaim liberty to fellow captives. "Just so, every good tree bears good fruit, and a rotten tree bears bad fruit" (Mt 7:17). Jude Abidemi-Asanbe weighs in: "Evangelization entails dialogue, co-operation, inculturation and contextualization."[89] Mwaura observes, "Dialogue has not been a common practice in the Church, yet we need to listen to each other in order to effectively proclaim good news. In the process of mutual listening, there is mutual learning and our common experience of God is deepened. This also facilitates common living, while respecting the dignity and difference of others."[90] It is time the Church genuinely ponders these observations.

A book published in 2017 from the Vatican's Congregation for Consecrated Life, *New Wine in New Wineskins*, highlights unsettling abuses experienced by religious men and women in the Church: "This is one of the reasons that seem to motivate numerous members to leave. For some, it is the only way to respond to situations that have become unbearable."[91] This revelation might be but a tip of the iceberg.

On this subject, Magesa contends, "The conflicts going on in

---

[89] Jude Abidemi-Asanbe, "Evangelization: Challenges and Prospects for the Church in Africa," *African Ecclesia Review (AFER)* 47, no. 3 (2005): 199–218.

[90] Mwaura, "Christian Identity and Ethnicity in Africa," 135.

[91] The Congregation for Institute of Consecrated Life and Societies of Apostolic Life, *New Wine in New Wineskins: The Consecrated Life and Its Ongoing Challenges Since Vatican II* (Nairobi: Paulines Publications Africa, 2018), no. 21.

Africa are a challenge to the whole Church in Africa and, in particular, to the way we evangelize."[92] He further observes:

> But honesty is needed here: people can live together, under one roof, year after year, without forming community, without there being communion between or among them. We see this daily in various families and...religious communities...A regulation or law can bring people together, but it will not necessarily bind people together in mind and heart...community life, such as one lived by consecrated people in the church, should constitute *care, concern,* and *presence.*[93]

The Church's success in conflict resolution challenges her to put her house in order before she can credibly fulfill Jesus' command: "Go, therefore, and make disciples of all nations, baptizing them in the name of the Father, and of the Son, and of the Holy Spirit, teach them to observe all that I have commanded you. And behold I am with you always, until the end of age" (Mt 28:19-20). This change has to begin with the Church leadership before it can be undertaken by all the individual faithful.

Proposals for Conflict Transformation in Africa

a). Re-evaluating Evangelizing Methods and Re-instilling African Traditional Values

Gospel values taught to African Christians resonate with most of the traditional African values. Commandments like you shall not kill, commit adultery, steal, lie, and lust after another's wife or property (Dt 5:16-21), are abhorred acts in traditional Africa. Gospel values such as love, unity, generosity, respect for parents and life, honesty, forgiveness and reconciliation, hard

---

[92] Magesa, *Rethinking Mission*, 86.
[93] Magesa, *Rethinking Mission*, 67.

work, hospitality, and sharing among others, are esteemed in traditional Africa. This is corroborated by Mbiti, who states, "Africans are notoriously religious"[94]

Mbiti is echoed by Nelson Mandela's concept of *Ubuntu* as stated by Steven McShane and Mary Ann Von Glinow: "Woven into the fabric of the African society is the concept of *Ubuntu*. The latter represents values, such as harmony, compassion, respect, human dignity, and unity. It is that profound African sense that each of us is human through the humanity of the other."[95]

The African-Christian synthesis of values has no room for violence. The Church should stress these values in its mission of evangelisation to root out violent conflict.

b). Adult Role Models for Dialogue and Conflict Resolution in Africa

Ilo writes, "The church in Africa must be the moral standard bearer of society and address herself to the historic problems of structures of sin in Africa. Christians in Africa must unite to articulate an Afro-Christian vision for a better Africa and provide moral leadership for the ordinary people of Africa."[96] I openly admit that role-model deficiency is a big challenge even within the internal structures of the Church. All Christians in Africa should exude the effects of the Gospel in their lives. This reality should be perceived in the way they live, and the ways they relate to each with love. "So by their fruits you will know them" (Mt 7:20).

---

[94] Mbiti, *African Religions and Philosophy*, 1.

[95] Steven L. McShane and Mary Ann Von Glinow, *Organizational Behaviour* (New York: McGraw-Hill, 2005), 43.

[96] Ilo, *The Face of Africa*, 291.

Corruption is the "exercise of official powers against public interest or abuse of public office for private gains."[97] In some African governments and even communities, corruption is defended and rewarded. Thus, the popular saying, a fruit does not fall far from the tree. Also, a goat eats the grass around the tree where it is tethered. This attitude ails and demeans Africa, putting many peoples' lives at stake. Ilo points out, "Western donors are constrained with the persistent begging by Africans… Poverty is perhaps the greatest insult to human dignity not only in Africa but also in the dark alleys of many cities in the world today."[98] He adds, "Poverty inferiorizes a person. It degrades a person and reduces self-confidence. Poverty closes a door to life. Poverty is the greatest weapon of mass destruction in the present world."[99]

I add to Ilo's words that poverty is what forces many Africans out of the continent. Poverty is what kills African immigrants on the high seas as they seek for green pasture. Poverty is what enslaves Africans in the so-called First World nations. Poverty subjects Africans to all sorts of abuses and even death, in and outside Africa. Yet, Africa is abundantly endowed with natural resources. Poverty is one of the leading causes of conflict in Africa, requiring the churches' urgent intervention.

Pondering this, Ilo laments:

> The face of Africa is contoured because of the failure in the management of her resources i.e., human, political, religious, cultural, economic and historical. The human capital has been badly managed making the African population a burden instead

---

[97] Anwar Shah, ed., *Performance Accountability and Combating Corruption* (Washington, DC: World Bank Publications, 2007), 234.
[98] Ilo, *The Face of Africa*, 129–30.
[99] Ilo, *The Face of Africa*, 129–30.

of a blessing. Today unemployment has become the greatest challenge facing young people in Africa.[100]

Poverty in Africa is evident in the sprawling scenes of street children and families, and surging crimes in urban and even rural Africa. Many of these children are involved in crime, just to survive. This is a serious social conflict, requiring the churches to persistently probe and convince their governments to address.

c) *The Holy Family as a Model for Conflict Resolution*

Many of the conflicts experienced in society could be managed in the family. The family in Africa could do better if it emulates the Holy Family's parenting prototype. For example, Mary and her husband Joseph lived in peace. They faithfully worked, earned a living, cared, loved, protected, and provided for their Son Jesus. They were available to their Son, and were concerned about his activities and whereabouts (Lk 2:41–52). Mary stood by her Son to the end (Jn 19:26). This is what is expected of parents or guardians to help stem conflicts in society.

d) *The Trinitarian Model*

Dialogue redirects humanity to its common origin and destiny (Wis 8:1; Acts 14:17; Rom 2:6–7: 1 Tim 2:4). The unity of the Holy Trinity is a powerful model of dialogue to be emulated by the churches in Africa. The Father is God, the Son is God, and the Holy Spirit is God. There are no distinctions in the Godhead, but only unity of purpose, as illustrated in Jesus' priestly prayer, "Holy Father, keep them in your name that you have given me, so that they may be one just as we are" (Jn 17:11). Jesus's disciples are expected to identify with God by practicing the unity of the Trinity.

---

[100] Ilo, *The Face of Africa*, 272.

e) The Incarnation Model

By the act of Incarnation, God became man and dwelt among us by dialogue (Lk 1:26–32). God humbled himself to dialogue with humanity, without losing his Godhead (Phil 2:6–11). Humility is important in dialogue and conflict resolution, among other attributes.

According to Teri Kwal Gamble and Michael Gamble, dialogue is "approval of one's self-concept by another."[101] Mary was free to accept or reject God's proposal, a sign that God created us with a free will and respects our choices, but for which we should be responsible. The angel patiently waits for Mary's "*FIAT*" ("YES"), and then he leaves (Lk 1:38).

Thereafter Mary visits her cousin Elizabeth not to lament but to share the good news through the song of praise, the Magnificat (Lk 1:46–55). Celebration and jubilation form a yard-stick for a well-resolved conflict.

Conclusion

The churches' role in dialogue and conflict resolution in Africa is commendable. Nonetheless, the struggle continues, owing to intermittent conflicts on the continent. A survey of conflict experiences, causes and methods of resolution in Africa reveals that Africa is richly endowed. Exacerbation of conflict comes from corruption, bad leadership and mismanagement, and ethnocentrism and nepotism. Some of these vices have unfortunately infiltrated the internal structures of the Church. Churches are challenged to lead by example, to rid themselves of counter-witness, to reclaim their prophetic role, to stand in solidarity with the poor and vulnerable, and to put their respective governments to account and reimbursement, where necessary.

---

[101] Teri Kwal Gamble and Michael Gamble, *Communication Works*, 7th ed. (New York: McGraw-Hill, 2000), 20.

Agents of evangelisation must re-evaluate their evangelizing methods, and incorporate African traditional values and strategies in dialogue and conflict transformation. The Church must pay attention to the family, since this is the cradle of individual and social values. Further, a lack of suitable role models is contributing to conflict in society. Ideal models are available from the Trinity, the Incarnation, and the Holy Family as dialogue and conflict resolution prototypes for Africa.

Bibliography

Abidemi-Asanbe, Jude. "Evangelization: Challenges and Prospects for the Church in Africa." *African Ecclesia Review (AFER)* 47, no. 3 (2005): 199–218.

Achermann, Eduard. *Cry Beloved Africa! A Continent Needs Help.* Munich: Kinshasa African University Studies, 1996.

AMECEA. *The African Synod Comes Home: A Simplified Text.* Nairobi: Paulines Publications Africa, 1995.

Berilengar, Antoine. "Advocacy for Just Distribution of Oil Revenues: The Case of Chad." In *Peace Weavers: Methodologies of Peace Building in Africa,* edited by Elias Omondi Opongo, 87. Nairobi: Paulines Publications Africa, 2008.

Bragotti, Joseph, et al. *We Pray and Sing to the Lord.* Nairobi: Paulines Publications Africa, 1990.

The Congregation for Institute of Consecrated Life and Societies of Apostolic Life. *New Wine in New Wineskins: The Consecrated Life and Its Ongoing Challenges Since Vatican II.* Nairobi: Paulines Publications Africa, 2018.

Dandala, Hamilton Mvumelwano. "The Challenges of Ecumenism in African Christianity Today." In *African Theology on the Way. Current Conversations,* edited by Diane B. Stinton, 104. London, UK: Society for Promoting Christian Knowledge, 2010.

Francis. *Address of Pope Francis, Meeting with the Brazil's Leaders of Society, Municipal Theatre, Rio De Janeiro.* Vatican web site, July 27, 2013. http://w2.vatican.va/content/francesco/en/speeches/2013/july/documents/papa-francesco_20130727_gmg-classe-dirigente-rio.html.

— — —. *Evangelii Gaudium.* Apostolic exhortation. Vatican web site, November 24, 2013. www.vatican.va/content/francesco/

en/apost_exhortations/documents/papa-francesco_esortazione-ap_20131124_evangelii-gaudium.html.

Gamble, Teri Kwal, and Michael Gamble. *Communication Works*, 7th ed. New York: McGraw-Hill, 2000.

Ghosh, Biswanath. *Human Resource Development and Management*. New Delhi: Vikas Publishing House, 2000.

Government of Kenya, "Report of the Commission of Inquiry into the Post-Election Violence." Nairobi: Government Printer, 2008.

Griffin, E. M. *A First Look at Communication Theory*. New York: McGraw-Hill, 2000.

Ilo, Stan Chu. *The Face of Africa: Looking Beyond the Shadows*. Bloomington, IN: AuthorHouse, 2006.

John Paul II. *Post-synodal apostolic exhortation Ecclesia in Africa of the Holy Father John Paul II to the bishops, priests and deacons, men and women religious and all the lay faithful on the Church in Africa and its evangelizing mission towards the year 2000*. Nairobi: Paulines Publications Africa, 1995.

— — —. *Sollicitudo rei Socialis*. Papal encyclical. Vatican web site, December 30, 1987. www.vatican.va/content/john-paul-ii/en/encyclicals/documents/hf_jp-ii_enc_30121987_sollicitudo-rei-socialis.html.

Kenyatta, Jomo. "Building Christian Communities," opening address to AMECEA Bishops' Plenary. *African Ecclesia Review (AFER)* 18, no. 5 (1976): 1.

Korir, Cornelius. *Amani Mashinani (Peace at the Grassroots): Experiences of Community Peacebuilding in the North Rift Region of Kenya*. Eldoret, Kenya: Catholic Diocese of Eldoret, 2009.

Magesa, Laurenti. *Rethinking Mission: Evangelization in Africa in a New Era*. Eldoret, Kenya: AMECEA Gaba Publications, 2006.

Maluleke, Tinyiko Sam. "A Postcolonial South African Church: Problems and Promises." In *African Theology on the Way: Current*

Conversations, edited by Diane B. Stinton, 157. London, UK: Society for Promoting Christian Knowledge, 2010.

Mbillah, Johnson A. "Interfaith Relations in Africa." In *African Theology on the Way. Current Conversations*, edited by Diane B. Stinton, 113. London, UK: Society for Promoting Christian Knowledge, 2010.

Mbiti, John S. *African Religions and Philosophy*. London: Heinemann, 1969.

McKenzie, John L. *Authority in the Church*. New York: Sheed and Ward, 1966.

McShane, Steven L., and Mary Ann Von Glinow. *Organizational Behaviour*. New York: McGraw-Hill, 2005.

Mefalopulos, Paolo. *Development Communication Source Book: Broadening the Boundaries of Communication*. Washington, DC: World Bank Publications, 2008.

Mwaura, Philomena Njeri. "Christian Identity and Ethnicity in Africa: Reflections on the Gospel of Reconciliation." In *African Theology on the Way: Current Conversations*, edited by Diane B. Stinton, 132–33. London, UK: Society for Promoting Christian Knowledge, 2010.

Nabushawo, Justin Clemancy. "Editorial." *African Ecclesial Review (AFER)* 51, no. 3 (2009).

Nyirabega, Euthalie. "Transitional Justice in Rwanda: The courts and challenges of reconciliation." In *Peace Weavers: Methodologies of Peace Building in Africa*, edited by Elias Omondi Opongo. Nairobi: Paulines Publications Africa, 2008), 225.

Odama, John Baptist. "Conflict Resolution, Peacebuilding and Reconciliation in Northern Uganda." *African Ecclesial Review (AFER)* 51, no. 3 (2009).

Okumu, Martha. "The Impact of Regional Networking in the Great Lakes Region: The PTN Experience." In *Peace Weavers:*

Methodologies of Peace Building in Africa, edited by Elias Omondi Opongo, 103–4. Nairobi: Paulines Publications Africa, 2008.

Opongo Elias Omondi. "The Church on the Road to Emmaus: Situational Analysis of Conflicts, Wars and Instability in AMECEA Countries." *African Ecclesial Review (AFER)* 51, no. 3 (2009).

Orobator, Agbonkhianmeghe E. "Catholic Teaching and Peacemaking in Africa: A Tale of Two Traditions." In *Peace Weavers: Methodologies of Peace Building in Africa*, edited by Elias Omondi Opongo, 39. Nairobi: Paulines Publications Africa, 2008.

Page, Don. *Effective Team Leadership: Learning to Lead Through Relationships*. Nairobi: Evangel Publishing House, 2008.

Rayudu, C. S. *Media and Communication Management*. Mumbai: Himalaya Publishing House, 1998.

Shah, Anwar, ed. *Performance Accountability and Combating Corruption*. Washington, DC: World Bank Publications, 2007.

Waliggo, John Mary. "The Synod of Hope at a Time of Crisis in Africa." In *African Theology on the Way: Current Conversations*, edited by Diane B. Stinton, 44–45. London, UK: Society for Promoting Christian Knowledge, 2010.

White, John. *IC's Role in Competitiveness and Innovation*. New Delhi: Maya Publishers, 2003.

CHAPTER THREE

Fraternal Solidarity and the Ethics of Care and Compassion in Church and State in Africa: A Theological Re-reading of *Things Fall Apart*[102]

Ikenna U. Okafor

Introduction

The centrality and pervasive presence of the ethic of care in the African social space is undeniable. In the Igbo language of the Southeast Nigeria, for example, the term for "poor man or woman" is a compound word, "*Ogbenye*," (*Ogbe* = clan + *nye* = give) which means "let the clan give." Here, the verb "give" is expressed as an imperative, a kind of moral injunction or commandment. This means that in the very concept of poverty lies an intrinsic communicated sense of obligation for the clan to cater for those who cannot cater for themselves.

The poor man or woman, therefore, is one whose wellbeing has become the responsibility of the clan. So imbedded was the ethic of care in the morphology of the Igbo language that the very idea of eradicating poverty was essentially seen as a common burden and a function of the polis. In this concept, the state or community is enjoined not merely with alleviating material

---

[102] *Things Fall Apart* is a classic African novel written by Chinua Achebe and first published in 1958, in which he plotted pre-colonial life in south-eastern Nigeria, the arrival of Europeans, and the socio-cultural impact the encounter had on the Igbo communities during the late nineteenth century. The edition of the book quoted in this chapter is (London: Everyman's library, 1992).

poverty but of providing all kinds of security especially to the weaker members of the society.

Now the questions begging for answers from the foregoing are: To what extent has the above understanding of the fundamental imperative to give attention to the needs of our weaker brothers and sisters permeated the consciousness of African political and religious institutions? How far does the awareness of the social responsibility to care influenced the behaviour of those invested with public authority and privileges in their day to day relationship with the poor and the vulnerable? How can theology today help contemporary African men and women to retrieve the importance of the social values of care, compassion, and fraternal solidarity, which are inscribed originally in some African languages and thoughts?

To answer these questions, we need to evaluate the African Church's appreciation of the ethic of care as well as appraise the heritage of that ethic that are found in African postcolonial literatures. In this chapter, I have chosen to evaluate the ethic of care in Africa from the point of view of Chinua Achebe's famous novel, *Things Fall Apart*. That narrative shows how this icon of modern African literature tried to illuminate African social morality to enable us to deplore the marginalisation of the ethic of care and compassion in African socio-political constitutions.

My understanding of care in this context derives from Joan C. Tronto's[103] exposition, in which caring presupposes a sort of compassionate engagement with the needs of others in such a way as to engender responsible actions toward supplying those needs or eliminating whatever obstacles that stand in the way of satisfying those needs. Achebe's narrative is a critique of the State which will help us to understand the undesirable consequences

---

[103] Tronto's ideas on the ethic of care, however, are from a feminist perspective which is not the focus of this chapter. Care and compassion are not, nor should they be relegated to the exclusive confines of "women's morality. See Joan C. Tronto, Moral Boundaries: A Political Argument for an Ethic of Care (NY: Routledge, 1993).

of the marginalisation of care and compassion. At the end, I will use a matrix framework to recommend what the Church in Africa should do to show a plausible engagement with the ethic of care in a continent populated with so many needy persons. A question we cannot avoid here though is: How important is this ethic to the Church's evangelical mission in Africa?

Ethic of Care and the First African Synod

The ethic of care and compassion as well as fraternal solidarity have always been the bedrock of Jesus' ministry on earth—a ministry of fraternal charity which he entrusted to his disciples with the imperative to spread and perpetuate it till the end of time (cf. Mt 28:20). The Lord's teachings accentuate the centrality of the social dimension of Christian spirituality, which are vividly illustrated with such parables as the Good Samaritan (Lk 10:25-37), the Good Shepherd (Lk 15:3-7; Mt 18:12-14) and the Last Judgment (Mt 25:31-46).

Fidelity to these teachings is the hallmark of Christian discipleship and one of the fundamental criteria for embodying the Church. For this reason, Africa's commemoration of the major milestones in her journey with the Lord compels us to undertake a reflective inventory that memorizes and appraises Africa's commitment to the evangelical mission of care, compassion, and fraternal solidarity by taking stock of the challenges and opportunities that have defined that journey of faith, hope and love, which the world celebrates as Christianity in Africa. One of the moments of hope that enlightened the path of that journey was the First Synod of Bishops for Africa, which set out, among other things, to "promote an *organic pastoral solidarity* within the entire African territory and the adjacent Islands"(*EIA*, 5, 16).

That First African Synod of April 10 to May 8, 1994 did well to identify Africa's problems, offer solutions, and propose those who should carry out these solutions. The outcome of the synod, published by Pope John Paul II in his apostolic exhortation,

Ecclesia in Africa (1995), demanded from theologians in Africa the task of working out "the theology of the Church as Family with all the riches contained in this concept [Family], showing its complementarity with other images of the Church" (*EIA*, 102).

It was envisaged then that such a theology of the Church as family should not ignore the harrowing conditions of African sons and daughters burdened by abject poverty. It must neither overlook the crushing debt, the currency devaluation, nor the selfish political interests tearing Africa asunder and fuelling fratricidal hate and wars (*EIA*, 13). The all-pervading despair in the continent was expected to serve as a springboard for a message of hope that the gospel promises. In fact, the synod understood itself as an occasion of hope and resurrection (*EIA*, 1).

To talk about a resurrection, however, presupposes that something died. What died, I argue, was solidarity. The Synod Fathers emphasised the missionary vocation of an African Church called to witness to Christ through prayer, sacrifice, and effective solidarity (*EIA*, 56). It is from this perspective of the synod's efforts and hope to revive the spirit of solidarity and thus salvage Africa from a socio-ethical death that this chapter evaluates the Church's engagement with the continent's social context. The synod commenced with a genuine concern about what the Church must do to be truly seen as a responsible mother to a family of hungry, ailing, and dying children whose wellbeing has become a great challenge and litmus test of Africa's witness to the gospel.

This concern has not been diminished more than 25 years later. Confronted today with Africa's ever-worsening social condition, the Church in Africa must ask herself the following questions: What can the Church do to translate the message of the gospel into concrete manifestations of abundant life in Africa? What has the Church been doing wrongly or neglected so far, and what has she learnt from the crucibles of African sociopolitical situation? What does it mean for the Church in Africa to be truly "salt and light" of the continent and its peoples? How can she appropriate the indigenous tools of knowledge and use them to lead and educate the people of Africa on their collective responsibility to restore the battered image of the continent?

In response to these questions, I think that the Church can invoke the legacies of the widely acclaimed father of modern African literature, Chinua Achebe, whose postcolonial narrative in *Things Fall Apart* has provided us an apt resource material for a hermeneutical phenomenology with which theologians can interpret and understand Africa's burden. Achebe's narrative is arguably a plausible interpretive tool for a moral and theological evaluation of the ethic of care in Africa's faith-pilgrimage. The need to revisit that narrative cannot be overemphasised, for he "who does not know where the rain began to beat him cannot say where he dried his body."[104] Achebe's critique of coloniality is at the same time a critique of Africa's marginalisation of her own ethic of care and compassion — a marginalisation which the colonial intruder has shrewdly exploited to disrupt and destroy the existing traditional structures of solidarity. African theologians who seek to develop a theology of the Church as family may need to tap into the wealth of that narrative.

Critique of Coloniality

We may ask what Achebe's postcolonial narrative has got to do with theology and the ethic of care and fraternal solidarity. First of all, we recall that the intellectual revolution that started in the seventies and eighties with the emergence of the phenomenon that came to be known in theological historiography as "the irruption of the third world"[105] was an offspring of the African

---

[104] Chinua Achebe, *There Was a Country*, (New York: The Penguin Press, 2012), 1. This is Achebe's adaptation of an Igbo proverb to underscore the importance of cultural and historical memory.

[105] See Fabella Virginia and Torres Sergio, eds. *Irruption of the Third World: Challenge to Theology* (Maryknoll, N.Y.: Orbis Books, 1983) This was the publication of the

decolonising literary critique from which Achebe emerged. The revolution, which is part of Africa's witness to the gospel, ushered in a new dialectical process that gave voice to African theology.

At no time in history has the Church's relationship with the poor and exploited in the modern world been more contentious than at this time of irruption when theologians from Africa, Latin America, and Asia aligned themselves together to challenge the legitimacy of the Western domination of theological hermeneutics. Contextual theologies of liberation, feminism, and inculturation, with unmistakable anti-colonial thrusts emerged. Their discourse challenged the structures of injustice that have been hitherto condoned or even exacerbated by the Church.

For example, economic exploitation of the poor, racial injustice, gender inequality, discrimination, and Western cultural imperialism gained new attention in theological discourse that deplored the ideological neutrality with which the Church tacitly endorsed the unjust social status quo. Anti-colonial criticism became a dominant topic in theology and numerous authors blamed Africa's ills on colonialism. The ethic of care, understood as a pathos and fundamental option for the poor, began to inspire a new social anti-hegemonic critique of a culture of dominance.

These nascent theologies criticised so-called Western knowledge for organising itself philosophically through "binary oppositions," which resulted in "demonising or denigrating" the other. This led to an eventual shift from anti-colonial to postcolonial discourse in African theology. The postcolonial critique and voice, understood as a critical stance,[106] and as language that

---

volume of the papers presented at the fifth conference of EATWOT held in New Delhi India from August 17 to 29, 1981.

[106] Sugirtharajah R. S., *Postcolonial Reconfigurations: An Alternative Way of Reading and Doing Theology*, (London: SCM Press, 2003), 13-16

gives voice to the marginalised[107] originated in the literature department, with its openness to "subjective" and "experiential" knowledge.[108]

Chinua Achebe, being among Africa's most prominent products of the literature department, became one of the most vociferous critics of coloniality and a tall beacon of Africa's cultural renaissance. His earliest and most influential works encapsulate the leading idea of postcolonialism and arguably provide a critical dialectic to the theological discourse on Africa's encounter with Christendom.

As a theory of social criticism, postcolonialism seeks to develop what is called the "third space:" where binary dichotomies like civilised/uncivilised, coloniser/colonised, man/woman, and master/slave are no longer starkly oppositional nor exclusively singular, but defined by their intricate and mutual relations. This "third space" is a sacred space characterised by social justice, equality, dignity of the human person, compassion, and hospitality. It finds expression in a theology of fraternal solidarity and inclusion which aims to undermine binary formulations of difference while considering the social maladies that afflict the people of God in Africa.

This post-colonial vision was articulated in the 1994 synodal ecclesiology of the Church as a "family of God" which emphasised care for others, solidarity, warmth in human relationships,

---

[107] See Heaney Robert S., *From Historical to Critical Post-Colonial Theology: The Contribution of John S. Mbiti and Jesse N. K. Mugambi*, (Oregon: Pickwick Publications, 2015), 15. Postcolonial critique, according to Robert Young, marks the moment where the political and cultural experience of the marginalized periphery developed into a more general theoretical position that could be set against western politics, intellectual and academic hegemony and its protocols of objective knowledge. See Young Robert, *Postcolonialism: An Historical Introduction*, (Oxford: Blackwell, 2001), 65.

[108] Ibid., 61-66. See Heaney Robert S., *From Historical to Critical Post-Colonial Theology*, (Oregon: Pickwick Publications, 2015), 15f.

acceptance, dialogue and trust.[109] African theologians' reception of that ecclesiology,[110] set the intellectual tone for the development of a theology of fraternity[111] and its corresponding Christologies[112] in Africa. The wisdom and enlightenment of the Synod Fathers in birthing that ecclesiological understanding of the Church cannot be overemphasized. It marked the Church's appreciation of authentic African theological development.

A glance at Africa's history indicates that there is a common denominator that connects the present day to the historical moment of the First African Synod and the earlier colonial times. That common denominator is the widespread awareness that "things are falling apart" in Africa. Africa's chronic inability to establish stable institutions that could guarantee human prosperity has become a recalcitrant albatross that makes it difficult for her to challenge her marginalisation in the world today. Achebe's critique helps to identify and analyse Africa's ailment in a constructive way that can benefit the Church in Africa.

We may not be able to give a comprehensive summary of Achebe's *Things Fall Apart* here but let us quickly note that the novel is divided into two parts. The first part showcases the values of enterprise, fearlessness, gallantry, which are personified in the chief protagonist, Okonkwo, and which are adjudged as *manliness*.[113] These were values which the precolonial Igbo so-

---

[109] John Paul II, *Ecclesia in Africa*, 63

[110] The Second African Synod which focused on reconciliation, justice, and peace, is seen as a reception of that ecclesiology.

[111] Ikenna Okafor, *Toward an African Theology of Fraternal Solidarity: Ube Nwanne*, (Eugene, Oregon: Pickwick Publications, 2014).

[112] Charles Nyamiti, *Jesus Christ, the Ancestor of Humankind: Methodological and Trinitarian Foundations. Vol. 1 of Studies in African Christian Theology* (Nairobi: Catholic University of eastern Africa, 2005); Benezet Bujo, *African Theology in Its Social Context* (Nairobi: Paulines, 1992); Diane B. Stinton, *Jesus of Africa: Voices of Contemporary African Christology*, (Maryknoll, NY: Orbis, 2004).

[113] Chinua Achebe, *Things Fall Apart*, ibid, 58. Here, in the eight chapter of the novel, Okonkwo's killing of Ikemefuna was referred to as "his latest show of manliness."

ciety of the novel appears to celebrate to the detriment of the values of compassion, care, and solidarity — the so-called "women's morality" whose marginalisation in political theories have been the cause of some feminists' grouse.

The first part of the novel, however, culminates in Okonkwo's banishment into exile while his friend Obierika muses sorrowfully over the cruelty of a traditional system that condones, in fact, legislates the killing of innocent twin babies, and metes out severe and disproportionate punishments for inadvertent offences.[114] Achebe attacks precisely this lack of sensibility which repudiates traditional humane ethos that are encapsulated in concepts like "Ogbenye." Hence, *Things Fall Apart* does not encourage an uncritical celebratory return to a glorious past whose growth was nipped at the bud by extrinsic forces.

On the contrary, Achebe blames the weakness of Africa's resistance to imperial power and the primary cause of her capitulation to colonial subjugation not on the invincibility of the colonial intruder, but rather on the internal social disintegration that arose in Africa in the wake of colonial intrusion, a disintegration exemplified in the loss of brotherhood, unity, and inclusion. What appears ostensibly to be a cultural criticism that seeks to contradict European prejudice against Africa, in fact, turns out to be an indictment of an endemic lack of fraternal solidarity as the root of social injustice, institutional collapse, and suffering in Africa.

As Stan Chu Ilo rightly observes, conversion of hearts and cultures are central to transforming society and removing the obstacles toward realising the divine purposes for a particular society and context. For, any community, whether it is as small as a clan or as large as a nation or the globe, that is not realising the purpose or mission for its existence ought to look into systems and structures as well as the ethical template on which that

---

[114] Cf. Chinua Achebe, *Things Fall Apart*, ibid., 110f

society is built and sustained.¹¹⁵ Achebe's postcolonial critique is thus invariably an eloquent reproach of the tragic theatre of modern African politics in a continent that has raised indifference to the plights of the poor, corruption, and bigotry to the status of culture, where the privilege of public office has ironically become sometimes an unholy opportunity to plunder the common wealth.

In that Achebe's critique, the vulnerable become unfortunate expendables whose ordeals exact from us a necessary moral condemnation of a system that appeases the capricious gods of fundamentalism, chauvinism, jingoism, and all the structural isms of an unjust society. Therefore, Achebe's classic novel, in addition to being a work of art in cultural and historical memory, provides a theological compass to a Church that genuinely wants to be family, to enable her pass a fair and unmitigated judgment on human hubris in African society.

Achebe's *Things Fall Apart*: A Phenomenological Commentary on the Ethics of Care and Compassion in African Society

> "That boy calls you father. Do not bear a hand in his death."¹¹⁶
>
> - Chinua Achebe, *Things Fall Apart*

It is important to understand what precipitated the above statement in *Things Fall Apart* to appreciate its significance in the context of an ethic of care and compassion in Church and State in Africa. The oracle of the land had decreed that Ikemefuna,¹¹⁷

---

¹¹⁵ Stan Chu Ilo, *A Poor and Merciful Church: The Illuminative Ecclesiology of Pope Francis* (Maryknoll, NY: Orbis Books, 2018) 166.

¹¹⁶ Chinua Achebe, *Things Fall Apart* (London: Everyman's library, 1992) 49.

¹¹⁷ Ikemefuna is the name of the boy Okonkwo killed in *Things Fall Apart*. He was a

a boy entrusted to Okonkwo's care, will be sacrificed to appease the gods. The above counsel came from an elder statesman, Ogbuefi Ezeudu, to restrain Okonkwo from participating in the ritual killing on the strength of the argument that a father should not kill his own son. In fact, the sagacious counsel summarises the moral principle that knits together the epic narrative of the African microcosm, the Umuofia clan, and her impetuous champion, Okonkwo.

The admonition discloses the obscure conflict of affectivity, of which the eventual outcome was doubly tragic. Being referred to as father is a recognition of special status, a conferment of honour to one as a guarantor of the highest form of filial affection. One is thus acknowledged as a provider of food, shelter, and security to one's dependents. Fatherhood is an honour, which only true love can confer. Okonkwo's rejection of that honour in favour of traditional loyalty was a tragic choice made on the presumption that he had no option. This is exactly what Achebe's implicit judgment contradicts. The narrative declares to us that there is always an option: To choose on the one hand a sterile dogmatism that celebrates uncritical loyalty to tradition, or on the other hand filial affection and humane concern for others and engagement with their needs, which the African ethic of compassion and care recommends. Unfortunately, it is the content of the latter—the ethic of care—that has become marginalised and denigrated as women's morality in the ideals of Okonkwo's political world.

Hence, what was at stake in the fictional colonial plot of Umuofia, as well as in the present socio-political situation of Africa, is the commitment to protect the most vulnerable of human society. Failure to do so is tantamount to destroying the very fabric of Africa's ethics of compassion and invariably the fountain of her communal vitality. Ezeudu's wise counsel

---

peace-oblation offered to avoid war between Umuofia and their neighbours.

underscores the inviolability of filial and fraternal love in African ethic. Ikemefuna, whose relationship to the man he calls father is more than putative, is like a son to Okonkwo. To betray that love and childlike trust is not only preposterous, it is a grave sin.[118]

Therefore, critics see Okonkwo's killing of Ikemefuna as an incredulous betrayal of a child's filial love and a repudiation of African family values.[119] The restraining counsel of Ezeudu presupposes that the African value system is more flexible than that of the missionaries. It is Okonkwo's failure to recognise the flexibility of that system and the sanctity of the autochthonous values it safeguards that brought his downfall. The resilience and potential universality of the African culture is thus tested by its affectivity to human vulnerability and suffering. That resilience lies in the humane ethic of care and fraternal solidarity that is documented in African pedagogy in such pithy sayings like "let no one ignore his/her brother's/sister's cry" ("*O nụrụ ube nwanne agbala ọsọ*") in the Igbo language. In other words, one can say that our culture encounters God not in the unbending dogmas and traditions, no matter how lofty and idyllic they may seem. Rather, our culture encounters God in the spirituality of compassionate response to the cry of another. Theology and religion do not have to choose between God and the poor, for in choosing the poor, we have already chosen God. This explains why the death of Ikemefuna became a negative turning point that marks a downward spiral in Okonkwo's rise to fame.

Again, it is important to note that the choice of the name "Ikemefuna" has a deep theological significance enshrouded in liminality. The name, which means "may my strength (or power) not be lost," arguably was deliberately chosen by Achebe in

---

[118] Okonkwo's friend, Obierika, chides him that "it is the kind of action for which the goddess wipes out whole families. See Achebe, Things Fall Apart, ibid., 58.

[119] Emmanuel Obiechina, "The Igbo Home in Achebe's Fiction," in Emenyonu Ernest N & Uko Iniobong I eds., *Emerging Perspectives on Chinua Achebe, Vol. 2* (Eritrea: Africa World Press, 2004) 179.

relation to Okonkwo, who Achebe determined to be the boy's foster father and caretaker. It could be interpreted as referring to Okonkwo's strength and invariably the strength of the traditions his character valorises. Hence, Africa, represented in this case by the microcosm of Umuofia town, is painted as a closed society struggling to guard its source of strength against the experience of a culture-shock of tremendous magnitude.

However, Africa's true strength or power [*ike*] ideally lies in the culture of inclusiveness and in the way in which she treats the weakest and the most vulnerable members of her society. This is true not only of Africa but of any human society. The strength of the social contract lies in the power of fraternal solidarity, which is the cohesive force of every community, and which Africans express variously with concepts such as "let no one leave his sister or brother behind" [*onye aghala nwanne ya*]; "I am because we are" [*ubuntu*]; or "familyhood or togetherness" [*ujamaa*].

It is a power whose potency derives from the community's own closeness to and harmony with the divine subject — a harmony expressed in ritualised forms of customs and ordinances. And whenever ordinances come into conflict with human affectivity, the human takes precedence over the religious. The dilemma involved in such a choice is the tension that runs through the entire narrative of *Things Fall Apart*. Okonkwo's refusal to cherish Ikemefuna's filial bond and affection to him as a treasure can be seen as Achebe's attempt at identifying the root of Africa's real problems and the explanation for the continent's abysmal weakness in the face of a colonial power.

Okonkwo's exiled condition after the killing of Ikemefuna is a metaphor for his desolate spirit. It is a sign of the rupture of divine-human relationship, which is a condition of sin. His inability or unwillingness to free himself from the shackles of an insensible tradition and show empathy to a child who calls him father thus marks the beginning of his own self-destruction. But beyond its damning implication for Okonkwo's personal destiny, the killing of Ikemefuna also represents for the African microcosm (Umuofia) the symbolical birth of Ichabod — the departure of the glory of God from the clan (cf. 1 Sm 4: 20-22).

As David Carroll rightly points out, "As we watch him [Ikemefuna] being taken unsuspectingly on this apparently innocent journey, the whole tribe and its values is being judged and found wanting."[120] Likewise, the demise of millions of innocent African daughters and sons who perish out of hunger and other preventable causes as a result of political and social irresponsibility indict African leaders of all cadres. So much is arguably exemplified in Okonkwo's exile. The lesson therein is that the politically privileged and the powerful do have a great responsibility in society to put the power of their political mandate in service of tearing down inhuman structures and practices and replacing them with more humane ones that foster justice, equity, and fraternity; otherwise, they would risk Ichabod, that is, they would risk emptying society and communal life of its divine element.

For, whatever will make a society appear cruel cannot be justified by law. Okonkwo's failure to rise to this responsibility despite his political influence and status in Umuofia sealed his tragic fate both as *pater familias* and as a political vanguard of an old order. Therefore, as Ato Quayson rightly points out, Okonkwo is at various times in the book "ironized by the text, suggesting the inadequacy of the values he represents and ultimately those of the hierarchy that ensures his social status. It is important to stress that it is not just Okonkwo's values that are shown as inadequate, but those of the patriarchal society in general; he represents an extreme manifestation of the patriarchy that pervades the society as a whole."[121]

---

[120] David Carroll, *Chinua Achebe, Novelist, Poet, Critic* (London: Macmillan Press, 1980) 45f.

[121] Ato Quayson, "Realism, Criticism and the Disguises of Both: A Reading of Chinua Achebe's Things Fall Apart with an Evaluation of the Criticism Relating to It" in Isdore Okpewho ed., *Chinua Achebe's Things Fall Apart: A Case Book* (Oxford

The tragic theatre of contemporary African politics (which includes Church politics) in a way reprises this unfortunate moment of *Things Fall Apart* in a continent that has raised corruption to the status of culture and where the *Ikemefunas* are directly and indirectly exterminated daily by the *Okonkwos* in deplorable acts of chauvinism, clericalism, sexism, fundamentalism, and/or jingoistic loyalties. A theological "re-cognition" of Africa's colonial past should pass judgment on such a socio-political derailment. Therefore, when interpreted from this perspective, *Things Fall Apart* actually laments the fact that it is the vultures of human hubris and not the doves of human fraternity and compassion who often dominate the theatre of history. African history could regain its nobility if it could become a history of salvation onto fraternal solidarity.

Sadly, a parallelism exists between Okonkwo's paternal role and the Church's maternal role and her ecclesial responsibility to provide succour to those who seek refuge under her maternal patronage of pastoral care. The thorny challenge of the African Church today is that of being a true witness of the good news to the poor. The Galilean ministry of Jesus Christ which was inaugurated on the foundation of the promise of Isaiah's prophecy (cf. Lk 4:18-19; Is 61:1-2) is yet to be re-enacted fully on African soil. The 2019 national multidimensional poverty rates in Sub-Saharan Africa, for example, range from 6.3 to 91.9 percent with an average rate of 57.5 percent.[122]

This means that the hope of liberation to the downtrodden which Jesus announced remains forlorn in Africa. And if we ask the question: "Who cares?", there is no doubt that the Church should care. The unfortunate tragedy of the African Church today, however, is the betrayal sometimes of the hopes of sons

---

University Press, 2003), 234.

[122] UNDP, "The 2019 Global Multidimensional Poverty Index (MPI)". Accessed Online 18.06.2020: http://hdr.undp.org/en/2019-MPI

and daughters who flock to evangelical ministries in desperate search for miracles to alleviate their suffering. Most end up being abused and fleeced by self-serving clerics who are no more than wolves in sheep's clothing.

The role of the Church as *Mater et Magister* (Mother and Teacher) in Africa requires a compassionate and caring intervention that will put reins on the infamous prosperity gospel whose exaggerated emphasis on paying tithes and "sowing seeds in cash" to reap the fruits of divine providence, is an example of some spiritual leaders' deplorable predatory greed, abuse, and turning of the gospel into an instrument of extortion. Such prosperity gospel is anchored on a "break-through" theology that presents God as a rewarder of laziness and mediocrity– a warped theology that was designed by pastors for the purpose of exploiting their gullible followers.

What Must We Do?

The fathers and mothers of the First African Synod already observed that the main question facing the Church in Africa consists of delineating as clearly as possible what it is and what it must fully carry out, in order that its message be relevant and credible. The synod believes that the answer consists in the African Church really believing what she proclaims: living what she believes and preaching what she lives. For the Church's "social doctrine will gain credibility more immediately from *witness of action* than as a result of its internal logic and consistency" (*EIA*, 21).

Against the backdrop of the foregoing analysis, the theme of the Pan-African Catholic Theological Congress was aimed at seeking practical solutions to the enormous challenges facing Africa: "What must we do to perform the works of God?" (Jn 6: 28). We must not forget that this question was preceded and, in fact, elicited by the miracle of the loaves. The synoptic accounts of that gratuitous miracle have an important element that theology and pastoral praxis should not ignore.

As his disciples asked him to send the hungry masses away so that they may fetch food for themselves, Jesus replied, "Give them something to eat yourselves!" (Mt 14:16; Mk 6:37; Lk 9:13). Therefore, what the Church in Africa must do must be modelled after what Christ himself did. I propose here a four Ps matrix-approach which corresponds to the actions of Christ himself, namely, proclaim, plan, pray, and provide. The gospel of Mark which is the oldest account of the miracle of the loaves reflects these four Ps adequately as we shall see in the matrix below.

Proclaim	Plan
"When he disembarked and saw the vast crowd, his heart was moved with pity for them, for they were like sheep without a shepherd; and he began to teach them many things" (Mk 6:34).	He asked them, "How many loaves do you have? Go and see." And when they had found out they said, "Five loaves and two fish." So he gave orders to have them sit down in groups on the green grass. The people took their places in rows by hundreds and by fifties (Mk 6: 38-40).
Pray	**Provide**
Then, taking the five loaves and the two fish and looking up to heaven, he said the blessing, (Mk 6:41).	[He] broke the loaves, and gave them to (his) disciples to set before the people; he also divided the two fish among them all. They all ate and were satisfied (Mk 6: 41b-42).

What must we do?
What Jesus did.

Proclamation

The most fundamental aspect of the ethic of care is a sense of being deeply moved by the encounter with situations of abject poverty and misery. It begins with identifying the problem(s) and experiencing a feeling of intimate and personal immersion in the condition of deprivation without which empathy and sincere engagement with the needs of the afflicted cannot be possible. The fruit of such empathy is the proclamation of the kingdom of God and healing (cf. Lk 9:11). The Church proclaims this kingdom by enkindling the light of hope in the hearts of the suffering masses, giving them the assurance that their miserable condition is not the final verdict of an omnipotent and merciful God.

This proclamation arises from the Church's awareness of her missionary discipleship which compels her to provide hope through education, food, and integral healing where hitherto ignorance, hunger, despair, brokenness, and diseases abound. The African Church must not fail to exercise her prophetic function in a way reminiscent of the prophecy of Ezekiel: "I will open your graves and have you rise from them, and bring you back to the land of Israel. Then you shall know that I am the LORD, when I open your graves and have you rise from them, O my people!" (Ez 37:12-13).

The First African Synod already captures this meaning in its description of its engagement with the African predicament as a moment of resurrection. The Church in African is already visibly present and active in the education sector of the society, especially at the primary and secondary school levels. She should in addition be well-equipped and evangelically committed to assume leadership in providing quality and affordable education capable of lifting the children of the poor from the graves of illiteracy and ignorance. She should also design food and healthcare programmes that are proactive in alleviating hunger and providing succour to the wounded and traumatised in Africa. These gestures of accompaniment constitute the proclamation of hope which the Church is called to witness to.

Planning

The awakening of hope and the consciousness of her prophetic mission should further compel the Church in Africa to go deeper than identifying problems and having the goodwill to act. Like her master Jesus Christ, the Church should always have an informed knowledge of problems, the resources available to her as well as a clear vision of what needs to be done in every context and a praxis on how to do it.

The text of Mark 6:38-40 in the matrix above clearly illustrates this in the actions that Jesus undertook. It is extremely important that every diocese, and by extension, every parish and church institution in Africa learn to prioritise the use of available technologies and theories of business management in making budgetary and other plans that will guide its activities in every fiscal year. The best guarantee of success in every venture is good planning. Planning will help the Church in Africa gain a good knowledge of the resources available and prevent her from underestimating her potentials or from wishful thinking and spiritualizing the problem.

For, it is such underestimation that had turned the African Church into a beggar-Church. The hope of self-sufficiency, which was one of the dreams of the first African synod (cf. *EIA*, 104), cannot be realised unless the Church learns to put the resources available to her to optimal use through a rigorous process of planning and strategic orderliness in executing the plans. Just like Jesus demanded from his disciples to go research what is available, and then gave orders to have the people sitted in groups of hundreds and fifties (cf. Mk 6:39-40), the Church in Africa should also pay attention to details in her projects and initiatives. Such details and planning will help the Church in risk management and avoidance of waste of resources or executing elephant projects which are beyond the carrying capacity of local resources or the poor faithful.

Wealth does not fall from the sky in such dramatic way the prosperity gospel preachers prefer reading and interpreting some Old Testament prophetic texts like Malachi 3: 10-12. True religion and true Christianity must produce productive youth. Before Africa could experience positive change in this regard, the way Christianity is preached in the continent must change. Once speaking about corruption in Africa, one-time Director-General of the European Centre for Development Policy Management (ECDPM), Dieter Frisch, noted: "Nothing is more destructive to a society than the pursuit of 'a fast and easy buck' which makes honest people who work hard appear naive or foolish."[123]

The idea that the gospel promises instant wealth has led Africa to a generation of people that thirsts for instant results without any regard to the importance of business planning, creativity, strategy, innovation, market and customer analysis, responsibility, and honesty. Hence, what we refer to as planning here involves a cultural revolution that will change the way things are being done in Africa. This requires enthronement of new values, like honesty; accountability; finesse; orderliness; punctuality, which is the soul of business, and modesty and simplicity in the church's structures and institutions. Wealth must be created through a culture of industry and then distributed through the spirituality of fraternal solidarity.

Prayer

A Church that looks up to heaven is always connected to the source of her spiritual energy. The Church's immersion in the condition of the poor must assume a new dimension through prayer, otherwise she runs the risk of degenerating into a kind

---

[123] Dieter Frisch, "The effects of corruption on development" in *The Courier* - No. 158 – July-August 1996 Dossier Communication and the Media - Country Report, Cape Verde. Accessed Online: 15.04.2020: http://www.unimig.tsu.edu.ge/greenstone/cgi-bin/library.cgi

of NGO or an ideological bastion of either conservative or liberal leftist agenda. The psalmist is clear on the outcome of such a disconnection: "Unless the LORD builds the house, they labor in vain who build" (Ps 127:1). The treasuries of compassion and care flow from the divine mercy of God who intimately partakes, more than the Church, in the sufferings of the poor. Prayer in this matrix consists of all tasks that signify the Church's trust in divine providence and her commitment to the ethics of care and compassion, which is the soul of Jesus' ministry.

Understood as an establishment of heavenly connection, prayer is an essential cultural and spiritual practice that compels the Church as a strong institution to put herself in the service of social transformation for human prosperity in Africa. Prayer reminds the Church that the ethic of care and compassion is not just about promoting material prosperity per se, but about restoring human dignity and advancing civilisation—a spiritual renewal of the earth. It is a journey with the Lord, which the African Church must be willing to make to salvage her mission and identity as a sacrament of salvation to the African people. Prayer also brings to our consciousness the importance of humility as an indispensable virtue of an ethic that is expected to serve the downtrodden and the victimised.

The failure of the African microcosm (Umuofia) in Achebe's narrative lies in the absence of such humility in the temperaments of the most dominant vanguards of the traditional pre-colonial society that is described in that narrative. Prayer is the ability to listen to the inner voice of conscience where God directs our actions, mitigates our imperfections and lacks, and blesses our efforts with success. Okonkwo's lack of this connection to the divine voice made him believe that he had no other option than to trump the ethic of compassion on the altar of religious fundamentalism. The Church in Africa must resist the temptation of sacrificing ethical principles that protects the poor for the sake of enjoying perceived privilege that compromises her prophetic mission.

Provision

The First African Synod urged us not to forget that a Church is able to reach material and financial independence only if the people entrusted to her do not live in conditions of extreme poverty (*EIA*, 104). This means that for the sake of her own survival the Church in Africa must provide for the material needs of her poor children, for the empowerment of the poor is invariably the empowerment of the Church. The inability to do so weakens the Church and perhaps even gives a lie to her message of liberation and abundant life.

In the imitation of her Lord who fed more than five thousand people with five loaves and two fish, the Church could create food programmes that would require every parish to establish small to medium-scale enterprises that can provide employment at the grassroots. Jesus' instruction: "Give them some food yourselves" (Mk 6:37), obliges the Church to assume leadership in the solution to hunger and poverty in the world. Crop and vegetable farming, poultry farms, piggery, fishery, other types of animal husbandry, and small-scale food-processing industries, etc. are some examples of low capital investment ventures which the Church can initiate to provide food and jobs for the teeming unemployed youths in Africa. Jesus has taught us that no matter the paucity of our resources we should never underestimate divine providence. This is exactly what was enacted by the miracle of the loaves when what was available was multiplied into surplus to the satisfaction and amazement of all.

Conclusion

In his message for the 2020 World Day of the Poor, Pope Francis quoted the book of Sirach, which says, "Stretch forth your hand to the poor" (*Sir* 6:7). Then he commented: "Generosity that supports the weak, consoles the afflicted, relieves suffering, and restores dignity to those stripped of it, is a condition for a fully human life. The decision to care for the poor, for their many different needs, cannot be conditioned by the time available or by private interests, or by impersonal pastoral or social projects."[124]

In this chapter, I have tried to shed light on this ethic of care, compassion, and fraternal solidarity which the book of Sirach and Pope Francis recommend to the world. I have shown how it is a core ethic in traditional African social space, and the abandonment of these values is Africa's failure at the modernisation project in both African Christian enterprise and in Africa's postcolonial states. A new collapse whose indices are seen in the social fragmentation that we see in such phenomena as intractable conflicts, insurgencies, terrorism, IDPs, the havocs of the HIV pandemic, hunger, and abject poverty, provides a challenge and another opportunity for the Church to consolidate her message of hope in Africa.

When things begin to fall apart, as they allegedly do in Africa today, it could be a *Kairos* moment that requires the Church to listen to the "presbyterial" counsel of Ogbuefi Ezeudu of Achebe's narrative: "That boy calls you father!...." It is the time for a Church that is known as mother to show that the exclusion, or worse still the victimization of the vulnerable is anathema to the very essence of being Church. The Church should neither put a hand in anything that could destroy the lives of her hapless children, nor be inert in the face of the heart-rending echo of the African cry. On the contrary, she is challenged to demonstrate with compassion that she is indeed a mother that cares.

The recommendations here are not in any way exhaustive. However, the excursus on Achebe's postcolonial narrative does more than merely locate the ethic of care at the core of what binds African societies together. It encourages home-bred theo-

---

[124] Pope Francis, "Message of Pope Francis for the 2020 World Day of the Poor", (Zenit, June 13, 2020 17:32) accessed online: https://zenit.org/articles/message-of-pope-francis-for-2020-world-day-of-the-poor/?utm_medium=email&utm_campaign=

logical reflections, whose material cause is from the repository of Africa's cultural and historical heritage—the deposits of values or what it means in Africa to be truly human. It calls on us to rethink not only the marginalisation of care as "women's morality" in political theology, but also to rethink the idea of inculturation which has hitherto been reduced to a shallow notion of liturgical dancing around the eucharistic altar. Theology in Africa must be willing to undertake an archaeological expedition that excavates new and relevant academic meanings from African literatures. It must embrace African literature and history as authentic sources of revelation of God's message and God's self-communication to the African mind.

Bibliography

Achebe Chinua, *Things Fall Apart* (London: Everyman's library, 1992).

—————, *There Was A Country. A Personal History of Biafra* (New York: The Penguin Press, 2012).

Bujo Benezet, *African Theology in Its Social Context* (Nairobi: Paulines, 1992).

Carroll David, *Chinua Achebe, Novelist, Poet, Critic* (London: Macmillan Press, 1980).

Fabella Virginia and Torres Sergio, eds. *Irruption of the Third World: Challenge to Theology* (Maryknoll, N.Y.: Orbis Books, 1983).

Heaney Robert S., *From Historical to Critical Post-Colonial Theology: The Contribution of John S. Mbiti and Jesse N. K. Mugambi*, (Oregon: Pickwick Publications, 2015).

Ilo Stan Chu, *A Poor and Merciful Church: The Illuminative Ecclesiology of Pope Francis* (Maryknoll, NY: Orbis Books, 2018).

John Paul II, *Ecclesia in Africa*, Post-Synodal exhortation (Yaoundé, Cameroon, September 14, 1995).

Nyamiti Charles, *Jesus Christ, the Ancestor of Humankind: Methodological and Trinitarian Foundations. Vol. 1 of Studies in African Christian Theology* (Nairobi: Catholic University of eastern Africa, 2005).

Emenyonu Ernest N &Uko Iniobong I ed., *Emerging Perspectives on Chinua Achebe, Vol. 2*, (Eritrea: Africa World Press, 2004).

Okafor Ikenna, *Toward an African Theology of Fraternal Solidarity: Ube Nwanne*, (Eugene, Oregon: Pickwick Publications, 2014).

Okpewho Isdore, ed., *Chinua Achebe's Things Fall Apart: A Case Book*, (Oxford University Press, 2003).

Stinton Diane B., *Jesus of Africa: Voices of Contemporary African Christology* (Maryknoll, Ny: Orbis, 2004).

Sugirtharajah R. S., *Postcolonial Reconfigurations: An Alternative Way of Reading and Doing Theology*, (London: SCM Press, 2003).

Tronto Joan C., *Moral Boundaries: A Political Argument for an Ethic of Care* (New York: Routledge, 1993).

Young Robert, *Postcolonialism: An Historical Introduction*, (Oxford: Blackwell, 2001).

Dialogue and Reconciliation
in the Christian Mission in Africa

CHAPTER FOUR

Engaging the Catholic and the Pentecostal-Charismatic Forms of Christianity in a Conversation: Towards An Authentic African Christianity

Lawrence Nchekwube Nwankwo

Introduction

Pentecostalism is a form of Christianity that is growing very fast in Africa. As the name implies, Pentecostalism highlights the centrality of the Pentecost event. Jesus promised his disciples that they would receive power from on high, the power of the Holy Spirit (Acts 1:8). The coming of the Holy Spirit on the day of Pentecost transformed the lives and actions of the disciples. Pentecostalism emerged as a movement set out to re-enact the experience of the Church at Pentecost. In the early days of Pentecostalism, *glossolalia* or speaking in tongues was seen as authentication of the Spirit's presence. The emphasis on *glossolalia* has waned but the expectation of the manifestation of the Holy Spirit through healing, prophecy and other gifts has remained as well as expectation of the imminent coming of the Lord.

Pentecostalism, as "a religion made to travel,"[125] soon crossed denominational boundaries and entered the mainline churches. This saw the birth in the Catholic Church of the Catholic Charismatic Renewal Movement in 1967 in South Bend, University

---

[125] This is the claim made in the subtitle of the collection of essays edited by Murray W. Dempster, Byron D. Klaus and Douglas Petersen, *The Globalization of Pentecostalism: A Religion Made to Travel* (Oxford: Regnum Books, 1999).

of Notre Dame, Indiana, U.S.A. Through the efforts of Cardinal Suenens, a group of eight theologians and leaders of the Charismatic movement who produced the Malines Documents, the Catholic Charismatic Renewal movement became mainstreamed.[126] However, the Catholic Charismatic Renewal movement and the Pentecostals share a lot in common especially with regard to their worldview. This commonality is the reason for hyphenating the terms.

The origin of the Pentecostal-Charismatic movement in West Africa has been placed by J.K Olupona in the 1970s. He also notes their organic connection to the prophetic Independent Churches initiated by Africans in the 19th century.[127] Without underrating the influence of the transnational Pentecostal movement especially from the United States of America, Olupona affirms that these movements are genuinely African in "origin and character" although their relations to the African traditional worldview is ambivalent.

They reject the traditional religion and culture as demonic. Yet they employ symbols from this tradition to understand and respond to the world.[128] Finally, Olupona presents three beliefs and practices at the heart of the theology of the Pentecostal-Charismatic form of Christianity: – belief in demons, the practice of healing, and *glossolalia*.[129] Apart from *glossolalia*, which is no longer as central as it used to be, the mainline Churches share

---

[126] See, Wilfried Brieven, "The Legacy of the Malines Documents," Paper delivered at the Golden Jubilee of the Catholic Charismatic Renewal, May 31-June 4, 2017, Rome. http://www.ccrgoldenjubilee2017.net/wp-content/uploads/2017/10/D3.2-FrWB-The-legacy-of-the-Malines-Documents.pdf. Accessed November 12, 2019.

[127] J.K Olupona, "Pentecostal-Charismatic Movement, Africa, West (Survey)" *International Dictionary of Pentecostal Charismatic Movements*, ed. Stanley Burgess and Eduard M. van der Maas (Grand Rapids, MI: Zondervan, 2002, 2003) 15.

[128] Ibid., 11, 14.

[129] Ibid., 17.

the same beliefs and practices as outlined. From the perspective of this reflection, however, the emphasis on power is the element that marks the Pentecostal-Charismatic form of Christianity out more clearly. This does not imply that there is no mention of divine power in the form of Christianity expressed in the mainline Churches. The emphasis makes the difference.

It is worthy of note that the Pentecostal-Charismatic form of Christianity resonates with an African traditional worldview that has been transformed. For example, Johannes Merz has shown that "witchcraft, which is traditionally believed to be an impersonal and usually internal power, is [now] misrepresented as an exorcisable evil spirit."[130] Similarly, in African traditional religion, the one God is not involved directly in the affairs of the world but through vicegerents – the deities, spirits, ancestors. History is the outcome of the interaction of these vicegerents and human beings. But divine providence, God's direct governance of the world is at the heart of Christianity.

Although the Pentecostal-Charismatic form of Christianity resonates with a transformed African traditional worldview, this form of Christianity can still be regarded as African Christianity *en route* to fuller appreciation and more adequate response to the African situation in creative fidelity to the Christian tradition. For this to happen, the underlying emphases and system of ideas behind the Pentecostal-Charismatic form of Christianity have to be brought into dialogue with the underlying schemes of other expressions of Christianity, especially the Catholic tradition. Such a conversation holds out the prospect of their mutual enrichment. This chapter aims at being such a conversation, listening empathetically to the traditions, seeking to understand them from within, looking for common grounds, highlighting

---

[130] Johannes Merz, "I am a Witch in the Holy Spirit: Rupture and Continuity in Witchcraft Beliefs in African Christianity," *Missiology* 36:2 (2008) 201-218.

strengths, weaknesses and differences and aiming at mutual enrichment for the emergence of a more authentic African expression of Christianity.

Experience and Power – the Dual Emphases of the Pentecostal-Charismatic Form of Christianity

Experience and power can be regarded as key emphases of the Pentecostal-Charismatic form of Christianity. These emphases are interrelated. The focus on the Pentecost and the experience of the power of the Holy Spirit immediately shows the interrelation. As Killian McDonnell remarked, sacramental grace in Catholic sacramental theological system is regarded as "beyond-consciousness reality" and "never experienced within the horizon of the existential facts of history."[131] In the Pentecostal-Charismatic form of Christianity, grace is conceived as palpable and experiential. This is the basis of the emphasis on 'endowment with power from on high.' This gives rise to what has been called "high voltage" rather than "flash-battery-voltage" Christianity.[132] This is the basis for what Nimi Wariboko terms a kinetic description of African Pentecostalism.[133]

The Origin of the Emphasis on Power in North-American Pentecostalism: Cursory View from History

The peculiar understanding and appreciation of divine power in the Pentecostal-Charismatic form of Christianity has

---

[131] Killian McDonnell, "The Ideology of Pentecostal Conversion," *Journal of Ecumenical Studies* 5 (1968) 108.

[132] Krister Stendahl, "The New Testament Evidence," *The Charismatic Movement*, ed. Michael P. Hamilton (Grand Rapids, Michigan: William Eerdmans, 1975), 56.

[133] Nimi Wariboko, "African Pentecostalism: A Kinetic Description," *Na God: Aesthetics of African Charismatic Power*, ed. Annalisa Butticci, Photography Andrew Esiobo (Padova: Grafiche Turato Edizioni, 2013) 21-23.

Engaging the Catholic and the Pentecostal-Charismatic

a historical and cultural origin. This is verified both in the historico-cultural setting of its emergence in Africa and in North America.[134] Let us briefly explore this historico-cultural setting first in North America and then in Africa in order to see what gave rise to the emphasis on power in this form of Christianity.

Pentecostalism is regarded as the third religious awakening in North America. The First Great Awakening is associated with Jonathan Edwards (1703-1758), an influential Puritan preacher in New England in the 18th Century, who combined elements of the Reformed tradition and the Puritan 'federal' theology. This federal theology is the outcome of the self-understanding of the Puritans who fled England to North America. Appropriating the imagery of Revelation 12:6, they saw North America as the desert prepared by God from which and through which God will renew the face of the earth. The new nation whose birth the Puritans midwifed was therefore considered the new Israel, a sanctuary administered by a priesthood of believers in which the Church and the civil polity have the duty of preparing people for righteous living.[135]

In line with the Reformed tradition, Edwards emphasized gracious election and justification apart from works. However, his puritanism and commitment to the 'federal' theology made him emphasize human agency. For example, he wrote, "if we would be saved, we must seek salvation. For although men do not obtain heaven by themselves, yet they do not go thither accidentally, or without any intention or endeavor of their own."[136]

---

[134] Cecil M. Robeck, Jr. "Pentecostal Origins from a Global Perspective," *All Together in one Place: Theological Papers from the Brighton Conference on World Evangelization*, ed. Harold D. Hunter & Peter Hocken (Sheffield: Sheffield Academic Press, 1993) 166-180.

[135] William Faupel, *The Everlasting Gospel: The Significance of Eschatology in the Development of Pentecostal Thought* (Sheffield: Sheffield Academic Press, 1996) 49.

[136] Jonathan Edwards, "The Manner in which the Salvation of the Soul is to be Sought," in Robert W. Jenson, *America's Theologian: A Recommendation of Jonathan Edwards* (New York & Oxford: Oxford University Press, 1988) 58.

The second religious awakening is linked to the Holiness movement influenced by John Wesley (1703-1791). Wesley accepted the Reformation doctrine of justification by faith but deemphasized the juridical and forensic understanding according to which, the justified were at once just and sinners (*simul justus simul peccator*). Wesley insisted on the possibility of total sanctification and the need to promote and foster holiness and perfection through special techniques applied during revivals.

The Holiness movement highlighted the social dimension of the Gospel so much so that Donald W. Dayton claims that it parallels "today's liberation theology" with the qualification that the commitment was not rooted in social analysis and careful strategy, but in the call to 'sanctification' of persons and society.[137]

The civil war in America (1861-1865) changed the religious mood and redirected the practices of the Holiness movement and gave birth to the Pentecostal emphasis. Donald Dayton sums up the shift in this way: "one of the most striking differences in mood between the antebellum advocates of Christian perfection, ... and the post-war proclaimers of Pentecostal sanctification is the earlier sense of 'ability' and the latter search for 'power'"[138] The war raised anew the question of evil and the understanding of total sanctification.

The disillusionment and pessimism caused by the war resulted in the appropriation of the apocalyptic vision and specifically a pre-millennial[139] view that expected things to grow from bad to worse until Christ returns to establish the millennial reign. In other words, there was little hope of improving or reforming the world through human effort and the expectation of an immi-

---

[137] Donald W. Dayton, "Yet Another Layer of the Onion or Opening the Ecumenical Doors to let the Riffraff in," *Ecumenical* 40:1 (1988) 87-110.

[138] Donald W. Dayton, *Theological Roots of Pentecostalism* (Peabody, Massachusetts: Hendrickson Press, 1987, 2000) 77.

[139] Steve Gregg, ed. *Revelation: Four Views, A Parallel Commentary* (Nashville: Thomas Nelson Pub., 1997) 27.

nent return of Jesus to "rapture" the saints. Social involvement was re-articulated in terms of rescuing sinners out of the world and enabling them to be among those to meet the Lord in the air when the trumpet would sound.

Another shift is from a Christocentric to a pneumatocentric pattern of thinking. Total sanctification was increasingly linked to the Holy Spirit. Spirit baptism became emphasized. The twofold division of history into two covenants (Old and New) was broadened to three in order to highlight the Pentecost as a distinctive dispensation. This resulted in a shift in exegetical foundations that gave new prominence to the Acts of Apostles and a consequent emphasis on 'pneumatic' themes such as 'power,' 'gifts of the Holy Spirit' and 'prophecy.'[140] These shifts created the disposition for and expectation of the replication of the experience of Pentecost through spirit baptism and speaking in tongues, *glossolalia*, and other experiences of divine action in history such as healing, prophecy, signs, and wonders.

The Roots of the Emphasis on Power in the African Reception of the Pentecostal-Charismatic Form of Christianity

The American civil war, as has been seen above, undermined what has been termed Wesleyan optimism, with its confidence in human ability and social engagement. Similarly, it was the advent of missionary Christianity and the massive transformation it brought about in the traditional cosmology, especially through vernacularization, that prepared the ground for the emergence of the African Initiatives in Christianity (AICs) with its pneumatic elements and emphasis on power. This empha-

---

[140] Donald W. Dayton, "Asa Mahan and the Development of American Holiness Tradition," *Wesleyan Theological Journal* 9 (1974) 60-69; Donald W. Dayton, "The Doctrine of the Baptism of the Holy Spirit: Its Emergence and Significance," *Wesleyan Theological Journal* 13 (1978) 114-126.

sis can be traced to how elements of African traditional religion were taken up into Christianity. We pay attention to two of such elements: the anthropocentricity[141] of the African traditional religion and the spirit world.

Before going into the elements of the African worldview, it is important to draw attention to the fact that the introduction of Christianity to Africa took place, especially from the point of view of the Africans, against a background of power contest. Missionaries were allotted land in the 'evil forests' with the expectation that the forests' sinister spirits and forces would kill them within days. The early converts also tried to prove to themselves the superiority of their new religion by breaking taboos which they had hitherto believed would attract vengeance from the deities.[142]

This is the background for understanding for example, the Braidist movement, founded by Garrick Sokari Braide (1882-1918), in the then Niger Delta Pastorate of the Anglican Communion in southern Nigeria. Braide was said to have performed many 'miracles.' These miracles were meant to confirm the superiority of Christian God and were followed by people burning their shrines and throwing away their charms and amulets.[143]

The anthropocentricity of African traditional religion refers to the fact that the traditional religion catered for human fulfilment in this present life. Fullness of life or abundant life in this world is the default setting.[144] Abundant life implies health,

---

[141] Chukwudum B. Okolo, *African Traditional Religion and Christianity: The Neglected Dimension* (Nsukka: Fulladu, 1995).

[142] Chinua Achebe, *Things Fall Apart*, (London: Heinemann, 1958).

[143] G.O.M Tasie, *Christian Missionary Enterprise in the Niger Delta 1864-1918* (Leiden: E.J. Brill, 1978) 175.

[144] Simon S. Maimela, "Salvation in African Traditional Religions," *Missionalia* 13:2

wealth, fertility and longevity. As Bernhard Udelhoven puts it, "a person is supposed to be healthy, prosperous, living in harmony with the community and a good influence on society."[145]

Every child is expected to live to a ripe old age, except those spirits who had decided to punish a family by being born into this family and dying repeatedly until something is done to remedy the situation. That is why in some communities, when people died young, they were disposed of in the evil forest. In others, dying before one's parents is still considered "unnatural" and such parents do not participate in the funeral.

The absence of fullness or abundance of life calls for explanation and remedy. In the traditional religious setting, diviners discern the cause and effort made to restore the cosmic balance through sacrifices. But religion is implicated in this search for fullness of life. The African initiatives in Christianity took this seriously. From the perspective of missionaries and those influenced by them, this was a distraction from Christianity. This was the view of Christian G. Baëta, a Ghanaian Presbyterian theologian, who writing in the 1950s, affirmed that "the Christianity taught by the historical churches is a message calling men to repentance from their sin and to a life of faith." In contrast, he continued,

> the Christianity offered by the separatist churches may be described as a power for overcoming the ills of the secular aspect of life. Human need is conceived almost entirely in terms of these ills. While such terms as 'sin', 'grace',... and other Christian themes are constantly spoken about, the central preoccupation is and remains how to cope effectively with the ills of worldly life. For

---

(1985) 63-77.

[145] Bernhard Udelhoven, *Unseen Worlds: Dealing with Spirits, Witchcraft, and Satanism* (Lusaka: FENZA, 2016) 65.

instance, 'sin' is really relevant only in so far as it is a potent cause of bodily, mental, and social disorders; the significance of 'the blood of Christ' resides in the fact that, by doing away with sin, it prepares the way for, or itself directly affects bodily healing; 'faith' is to entertain no inward doubt whatsoever that the particular help sought will be received.[146]

From the above, one can distinguish between the quest for power to overcome sin which Baëta would subscribe to and the quest for power to overcome the challenges and ills of everyday living or what Baëta called the "secular aspect of life" in the quotation seen above. The quest for power to overcome the "secular aspect of life" leads up to the traditional African understanding about the spirit world and about history. According to Elochukwu Uzukwu, the universe for the Igbo is divided into the human (*ana mmadu*) and the spirit world (*ana mmuo*). There is however "incessant commerce" between them.[147] Emefie Ikenga Metuh writes of an overcrowding in the traditional Igbo worldview of the human world by

spirits of all sorts, deities, *Arusi*, evil spirits and so forth. The deities, *Mmuo*, are indeed, numerous, but they are few enough to be known to the ordinary Igbo believer. On the other hand, the *Arusi* are so great in number that nobody is expected to know them all. Moreover, as new *Arusi* and other powerful mystical forces are invented, old ones fade into oblivion and yet any worshipper should be prepared to placate both the new and the old. This leaves a believer subject to constant fear because he does not know from where to expect the next problem. Because of the great number of these spirit-forces, and the fact that their spheres of influence and taboos overlap, it takes an expert to know which spiritual force is

---

[146] Christian G. Baëta, "Conflict in Mission, Historical and Separatist Churches," *The Theology of the Christian Mission*, ed. Gerald H. Anderson (New York: McGraw-Hill, 1961), 293.

[147] Elochukwu Uzukwu, "Igbo World and Ultimate Reality and Meaning," *Ultimate Reality and Meaning* 5 (1982) 195.

responsible for any given misfortune and therefore which are the appropriate remedies to take. This enhances the role of the *dibia afa*, diviner, and the oracles.[148]

In the light of this, Ogbu Kalu concludes that "life is precarious"[149] in the traditional society although they had ritual experts who helped them to navigate it. Christianity added to the precariousness of the life of the early converts. It not only banned visits to the diviners and oracles but provided no alternatives. Above all, it added to the population of the evil spirits. In the African traditional worldview, many of the deities and spirit forces are ambivalent. In Christianity, if a spirit is not the Holy Spirit, it is evil spirit and was assimilated to the minions of Satan.

This is the setting in which emerged the prophets and founders of the AICs who saw themselves as engaged in a power encounter; assaulting the spiritual gates of the traditional religion. An example is the belief in the traditional worldview that the world is populated by spirit forces and the view that these influence events in the world imply that events can be explained in terms not only of inner-worldly chain of causes but also as caused by the spirit forces and beings. There is an openness to the involvement of spirit forces and beings in all events of human life.

While this is at the roots of John Mbiti's assertion that Africans are notoriously religious,[150] it also gives rise to ways of interpreting negative experiences in terms of the interference of spiritual forces – witchcraft, ancestral curses, etc. Indeed, a stream of thought within the Pentecostal-Charismatic form of Christianity claim that before anything happens in the physical

---

[148] Emefie Ikenga-Metuh, *God and Man in African Religion* (Enugu: Snaap, 1999) 107-108.

[149] Ogbu U. Kalu, "Ethical Values in Igbo Tradition of Politics," *The Igbo and the Tradition of Politics*, ed. U.D Anyanwu & J.C.U Aguwa (Enugu: Fourth Dimension Publishers, 1983) 13-14.

[150] John Mbiti, *African Religions and Philosophy* (Nairobi: Heineman, 1969).

world, it has been decided in the spirit world. This indicates a preference for explanations of events in terms of conscious spiritual beings with intentions, desires and purposes rather than simply in terms of inner-worldly causation.

This line of interpretation was initially discountenanced by the mainline Churches as seen in the vituperation of Baëta but taken up in the AICs and in the Pentecostal-Charismatic forms of Christianity. Since negative experiences are explained in terms of the interference of spirit forces, spiritual solutions must be sought for them. Such spiritual solutions entail power encounter between the offending spirit or spirits and the Holy Spirit of God.

In what is called Prosperity Message or Prosperity Gospel, one sees a combination of the ideas seen above about fulness of life and the conceptualization of negative experiences in terms of the spirit world. The Prosperity Message is a stream within the Pentecostal-Charismatic form of Christianity which interprets salvation mainly in terms of prosperity.[151] Here one sees clearly the demonization not only of the spirit world but of people's life world and the construction of the subjectivity of the believer and ascription to him or her of divine powers so much so that things are supposed to work out almost magically.

David Oyedepo of the Christ Living Church, a.k.a Winners' Chapel, can be classified as an exponent of the Prosperity Message. According to him, the Jesus event has restored humanity to fullness of life. This, notwithstanding, humanity still lives in the

> magnetic field of wickedness. Here, Satan, his demons and sometimes human extensions carry out their wicked acts by remote control. Diseases, frustrations and all kinds of human afflictions originate here. Spells and curses that upturn people's destinies come from this negative pole of evil. A satanic influence

---

[151] Lawrence Nwankwo, "African Christianity and the Challenge of Prosperity Gospel," *Ministerium* 5 (2019) 11-27.

is almost always behind the stagnations, failures and losses people experience in life.[152]

Oyedepo further writes: "I want you to know that the prosperity God has planned for you has nothing to do with your profession, your career or your family background ... Your covenant alignment is the issue."[153] This covenant alignment or re-alignment as the case may be, comes through being born-again. This not only grafts one unto a new community of believers, guarantees access to covenant blessings spelt out in Deuteronomy 28 and Leviticus 26, but also enables one to become "rooted in the supernatural" with the attendant discovery that one is "a spirit after the order of God."[154]

According to Oyedepo, sons of God "can operate like God," with the ability "to exercise total dominion over all issues of life, bringing deliverance to many. They will think, talk, and live in the realm of dominion where, all things shall be possible with them. They will have it, the way they want it, according to the Word of God."[155] More succinctly, Oyedepo claims that "the cardinal mark of sonship is power, power to reign, power to exercise authority. ... Understanding your sonship power, rights and privileges is the master key to freedom and a life of fulfilment. That is what puts you over and puts the enemy on the run."[156] It is what makes one a winner.

Put in a different way, Oyedepo re-articulates *theosis* and makes a link between being born-again and being in the status of God. This is in the service of constructing the subjectivity

---

[152] David Oyedepo, *Releasing the Supernatural: An Adventure into the Spirit World* (Lagos: Dominion, 1993) 19.

[153] David Oyedepo, *Understanding Financial Prosperity* (Lagos: Dominion House, 1997) 11-12.

[154] Oyedepo, *Releasing the Supernatural.*, xi.

[155] Ibid., 45.

[156] Ibid., 48.

of the believer as a winner. In other words, being born-again implies being sovereign like God. As he puts it, "as far as God is concerned, a believer is not an ordinary man and since with God nothing is impossible, then nothing is impossible for the believer (Mk 9:23; 10:27). Since all things are possible with both God and the believer, then the believer is in the class of God and can exhibit the character of God and work miracles and signs, as long as he is aware of his position."[157]

This shows the height of the quest for power – identification of the human and the divine in order to be able to claim unlimited power for the human being who believes.

In sum, we have explored the key emphasis of the Pentecostal-Charismatic form of Christianity especially from the point of view of the emphases on experience and on power. We have seen how this emphasis is rooted in the history of Pentecostalism, the encounter with African traditional religion, the appropriation and transformation of elements of the primal African worldview, especially the anthropocentricity and the belief in the spirit world.

Engaging the Pentecostal-Charismatic Form of Christianity

The Pentecostal-Charismatic form of Christianity appropriated the anthropocentricity and the focus on abundant life of African Traditional Religions. The scheme of its appropriation, however, fails to take note of the transformation of the African life context on the one hand, while committing it to view the significance of the Jesus event in terms of a return to paradise. This form of Christianity does violence to the primal view of the Spirit world with the consequence that it has increased existential angst. While celebrating power, it has left human

---

[157] David Oyedepo, *Releasing the Power of the Supernatural*, 39.

beings powerless, whose agency is limited to magically mobilizing divine power to deal with everyday problem. This is due to its scheme for conceptualizing negative experiences.

The emphasis on abundant life in African traditional religions was supported by the socio-cultural and economic system, which obtained at that time. The lifestyle and environment of the people was healthier than what obtains presently. Wealth was reckoned in terms of goods and services locally produced and any hardworking person could accumulate enough. There was no joblessness because there was no wage labour.

Infertility had a cultural and not a technical solution. Just as Sarai gave her servant girl Hagar to Abram so as to remove the shame of barrenness (Gn 16:2), in the same way women 'married' wives in traditional African family. In sum, in as much as the expectation of abundant life was not always fully met in everyone, there were cultural arrangements to handle this situation through communal solidarity. The diviners took care of the remnants in terms of identifying the offending spirits and prescribing what was needed to appease them. Contact with Europe and the plugging of Africa onto modernity and the global capitalist system introduced profound changes.

The colonial and postcolonial state have become the structure for socio-economic and political organisation. The introduction of paper money brought about wage labour and the possibility of unemployment; rapid urbanisation and the gradual dissolution of communal bonds. New consumer goods and the pressure of advertising make people to consume foreign goods and services. The underperformance of the states in Africa has given rise to poverty, disease, criminality, and a sense of hopelessness. In this changed context, abundant life can be the ideal towards which people work rather than a given.

By postulating abundant life as a given, the Pentecostal-Charismatic form of Christianity presents the significance of the Jesus event in terms of a restoration of the paradisal state. The personal and social challenges that face the majority of people are explained in terms of the interference of evil spirits. This abstracts from and transposes onto the cosmic sphere the socio-economic, political and cultural factors at the root of the challenges people go through. Such a vision projects prayer, fasting, and recourse to the powerful (wo)man of God as the sure means to ensuring the flow of abundance. This attenuates the role of human agency in social transformation and misses the opportunity of re-articulating Jesus' invitation to carry one's cross in terms of self-denial and commitment to the common good.

A more explicit theological engagement of the Pentecostal-Charismatic form of Christianity has to address its underlying apocalyptic framework. This is as much responsible as the belief in spirits in the primal African worldview for the view that cosmic forces are implicated in the negative experiences people go through. In the Bible, one notices a remarkable difference between the books of the prophets and the apocalyptic books. The prophets carried out their ministry in line with Deuteronomistic theology. This theology links divine blessings with covenant fidelity and vice versa (Dt 28, Lv 26).

In the apocalyptic writings, the persecuted Israelites and early Christian communities were encouraged to remain steadfast in their faith in the sure hope of a definitive intervention by God and a reward in the afterlife. The style of apocalyptic writings, the visions, the 'heavenly guides,' the elaborate angelology and the grotesque images of animals give the impression that history is the outcome of the battle between good and bad cosmic spiritual beings.[158] God's definitive intervention on the side of the good is assured. Pentecostals and Charismatics espouse Deuteronomistic theology within a pre-millennial context.

---

[158] John J. Collins, *The Apocalyptic Imagination: An Introduction to Jewish Apocalyptic Literature* (Grand Rapids, MI, W. B. Eerdmans, 1998).

Pre-millennialism is an apocalyptic interpretation of history based on Revelation 20 which makes reference to the millennial or the one-thousand-year-reign of Christ. For pre-millennials, the one thousand years of universal peace will be preceded by increased activities of forces aligned against God and God's kingdom.[159] The many challenges of modern life – the wars, the diseases like COVID-19 pandemic, the gross inequality between peoples and nations, etc – are taken as evidence that that present age precedes the millennial reign of Christ and thus witnesses an increased activities of negative forces.

There are four insights with which to build up a response to pre-millennialism. First, Jesus enjoins all to vigilance but abstained from naming the end-time because "as for that day and hour, nobody knows it, neither the angels of heaven, nor the Son, no one but the Father alone" (Mt 24:36; Mk 13:32). Identifying the present generation as preceding the end presumes knowledge that Jesus ascribes to the Father alone. Second, many epochs in history, such as during the bubonic plague in Europe,[160] had been identified as heralding the end.

This cautions against identifying any period in history because of any challenges being faced as "end-time" and thus as besieged by negative spirit forces to be countered through spiritual warfare. The third insight comes from the fact that there are other ways of interpreting Revelation 20. While a-millennials hold that the one-thousand-year-reign of Christ in Rev. 20 is symbolic, post-millennials see the death of Jesus on the cross as that definitive intervention that defeated the devil and inaugurated

---

[159] Steve Gregg, ed. *Revelation: Four Views, A Parallel Commentary* (Nashville: Thomas Nelson Pub., 1997) 27.

[160] Carter Lindberg, *The European Reformations* (Oxford, UK: Blackwell, 1996) 25-34.

the Kingdom of God.¹⁶¹ Through her ministry, the Church is extending this reign of Jesus Christ till the second coming of Jesus which would take place at a time known to the Father alone.

The last point to dislodge the pre-millennialian interpretation of history has to do with the provision of an alternative account for the suffering and calamities in the world which pre-millennialism sets out to make sense of. In this regard, it is important to note that many layers of the Biblical tradition as well as primal African worldview factor in human agency and natural processes in the explanation of events in history. The exclusive use of herbs or a combination of this with divination in traditional African healing practices show recognition of natural causes of illnesses just as insistence on reconciliation[162] indicate an awareness of the social dimension in the aetiology of illnesses.

In the primal African worldview and in large section of the Biblical tradition, history is not interpreted simply as the outcome of the struggle between the cosmic forces of good and evil as pre-millennialism presents it. Indeed, as Meinrad Hebga argues in what he calls *"la philosophie de l'immanence du mal,"* (the Philosophy of the Immanence of Evil), *"les Africains n'ont pas assigné au mal une origine extra-humaine .... Ils ont eu le courage d'en reconnaître la source en eux-mêmes, dans leur ventre, comme ils dissent de façon pittoresque."*[163]

In a similar vein, Herman Beseah Browne speaks of the "victim as culprit" thesis.[164] Thus, in spite of the population of the

---

[161] Steve Gregg, ed., *op. cit.*, 28.

[162] Eric de Rosny, *Healers in the Night*, trans. Robert R. Barr (Eugene, Or: Wipf & Stock, 2004) 128-149.

[163] "Africans have not assigned an extra-human origin to evil.... They had the courage to recognise the source of evil in themselves, to use an imagery, in their belly" – my translation).Meinrad Hebga, *Sorcellerie: chimere dangereuse...?* (Abidjan: Inades Edition, 1979) 261-262.

[164] Herman Beseah Browne, *Theological Anthropology: A Dialectical Study of the*

African traditional world by deities and spirits, it is the human being who renders himself or herself open to their interference. It is also the task of human beings to ritually restore the cosmic balance when broken. From this perspective, the centrality of human agency both in the causation and amelioration of negative experiences is highlighted.

Having retrieved human agency, the corollary target is to secure the regularity of natural processes while keeping these processes open to what is beyond the natural. This is necessary to overcome the magical mentality of the Pentecostal-Charismatic form of Christianity. The Christian tradition had faced similar challenge earlier and had produced a distinction between two ways of speaking about divine power - *potentia dei absoluta* and *potentia dei ordinata*.[165] *Potentia dei absoluta* refers to God's power considered absolutely, without any limitation from creation while *potential dei ordinata* refers to that power which by creating has set limits to itself. From the point of view of the former, no limitation is placed on divine power and thus on the possibility of miracles. However, from the point of view of the second, the stability and regularity in creation is secured because God at creation has freely ordained his powers to flow in a certain way. Divine sovereignty does not mean divine arbitrariness.

In the light of the above re-articulation of the key elements that underpin the Pentecostal-Charismatic form of Christianity, a shift is needed from an emphasis on power or love of power to an emphasis on the power of love. Retrieving human agency and the role of natural as well as social-cultural processes in the determination of the process of history require love as the wellspring of action for the amelioration of the human situation. Such power can then move human beings to exercise agency in

---

African and Liberation Traditions (London: Avon Books, 1996) 59.

[165] See St. Thomas Aquinas, *De Potentia Dei* 1, 3, trans. Linwood Urban in *The Power of God: Readings on Omnipotence and Evil*, ed. Linwood Urban Douglas N. Walton (New York: Oxford University Press, 1978) 41-46.

such a way as to bring about social processes that lead to human promotion and enthronement of the values of truth, justice, fraternity and sorority.

Recalibrating Some Catholic Practices and Emphases

According to Uzukwu, part of the history of the Catholic Church in Africa is that she was born old with theologies and pastoral practices that were honed in a world with a different socio-cultural history.[166] This is to be celebrated as well as regretted. It is to be celebrated because she became heir to the wealth of experience built over centuries. It is however to be regretted on two counts. First, it means the reproduction of any blind spots or narrowness of vision that had crept into the tradition. Second, it implies the possible loss of a new understanding that could have arisen from the 'translation'[167] of the Christian message into the African cultural context. The Pentecostal-Charismatic form of Christianity is a recent phenomenon which according to J.K Olupona can be dated to the 1970s.[168] It does not have a central teaching authority.

One can, therefore, claim that it is more likely to engage the popular aspirations, religious sensibility and visions. Things are, however, much more complex than presented. Suffice it to say that the Pentecostal-Charismatic form of Christianity has some emphases that the Catholic Church in Africa needs to engage with. Interestingly, some of these emphases corroborate the direction that the documents of the Special Assembly for Africa of the Synod of Bishops (1994, 2009) point to.

---

[166] Elochukwu Uzukwu, "The Birth and Development of a Local Church: Difficulties and Signs of Hope," in *The African Synod: Documents, Reflections, Perspectives*, ed. Maura Browne (Maryknoll, New York: Orbis, 1996) 3.

[167] Lamin Sanneh, *Translating the Message: The Missionary Impact on Culture* (New York: Orbis Books, 1989).

[168] J.K Olupona, "Pentecostal-Charismatic Movement, Africa, West (Survey)" 15.

The first element of the Pentecostal-Charismatic form of Christianity worth mentioning is the emphasis on the believer as formed in the image of God. As seen above, the extreme articulation of this idea in the thoughts of David Oyedepo, presents the believer as being in the class of God and thus capable of exercising dominion over all the world's troubles. More balanced presentations underline the intimate relationship of adoptive sonship and daughtership that Christians enter into with God that constitutes them into a special people separated from the rest and exempts them from some of the regulations of the community. Catholics tend not to emphasise difference and separation from the community with the result that it is possible to be a nominal Catholic.

These are Catholics whose Catholicity is limited to the fact that they are baptised and probably have their names registered with a parish. A way to combine both emphases is to highlight the import of receiving the Eucharistic Lord who sends all on the mission of being salt and light in the community.

Corollary to the emphasis on specialness is the stress in the Pentecostal-Charismatic form of Christianity on building up a personal relationship with Jesus Christ, accepting him as one's personal lord and saviour. In contrast, the Catholic Church often emphasise membership of the Church as the mystical body of Christ. These emphases are not exclusive. They entail each other. However, invitation to union with Jesus Christ is more direct in its presentation of the goal of the Christian life and could lead to an acceptance of the Church as the sacrament of Jesus' presence and the community commissioned to teach and sanctify her members through the celebration of the sacraments.

By presuming the personal encounter with Jesus, the emphasis on the Catholic Church risks gathering people into the community of the Church who are not touched by the Spirit of the Son. By focusing on the encounter with Jesus Christ and the Spirit as foundational, at least in its rhetoric, the Pentecostal-Charismatic form of Christianity constantly present this challenge.

Experience that is in line with the sensitivity of African is the third element that the Pentecostal-Charismatic form of Christianity has brought to the fore. Religions seek to evoke in their members an experience of the divine. This is what symbols are supposed to do in the celebration of the sacraments and in liturgical celebrations. Yet experience is culture specific. More Africans than Europeans are likely to be moved by a drumming session than by a solo presentation in an opera and vice versa. It is to the credit of the Pentecostal-Charismatic form of Christianity that they work with an aesthetic model which resonates with Africans.

Reference has been made to Nimi Wariboko's kinetic description of the Pentecostal-Charismatic form of Christianity in Africa and this can be correlated to the prevalence of drumming in the traditional African healing practices.[169] This points to the fact that the dominant approach to the transformation of consciousness in Africa involves kinesis, movement of the whole body. It has however to be noted that dancing in the Church may have cathartic effect without bringing those involved any nearer to God. Therefore, this can only be one among other adjustments aimed at fostering a personal experience of the God of Jesus Christ.

The engagement of the Pentecostal-Charismatic form of Christianity with elements of primal African cultures has been noted. As has been seen, this engagement is not always successful. But this is a pointer to the urgency of the task. The way the Christian message was preached in Africa gave rise to what Bernhard Udelhoven, termed "uprooted Christians."[170] Although inculturation is an ongoing task because culture is dynamic, its urgency in the Church in Africa, as insisted upon in chapter three of the Post-Synodal Apostolic Exhortation of Pope St John Paul II,

---

[169] Eric de Rosny, *Healers in the Night*, 128-149.
[170] Bernhard Udelhoven, *Unseen Worlds*, 62.

Ecclesia in Africa, stems from the need to undertake evangelisation as a way of re-rooting African Christians into the African soil.[171]

For example, what is known in the Pentecostal-charismatic discourse as generational curses[172] is an attempt to interpret negative experiences in line with a scheme in traditional African culture in which individuals can suffer as a result of the misdeeds of their forebears. This flies in the face of the insistence on individual responsibility in the book of Ezekiel (Ez 18:1-20)[173] and sets the stage for rediscovering an aspect of the traditional anthropology in which the human being is a nodal point in a vast network extending backwards into the past and forward into the future. This can be a helpful framework in the engagement in human promotion understood as intervening positively in the present so as to rewrite the past and redirect the flow into the future.

Finally, the Pentecostal-Charismatic form of Christianity harnesses more fruitfully information, communication technologies. In Nigeria, dealers on public address systems distinguish between Catholic and Pentecostal public address systems. The Catholic system does not function as well as the Pentecostal one and is often cheaper. Although this may be exaggerated, but it says a lot not only about the perception of Catholics but also of the commitment of Catholics to quality as regards their communication strategies.

Conclusion

We have engaged the Catholic tradition and the Pentecostal-Charismatic form of Christianity in a conversation. The Pente-

---

[171] Pope St. John Paul II, *Ecclesia in Africa*, (Vatican: Editrice Libreria, 1995).

[172] Stephen Uche Njoku, *Curses, Effect and Release* (Enugu: Christian Living Publications, 1993).

[173] See Paul M. Joyce, "Ezekiel and Individual Responsibility," *Ezekiel and His Book: Textual and Literary Criticism and their Interrelation*, ed. J. Lust (Leuven: Leuven University Press, 1986) 317-321.

costal-Charismatic form of Christianity emerged in history. It represents a shift towards the search for power so much so that some groups may be rightly accused of extolling a love of power. Power is in the service of having dominion over all negative experiences.

Engaging this form of Christianity by retrieving what it tends to downplay such as human agency, the socio-economic, political and cultural process at the root of the challenges faced by the people demand a shift of emphasis on the power of love. Despite the shortcomings of the underlying scheme of the Pentecostal-Charismatic form of Christianity, there are some of their emphases and practices that can enrich African Catholicism. Paradoxically, some of those elements capture aspects of the insights of the Special Assemblies for Africa of the Synod of Bishops.

Bibliography

Aquinas, St. Thomas. *De Potentia Dei* 1, 3, trans. Linwood Urban in *The Power of God: Readings on Omnipotence and Evil*, ed. Linwood Urban Douglas N. Walton, 41-46. New York: Oxford University Press, 1978.

Baëta, Christian, G., "Conflict in Mission, Historical and Separatist Churches." *The Theology of the Christian Mission*, edited by Gerald H. Anderson, 290-299. New York: McGraw-Hill, 1961.

Brieven, Wilfried. "The Legacy of the Malines Documents," Paper delivered at the Golden Jubilee of the Catholic Charismatic Renewal, May 31-June 4, 2017, Rome. http://www.ccrgoldenjubilee2017.net/wp-content/uploads/2017/10/D3.2-FrWB-The-legacy-of-the-Malines-Documents.pdf accessed November 12, 2019.

Browne, Herman, Beseah. *Theological Anthropology: A Dialectical Study of the African and Liberation Traditions*. London: Avon Books, 1996.

Collins, John, J. *The Apocalyptic Imagination: An Introduction to Jewish Apocalyptic Literature*. Grand Rapids, MI: W. B. Eerdmans, 1998.

Dayton, Donald, W. "Asa Mahan and the Development of American Holiness Tradition." *Wesleyan Theological Journal* 9 (1974): 60-69.

Dayton, Donald, W. "The Doctrine of the Baptism of the Holy Spirit: Its Emergence and Significance." *Wesleyan Theological Journal* 13 (1978): 114-126.

Dayton, Donald, W. "Yet Another Layer of the Onion or Opening the Ecumenical Doors to let the Riffraff in." *Ecumenical* 40 no. 1 (1988): 87-110.

Dayton, Donald, W. *Theological Roots of Pentecostalism* Peabody, Massachusetts: Hendrickson Press, 2000.

de Rosny, Eric. *Healers in the Night,* translated by Robert R. Barr. Eugene, Or: Wipf & Stock, 2004.

Dempster, Murray, W., Byron D. Klaus and Douglas Petersen, ed. *The Globalization of Pentecostalism: A Religion Made to Travel,* Oxford: Regnum Books, 1999.

Edwards, Jonathan. "The Manner in which the Salvation of the Soul is to be Sought," in Robert W. Jenson, *America's Theologian: A Recommendation of Jonathan Edwards.* Oxford: Oxford University Press, 1988.

Faupel, William. *The Everlasting Gospel: The Significance of Eschatology in the Development of Pentecostal Thought,* Sheffield: Sheffield Academic Press, 1996.

Gregg, Steve. ed. *Revelation: Four Views, A Parallel Commentary.* Nashville: Thomas Nelson Pub., 1997.

Hebga, Meinrad. *Sorcellerie: chimere dangereuse...?* Abidjan: Inades Edition, 1979.

Ikenga-Metuh, Emefie. *God and Man in African Religion* (Enugu: Snaap, 1999).

John Paul II, *Ecclesia in Africa,* (Vatican: Editrice Libreria, 1995).

Joyce, Paul, M. "Ezekiel and Individual Responsibility," *Ezekiel and His Book: Textual and Literary Criticism and their Interrelation,* edited by J. Lust, 317-321. Leuven: Leuven University Press, 1986.

Kalu, Ogbu, U. "Ethical Values in Igbo Tradition of Politics," *The Igbo and the Tradition of Politics,* edited by U.D Anyanwu & J.C.U Aguwa, 9-19. Enugu: Fourth Dimension Publishers, 1983.

Lindberg, Carter. *The European Reformations.* Oxford, UK: Blackwell, 1996.

Maimela, Simon, S. "Salvation in African Traditional Religions," *Missionalia* 13, no. 2 (1985): 63-77.

Mbiti, John. *African Religions and Philosophy*. Nairobi: Heineman, 1969.

McDonnell, Killian. "The Ideology of Pentecostal Conversion," *Journal of Ecumenical Studies* 5 (1968): 105-126.

Merz, Johannes. "I am a Witch in the Holy Spirit: Rupture and Continuity in Witchcraft Beliefs in African Christianity," *Missiology* 36, no 2 (2008): 201-218.

Njoku, Stephen, Uche. *Curses, Effect and Release*. Enugu: Christian Living Publications, 1993.

Nwankwo, Lawrence, N. (2019) "African Christianity and the Challenge of Prosperity Gospel," *Ministerium* 5 (2019) 11-27.

Okolo, Chukwudum, B. *African Traditional Religion and Christianity: The Neglected Dimension*. Nsukka: Fulladu, 1995.

Olupona, J.K. "Pentecostal-Charismatic Movement, Africa, West (Survey)" *International Dictionary of Pentecostal Charismatic Movements*, edited by Stanley Burgess and Eduard M. van der Maas, 11-21. Grand Rapids, MI: Zondervan, 2003.

Oyedepo, David. *Releasing the Supernatural: An Adventure into the Spirit World*. Lagos: Dominion, 1993.

Oyedepo, David. *Understanding Financial Prosperity*. Lagos: Dominion House, 1997.

Robeck, Cecil M., Jr. "Pentecostal Origins from a Global Perspective," *All Together in one Place: Theological Papers from the Brighton Conference on World Evangelization*, edited. Harold D. Hunter & Peter Hocken, 166-180. Sheffield: Sheffield Academic Press, 1993.

Sanneh, Lamin, *Translating the Message: The Missionary Impact on Culture* (New York: Orbis Books, 1989).

Stendahl, Krister. "The New Testament Evidence," *The Charismatic Movement*, ed. Michael P. Hamilton, 49-60: Grand Rapids, MI: William Eerdmans, 1975.

Tasie, G.O.M. *Christian Missionary Enterprise in the Niger Delta 1864-1918*. Leiden: E.J. Brill, 1978.

Udelhoven, Bernhard. *Unseen Worlds: Dealing with Spirits, Witchcraft and Satanism*. Lusaka: FENZA, 2016.

Uzukwu, Elochukwu. "Igbo World and Ultimate Reality and Meaning," *Ultimate Reality and Meaning* 5 (1982): 188-209.

Uzukwu, Elochukwu. "The Birth and Development of a Local Church: Difficulties and Signs of Hope." in *The African Synod: Documents, Reflections, Perspectives*, edited by Maura Browne, 3-8. New York: Orbis, 1996.

Uzukwu, Elochukwu. *God, Spirit, and Human Wholeness: Appropriating Faith and Culture in West African Style*. Eugene, Or: Pickwick, 2012.

Wariboko, Nimi. "African Pentecostalism: A Kinetic Description," *Na God: Aesthetics of African Charismatic Power*, edited Annalisa Butticci, Photography Andrew Esiobo, 21-23. Padova: Grafiche Turato Edizioni, 2013.

CHAPTER FIVE

Dialogue in Cultural Conflicts between the Church and African Traditions: Lessons from Biblical Traditions

Cosmas Uzowulu OFMCap

Introduction

Since the Second Vatican Council, there has been a renewed effort by the leadership of the Church to advance good rapport between Christians and those who belong to other religious traditions. Such dialogue is conceived as a meeting of people of differing religions, in an atmosphere of freedom and openness, in order to listen to the each other, to try to understand the person's religion, and hopefully to seek possibilities of collaboration.

This position cannot be clearer in the Post-Synodal Apostolic Exhortation of John Paul II which states that "authentic dialogue, therefore, is aimed above all at the rebirth of individuals through interior conversion and repentance, but always with profound respect for conscience and with patience and at the step-by-step pace indispensable for modern conditions."[174] Dialogue in our modern society of different religions is an important component of the mission of the Church in the world. The then Pontiff John Paul II refers to it as "a part of the evangelizing

---

[174] John Paul II, *Post-Synodal Apostolic Exhortation: Reconciliation and Penance* of John Paul II On the Reconciliation and Penance in the Mission of the Church Today (no.25).

mission of the Church."[175] And Pope Benedict the XVI stresses that it is "*caritas Christi*" that urges the Church to reach out to other believers.[176]

It is good to know at this point that the Church, *ab initio*, has been very positive with dialogue with Christians of other denominations and members of other Religions. This will be made clearer by the Magisterial Documents and other Biblical Documents that will be used in the course of this research. Unless indicated otherwise, New Reversed Standard Version, Catholic Edition is the version to be used in this paper.

Among the many fruits of the Council was the directive on the positive approach of the Church to people of other religions and traditions. The main Conciliar document for this novel approach was *Nostra Aetate* (1965) which set out the initial guidelines for interreligious relations. Even before the document was signed and approved by the Council Fathers, Pope Paul VI, in his very first encyclical letter, *Ecclesiam Suam* (1964), detailed the needs for the Church to reach out in dialogue to different institutions and persons in the world.

On Pentecost Sunday 1964, the same Pontiff announced officially the establishment of a special department of the Roman Curia for relations with the people of other religions and traditions. This department was first known as the Secretariat for Non-Christians, but in 1988 was renamed Pontifical Council for Interreligious Dialogue. In the course of time, this Pontifical Council for Interreligious Dialogue among other things articulated its responsibilities: to promote respect, mutual understanding and collaboration between the Church and followers of other religious traditions.

---

[175] See John Paul II, *Redemptoris mission*, 55.

[176] Benedict XVI, *Address to the Plenary Assembly of the Pontifical Council for Interreligious Dialogue*, 7 June 2008.

It is in this context and under this background of dialogue that we are launching into this interesting topic: dialogue between the Church and the African Traditions. We shall furnish our findings with insights and lessons from Biblical Traditions. The work will be in two parts. In Part One, we shall elaborate on the concept of dialogue and the witness of the Church in this regard. The biases from the part of the Church on African Traditions and the challenges the Church encountered will be highlighted. Progress made in dialoguing will be presented. The Second Part will be dedicated on the Lessons from the Biblical Traditions. In the final analysis, this will strengthen the desire for dialogue as an important vehicle of resolving conflicts by people of different creed and culture.

Witness in Dialogue

Christianity as a Religion was established in the midst of other existing religions and Traditions including African Traditions. From the very beginning, the followers of the Man of Nazareth had the challenge of establishing their presence in the midst of these other Traditions and Religions. For about three decades the Church has vigorously championed dialogue with other Traditions and Religions. Often this effort had been frustrated by these same Traditions and Religions on the Church through attacks in her places of worship and unhealthy and unnecessary conflicts.

In recent times, such violent attacks on the Church have been recorded in Egypt, India, Kenya, Nigeria, Iraq and in hosts of other places. The Church in the Middle East is under attack, and many Christians from that part of the world are now migrants. In Nigeria, especially in the Northern part of the country the story is the same. In the midst of all these events and sad stories and experiences, one cannot but wonder if there is still any need for any form of dialogue with these other traditions and religions.

With this dilemma on the witness in dialogue, the then Pontiff came up with one of the shortest but ground breaking documents of the Second Vatican Council, *Nostra Aetate*. This important document calls on all Christians to build a relationship of dialogue with those who form part of other religions: "The Church, therefore, exhorts her sons (and daughters), that through dialogue and collaboration with the followers of other religions, carried out with prudence and love and in witness to the Christian faith and life, they recognise, preserve and promote the good things, spiritual and moral, as well as the socio-cultural values found among these men."[177]

What Is Dialogue?

The term dialogue is employed to describe relations between folks of different religions and traditions. Cardinal Arinze opines that it is "a meeting of people of differing religions, in an atmosphere of freedom and openness, in order to listen to the other, to try to understand the person's religion, and hopefully to seek possibilities of collaboration."[178] At the purely human level, it means "reciprocal communication, leading to a common goal or, at a deeper level to interpersonal communion;"[179] and it is "attitude of respect and friendship, which permeates or should permeate all those activities constituting the evangelizing mission of the Church."[180]

---

[177] Cf. A. Flannery, ed., Vatican Council II: The Conciliar and Post Conciliar Documents – *Nostra Aetate*, 1 and 3.

[178] Cf. F. Arinze, *Meeting Other Believers* (Leominister, 1997), 5

[179] C. D. Isizoh, *Sharing the Good News of Christ in Dialogue: Crossing Religious Paths in Sub-Saharan African* (Onitsha: Trinitas, 2013) 21.

[180] Isizoh, *Sharing the Good News of Christ in Dialogue*, 21.

Experiences and exigencies of life have shown that any individual or society that learns to dialogue, lives to appreciate tomorrow.[181] The word has become a popular and household word. Dialogue is a matter of not criticizing another's opinion or defending one's position and ideology. It does not aim primarily on reaching a consensus.

Indeed, dialogue is a course of action of finding the midway by which people will meet themselves. "It is a conversation on a subject between two or more partners holding different views",[182] "working together in order to enrich one another thereby promoting greater unity among the people as well as religions."[183] We can call it a process of communicating differences. Hence it is a wonderful forum whereby people with differences come together to iron out their divergent worldviews. "In general, dialogue here means any form of getting together and communication between persons, groups, communities, in a spirit of sincerity, reverence for peace and a certain trust, in order to achieve either a greater grasp of truth or more human relationships."[184]

---

[181] Cf. A. Ezeonyiwara, "Promoting the Culture of Dialogue as a Panacea to the Prevalence of Disunity and Agitations in Many African Countries", in *The Church in Africa and the Challenges of Culture* (Nacaths Journal of African Theology, vol 27 March 2018) 32; similarly, N. I. Mbogu, *Jesus in Post-Missionary Africa: Issues and Questions in African Contextual Christology* (Enugu: San, 2012) 79-81; likewise, O. J. Amaegwu, *Dialogue with Culture: A New Method of Evangelization in Igboland* (Enugu: San, 2011)127-128; also, O. A. Onwubiko, *The Church in Mission: In the Light of Ecclesia in Africa* (Nairobi, Kenya: Pauline Publications Africa, 2001) 183-185.

[182] Cf. L. Swidler – J Cobb, et ali., *Death or Dialogue: From the Age of Monologue to the Age of Dialogue* (London: SCM Press, 1990) 57.

[183] Cf. M. Amaladoss, *Walking Together: The Practice of Inter-Religious Dialogue* (India: Gujarat Sahitya Prakash, 1992) 4.

[184] Cf. A. Flannery, ed., Vatican Council II: The Conciliar and Post Conciliar Documents – *Humanae Dignitatem*, 882.

Dialogue and Changing Attitude of the Church to African Traditions

It is a documented fact that Christianity reached sub-Saharan Africa through explorers, traders, colonial administrators and missionaries.[185] Pope Benedict XV[186] knew about this, hence he admonished the missionaries to be ambassadors of Christ not of their own country. Unfortunately since some of these missionaries travelled with their countrymen (the explorers), some of these missionaries were anxious to increase the power of their own countries rather than that of the kingdom.[187] The movement and activities of these fervent and early *angeloi* ("messengers") of the Gospel into different parts of the continent of Africa are documented in many of the international journals.[188]

It is a known fact that the early missionaries from Europe to Africa did not meet pagans, barbarians without any religion. The historian Herodotus had already observed how pious and creatively religious the Egyptians were before the Europeans brought Christianity to them. They were the "first who brought into use the names of the twelve gods, which the Greeks adopted from them; the first who erected altars, images, and temples to the gods; and also the first who engraved upon stone the figures

---

[185] The position and arguments expressed above could be assessed in the following authors: L. Layden, "Early Work of the Irish Province", in *Go Teach All Nations: A History of the Irish Province of the Congregation of the Holy Spirit* (ed. E. Watters; Dublin: Paraclete Press, 2000) 93-100; similarly, H. J. Koren, *To the Ends of the earth: A General History of the Congregation of the Holy Ghost* (Pittsburgh: Duquesne University Press, 1983) 24-38. But a more detailed documented facts are expressed and contained in a book by C. A. Ebelebe, *Africa and The New Face of Mission: A Critical Assessment of the Legacy of the Irish Spiritans Among The Igbo of SouthEastern Nigeria* (Lanham, Maryland: University Press, 2009) 59-82.

[186] We shall discuss the document of this Pontiff later in this work.

[187] Cf. Ebelebe, *Africa and the New face of Mission*, 71.

[188] Cf. Isizoh, *Sharing the Good News of Christ in Dialogue*, 78.

of animals",[189] this religious piety was and is still evident in the sub-Saharan Africa, as many African scholars, especially John Mbiti[190] and Edmund Metuh,[191] have pointed out. Paris opines that in spite of the variety of religious system, "the ubiquity of religious consciousness among African peoples constitutes their single most important common characteristic."[192]

The African person is deeply religious and has a very high sense of the sacred. Everything about him, around him and in him is deeply religious, since he eats, drinks, sleeps, works, and does practically everything religiously. Indeed, an African is a religious being by nature.

Early Difficulties

The first missionaries who first came to Africa for missionary activities had good intentions but unfortunately, they came with their own languages and cultures. Without serious regard to the cultural systems and religious traditions of many African ethnic groups and communities, some of the missionaries imposed their own categories of thought and religious worldviews on many African communities. Some of the major Church documents of later part of the 19th century and the first half of the 20th century, reflect a disrespect for African cultures and many of the cultural conflicts and divisions in many local churches in Africa today reflect the unresolved tension of these early beginnings of the faith in Africa.

The Church had no problem with the customs, rites and traditions of other people when they were not perceived as being in

---

[189] Herodotus, *The History of Herodotus – Book II* (tr. G. Rawlinson; New York: Tandy-Thomas Company, 1909) 49.

[190] Cf. J. S. Mbiti, *African Religions and Philosophy* (London: Heinemann, 1969),1.

[191] E. I. Metuh, *God and Man in African Religion* (London: G. Chapman, 1981)20-40

[192] P. J. Paris, *The Spirituality of African People: The Search for a Common Moral Discourse* (Minneapolis: Kindle, 1995) 12-20.

conflict with "divine laws." Pope Pius XII in his address to the directors of the Pontifical Mission Works put it very clearly: "The specific character, the traditions, the customs of each nation must be preserved intact, so long as they are not in contradiction with the divine law. The missionary is an apostle of Jesus Christ. His task is not to propagate European civilization in mission lands..... rather it is his function so to train and guide other peoples, some of whom glory in their ancient and refined civilization, as to prepare and dispose them for the willing and hearty acceptance of the principles of Christian life and behaviour......"

The situation was completely different when it came to the attitude towards other religions and other religious traditions. Non-Jews in the Bible were considered as pagans whose "gods are idols, silver and gold, the work of human hands" (Ps 134:15-18). Verses 15-18 of Psalm 134 consist of a polemic against idols. Remarkable is the fresh use of the material in the aforementioned verses to function no longer as a negative confession of trust with a final wish but an implicit praise of Yahweh matching the explicit praise of vv. 5-7. The satire on heathen religions promotes the exclusiveness of Yahweh. These Jewish in-jokes about the powerlessness of cultic images serve to contrast the made with the divine maker of vv.6-7. The logical conclusion concerning the prediction of doom for their devotees who will end up like them stresses the welfare of Yahweh worshipper. This biblical attitude influenced the kind of negative characterization of African cultures and way of life by many missionaries who brought Christianity to Africa.

The framing of non-Christian religions and especially African traditions in some of the Church's documents and expressions of the pre-Vatican II Council was not generally positive. When one looks at the different archives of the reports sent to "Mother-houses" by the early missionaries that came to Africa one can see numerous documents which ooze with these negative characterizations of Africans. But the more disturbing is the official position of the Church towards these other religions and their traditions expressed in some of her official documents. I will briefly discuss three of such well-known documents which came to light during the years of implantatio of the Gospel in the Africa soil. These documents are two encyclicals and one Apostolic Exhortation. These documents came from the highest authority of the Church on earth. They gave direction to the missionaries coming to Africa on how to treat the traditions of these people.

The encyclical of Pope Leo XIII, Catholicae Ecclesiae of 1890 among other things told the missionaries in Africa apart from working hard to stop the slave trade that they should try to "bathe those inhabitants living in darkness and blind superstition with the light of divine truth, by which they can become co-heirs with us of the kingdom of God."

In Maximum Illud, Pope Benedict XV referred to the followers of non-Christian religions as "the numberless heathen who are still sitting in the shadows of death. According to recent statistics their number accounts to a thousand million." These people stood in need of the "benefits of divine redemption." These native folks were in need of the "benefits of divine redemption." It was the task of the bishops "to light the torch for those sitting in the shadows of death, and open the gate of heaven to those who rush to their destruction." Major Superiors whose members were engaged in missionary work in Africa were mandated after having "successfully accomplished their task and converted some nations from unhallowed superstition to Christian faith and have founded there a Church with sufficient prospects, they should transfer them, as Christ's forlorn hope, to some other nation to snatch it from Satan's grasp."

In the Rerum Ecclesiae, Pope Pius XI thought it a great act of charity on the part of the European missionaries to withdraw "pagans...from darkness of superstition" in order to instruct them "in the true faith in Christ." Each missionary is encouraged to "bravely face all hardships and difficulties, as long as he can snatch a soul from the mouth of hell."

Furthermore, Pope Pius XI encouraged vocation to the priesthood especially for "heathens particularly those who are still savages and barbarians." The Pontiff encouraged European missionaries to have patience, saying: "if you find extreme slowness of mind in the case of men who live in the very heart of barbarous regions, this is due to the conditions of their lives, for, since the exigencies of their lives are limited, they are not compelled to make great use of their intelligence."

The missionary zeal to instruct and save the Africans from the "darkness of superstition" went beyond catechizing them in the true faith in Jesus Christ to an overall cultural advancement and civilization of the uncivilized and uneducated and illiterate people. Hence the zealous missionaries preached and taught the theology of discontinuity. They urged the Africans to break up with their traditions which were evil. As if this were not enough, they tabulated as mortal sins some of the African traditions and practices which were different from Western way of life. Unfortunately, this is the image of Africa and African religions and people before the Second Vatican Council.

Positive Attitudes of the Church towards Other Traditions

With the advent of the Second Vatican Council, the Church scored a major breakthrough with other religions and traditions. In one of its earliest documents of this period, Lumen Gentium, the Church makes it clear that salvation is possible for other believers outside the visible Christian fold:

> The plan of salvation includes those also who acknowledge the Creator... with us, adore the one and merciful God who will judge mankind on the last day. Nor is God far from those who in shadows and images seek the unknown God; for he gives to all men life and breath and all things, and as Saviour desires all men to be saved. For those also can attain eternal salvation who without fault on their part do not know the Gospel of Christ and his Church,

but seek God with sincere heart, and under the influence of grace endeavor to do his will as recognised through the promptings of their conscience.

In another Church document, Gaudium et Spes, the Council Fathers encouraged dialogue among all people. This dialogue should spring from mutual respect and love which should be found in all spheres of human interaction. Furthermore, the Council's fathers in *Nostra Aetate*, urged all Christians "to enter with prudence and charity into discussion and collaboration with members of other religions." The document continues that "while witnessing to their own faith and way of life, acknowledge, preserve and encourage the spiritual and moral truths found among non-Christians, also their social life and culture."

In his first encyclical letter, *Ecclesiam Suam*, Pope Paul VI mentioned by name "followers of the great religions of Africa and Asia." It is also significant to note similar positive sentiments towards African cultures in *Africae Terrarium* where Pope Paul VI praised the numerous valuable elements found in the African worldview which the Church appreciates and respects. This Pontiff in order to make concrete his intention, established the Pontifical Council for Interreligious Dialogue and mandated it with the specific duty to "become a means by which to arrive at a sincere and respectful dialogue with those who still believe in God and worship him."

More understanding, appreciation and direct contact with the practitioners of African Traditional Religions with their traditions had to wait until the pontificate of John Paul II. This Pontiff praised the many positive values found in African traditions and cultures that can help the African person to be open to the Gospel of Jesus Christ. This particular Pope introduced a new dimension to the dialogue with the followers of African traditions, that on 4 February, 1999 he met and addressed the followers of this Tradition in the Republic of Benin.

In his dialogue with them, the Pope made it clear that African Traditional Religion is not an archaic religion of primitive people, but rather a religion of the vibrant and living people. It is also remarkable that as recently as 24 November, 2013, the present Pontiff, Pope Francis, in his Apostolic Exhortation Evangelii Gaudium made an important contribution in this area. Among other things the Pontiff said that "dialogue is in first place a conversation about human existence." He continued by saying that "in this way we learn to accept others and their different ways of living, thinking and speaking." This kind of dialogue will lead to an openness in understanding the other party, which will eventually enrich each side.

Second Part – Lessons from Biblical Traditions

In this second part of our study, we shall employ some passages from the Sacred Text to achieve our aim, that is, to see how our Holy Book dialogued with other traditions and cultures and how it can help us in developing practices of dialogue between Christianity and African religions and cultures in our times.

Salvation is from the Jews (Jn 4:22)

Here, we see how a Jew, born into the Jewish religion leaves his abode and his religion and tradition and moves to the periphery of Judaism, to Samaria, and here he not only meets a woman from a different religion and tradition, but he shows the woman that his religion and tradition are far better than hers. But despite this apparent and negative evaluation of the woman's religion and tradition, Jesus was able to dialogue with her and convince her too of the beauty of her own religion and tradition. This methodology of Jesus is a right approach to meeting with another religion or tradition.

One of the challenges put before the Samaritan woman is for her to unravel the mystery of Jesus' words as he replaces the very well she reveres and in this context her ancestral tradition.

Dialogue in Cultural Conflicts

The Jewish Master has a religion that the Samaritan woman has never known, even in her home religion and she must discern how to get enter into this new religious space. This Jewish Messiah broke every barrier to be able to positively influence a person of another religion and tradition. In our world of today where religious conflict is on the increase, the methodology of Jesus with the Samaritan woman should be used to address the tension in a world of religious conflict.

This invites different practices of dialogue enriched by a convinced and exemplary way of life which rejects all forms of extremism and language of aggression and negative judgement which often demeans other people's religions. With this, the entire world with its different religions should live in peace and not in conflict. How can we employ the Samaritan narrative in developing a methodology for dialogue?

Many modern readers, who correctly observe that Jesus surmounts the Jewish-Samaritan chasm in this story may be surprised that before Jesus does so, he does take sides, and he plainly announces that the Jewish side was correct on the central matter of salvation history. This affirmation surprises us, however, only if we assume that the Johannine community had broken completely with its Jewish heritage and regards that heritage in a negative manner. In the opinion of many learned scholars, such an assumption stems from a misreading of John's usual use of the title "Jews." "We" in this context, can only mean the "Jews", and Jesus remains a faithful Jew in the Fourth Gospel even if not regarded as such by the leaders of his people. Contrary to the usual Gentile Christian reading of the Gospels, the Synoptic Jesus likewise required Gentiles to recognise Israel's priority and preeminence (Mk 7:27-29? Mt 15:24-28; Mt 8:7-8; Lk 7:6-7). Dialogue with other traditions and cultures does not mean denying the truth. It simply means recognizing and affirming the truth without making the other feel rejected.

Because the Samaritans accepted only Moses but rejected the Judean aspect of salvation history, including the Davidic messiah, they necessarily held an incomplete view of salvation history by both Jewish and Christian standards. Some regard "salvation" in John as eschatological messianic deliverance. Some other scholars are of the opinion that it functions as a Christological title here.

In the context of the entire Fourth Gospel, it embraces Jesus' mission of transforming citizens of the world into people born from above, and locates Jesus himself, the bringer of salvation, squarely within the salvation history of Israel (see esp. 3,17 in context; cf.4,42). "Quite simply, Judea is conceived as the country of origin of Jesus the Messiah (Jn 1:41; 4:25) and as such the source of salvation." Jesus recognised this but at the same time he was able to affirm what is good in the woman's religion and tradition.

In the end, however, Jesus challenges both Jewish and Samaritan traditions, calling for a higher worship that transcends geographical – in this context also ethnic – particularities (4,21) and traditions. Here, we see how Jesus coming from a different tradition was able to dialogue with another person different from him and coming from a different tradition to accept his own new teaching and tradition.

African Traditions Insight from the Areopagus Speech in Athens

Athens (like Corinth) was in the province of Achaia and it is the capital of modern Greece. Today the heart of the city is "sufficiently cleared for the great monuments of its classical past to be conspicuously visible." In this section (Paul in Athens 17, 16-32), I will focus mostly on those areas of Paul's Areopagus speech that are especially relevant to my interest and the discussion of approaches to dialogue. Where necessary I provide, as I go along, commentaries on some relevant verses. When Paul saw the exquisite works of pagan arts, he was "greatly distressed" (v.16). Though Paul was in a rage when he saw the idols, he acted with restraint and respect in his outward behaviour among the idolaters. The Areopagus was the main administrative body and the chief court of Athens. Here, Paul delivered a speech that "could be considered as one of the earliest presentations of a Comparative Theology of Religions in the New Testament."

In this speech in Athens (Acts 17:16-32), Paul rendered the concept of God among the non-Jews in a positive light. The God worshipped in the pagan territory is the same creator whom the apostle had come to announce. The speech, then, provides the theological basis for the missionary adventure among non-Jews and non-Christians. God is not tied down to a particular geographical ambient. God is acknowledged and worshipped by all people everywhere. No particular religion or Tradition has a monopoly of this God.

This speech of Paul remains a model of sensitive but forthright confrontation of an intellectual audience with the claim of the Gospel. "Very Religious" in Paul's opening remarks (v.22) is a general word that can mean different things depending on the context. It could be a criticism, as is implied by the KJV translation: "Ye are too superstitious" though this is an unlikely way to start an evangelistic speech. It was most likely not a compliment, for according to an ancient writer Lucian, "complimentary exordia [beginnings] to secure the goodwill of the Areopagus court were discouraged." Obviously, it seems to be a simple observation, opening the way for Paul's comment about the altar to the unknown god (v.23a).

In the city of Socrates, Paul adapted his message to his audience both in style and content. His speech to the philosophical members of the Areopagus was perceived as a divinely philosophical discourse. He commenced by alluding to a need his audience was conscious of (which brought about setting up a temple to an unknown God). Though his substance was entirely biblical, he did not quote from the Scriptures as he did when he spoke to Jews and God-fearers. In fact, he quoted from the writings of their own philosophers (v.28). We call such adaptation or translation of meaning a form of contextualization. Contextualization occurs when the presentation and the outworking of the gospel is done in a manner appropriate to the context in which it is found.

People of Deep Religion

"I perceive that in every way you are very religious (v.22). "Africans are notoriously religious." This affirmation can be verified in the lives of most Africans. Religion permeates every aspect of African life. Mbiti expresses the religiosity forcefully when he affirms that wherever the African is, his or her religion is there with him or her in whatever he or she does, whether he or she is in business or in politics. Indeed, everything about the African person is religious. Holloway elaborates further by saying that religion for an African is a way of life. Right from the womb till death, many African societies have religious ritual for each phase of life.

For the fact that religion is deeply rooted in the life of an African, this could explain why a good number of Africans migrate from African Traditional Religion to Christianity or to Islam. This can as well explain the reason behind the spreading and founding of many religious groups in the land of Africa. Barrett has recorded a long list of religious groups operating in Africa. The number is growing every day. Africans are always aware of the presence of divine in their lives. The African's strong religious instinct is a proof that no amount of human or scientific endeavor can solve the problem of the human person without divine intervention.

Religious Items in Worship

"For as I passed along, and observed the objects of your worship" (v.23a). Generally, the term "worship" is not found in the vocabulary of many African societies. In some sections of the African society, when such a term is employed, it most likely refers to religious acts which are directed to God. The terms we hear often among the Africans are "offering" and "worship." The objects employed in the worship include: animals, foodstuffs, drinks and incense. A place, shrine or temple is always set apart for the offering and sacrifices. The sacred spot where sacrifices are made is the altar. All these objects of worship are seen in the Traditions of the African. Hence, there should not be any conflict between the Church and the African Traditions.

The Profundity of God

"I found also an altar....to an unknown god....this I proclaim to you" (v.23b). Traditions of Africa and its religions had been variously described as monotheistic, pantheistic, polytheistic and recently a learned author has added henotheistic. The divinities are broadly divided into two. This division is not on the basis of equality of status. The Tradition has the Supreme deity and the subordinate deities. The missionaries who came to Africa did not meet a people without the knowledge of God. They equally did not encounter pagans. The missionaries did not invent the names and various attributes given to God. They employed what was already available among the people in their traditions.

When the Apostle Paul spoke about an "Unknown god", many Africans would have recognised the phrase as the title they give to the Supreme deity (God). The Igbo will not find it hard to understand that Chukwu (God) is Amama-amasiama (the Known who cannot be sufficiently known).

It is very clear from the above discussion that the important concepts and religious ideas expressed in the Areopagus speech are not strange to Africans in their traditions. If this speech originally were addressed to Africans in their traditions, it would have been well received. Paul adopted a wonderful methodology of presenting the Good News in the context of the Greek religious establishment. He was respectful of the traditions of his audience. This very methodology of contextualizing the Gospel is most admired. If the missionaries who came to Africa had applied this text in the context of evangelisation, it would have created the right structure and foundation for the flourishing of Christianity in Africa without so much of the tensions and conflicts which seem to be increasing amidst the contending narratives of modernity and the new narratives of religions in Africa.

Implications

The great Apostle Paul reasoned with the Athenians he met. He expressed what I might call 'Restrained Provocation.' He studied this religion and traditions of the Athenians and was familiar with the way of life and thought of the people whom he sought to lead to Christ. This ought to have been the attitude of the early missionaries in Africa.

The issue of studying other religions and traditions has come into special focus in recent times. These past years have seen a fresh discovery in the Western world of the cultural and religious heritage of many non-Christian cultures. As Stephen Neil puts it, "as these 'treasures of darkness' penetrated the consciousness...something of a gasp of astonishment arose. Surprise was followed by appreciation and even admiration."

The negative reaction to non-Christian religions and traditions which we find today not only in the attitude of Westerners to African cultures, but also in the hostility and intolerance which we find among some African Church leaders in our local churches does not seem to accord with this biblical tradition represented by the evangelist, Paul. It borders on paranoia in that it sees non-Christians only as being under the grip of demonic powers, thus making inter-cultural and inter-faith exchanges impossible.

When we meet non-Christians and find things that we can admire in them, we should not be afraid to acknowledge it. Our measure of truth must always be the Scriptures. If the Bible agrees with something that another religion or tradition teaches, we do not need to be afraid about affirming it. But if Scripture disagrees, we must respectfully say so and seek to show why it is wrong, as Paul did in Athens.

I will propose by way of concluding this biblical theological appropriation that when theology and philosophy dialogue with cultures and traditions in creative ways, they become a powerful and inspiring tool for renewing humanity with the Word of God. This is in agreement with the statement of Pope Francis at the 2019 Ratzinger Prize's Award ceremony at the Vatican. According to Pope Francis: "This is true for all cultures: access to redemption for humanity in all of its dimensions should be sought with creativity and imagination." He quoted Pope Paul VI's apostolic exhortation, Evangelii Nuntiandi, which says, "Evangelizing means bringing the Good News into all the strata of humanity, and through its influence transforming humanity from within and making it new." In this regard, Pope Francis affirms that, "It is a duty for theology to be and remain in active dialogue with cultures, even as they change over time and evolve differently in various parts of the world…It is a condition necessary for the vitality of Christian faith, for the Church's mission of evangelisation."

Conclusion

A Church that seeks to be faithful to Christ's call to go to the unreached must take the challenge of contextualization seriously. What the Church should do is to enter into dialogue with those local traditions especially with a view to translating what is good and true in them into the Gospel message. Indeed, whatever goodness there is found in people and the traditions to which they belong are sources for God's continued revelation in history. The guiding principle for church leaders in Africa today should be the same central message which has governed the work of evangelisation and translation: "let not the Gospel on being introduced into any new land destroy or extinguish whatever its people possess, that is naturally good, just or beautiful."

For the Church, when she calls men and women to a higher and a better way of life under the inspiration of the Christian religion, does not act like one who recklessly cuts down and uproots a thriving forest. No, she grafts a good scion upon the wild stock: that it may be a crop of more delicious fruit.

Bibliography

Allen, L. C., *Psalms 101-150*. WBC 21; Nashville: Thomas Nelson, 2002.

Amaegwu, O. J., *Dialogue with Culture: A New Method of Evangelization in Igboland*. Enugu: San, 2011.

Amaladoss, M., *Walking Together: The Practice of Inter-Religious Dialogue*. India: Gujarat Sahitya Prakash, 1992.

Arinze, F., *Meeting Other Believers*. Leominister, 1997.

Barrett, D. B., ed., *World Christian Encyclopaedia*. Oxford: Oxford University Press, 2001.

Basden, G. T., *Among the Ibos of Nigeria*. Lagos: 1983.

Benedict XV, Apostolic Letter, *Maximum Illud* (The Latin text of Maximum Illud is found in AAS 11 (1919) 440-55.

Benedict XVI, *Address to the Plenary Assembly of the Pontifical Council for Interreligious Dialogue*, 7 June 2008.

Bernard, J. H., *A Critical and Exegetical Commentary on the Gospel according to St John*. ICC; Edinburgh: T & T Clark, 1928.

Ebelebe, C. A. *Africa and The New Face of Mission: A Critical Assessment of the Legacy of the Irish Spiritans Among The Igbo of South-Eastern Nigeria*. Lanham, Maryland: University Press, 2009.

Ezeonyiwara, A.,"Promoting the Culture of Dialogue as a Panacea to the Prevalence of Disunity and Agitations in Many African Countries," in *The Church in Africa and the Challenges of Culture* (Nacaths Journal of African Theology, vol 27 March 2018).

Fernando, A., *Acts: The NIV Application Commentary*. Grand Rapids, Michigan: Zondervan, 1998.

Flannery, A., ed., *Vatican Council II: The Conciliar and Post Conciliar Documents – Nostra Aetate*, 1 and 3.

Flannery, A., ed., *Vatican Council II: The Conciliar and Post Conciliar Documents – Humanae Dignitatem*.

Francis, *Evangelii Gaudium* – Apostolic Exhortation.

Holloway, J. E., ed., *Africanisms in American Culture*. Indiana: Indiana University Press, 1990.

Herodotus, *The History of Herodotus – Book II*. tr. G. Rawlinson; New York: Tandy-Thomas Company, 1909.

Idowu, E. B., *Olodumare: God in Yoruba Belief*. London: SCM, 1962.

Isizoh, C. D., *Sharing the Good News of Christ in Dialogue: Crossing Religious Paths in Sub-Saharan African*. Onitsha: Trinitas, 2013.

Jeremias, J., *Jesus' Promise to the Nations*. tr. S. H. Hooke SBT 24; London: SCM, 1958.

John Paul II, Post-Synodal Apostolic Exhortation: Reconciliation and Penance of John Paul II On the Reconciliation and Penance in the Mission of the Chruch Today.

Keener, C. S., *The Gospel of John A Commentary*. Grand Rapids, Michigan: Baker, 2003.

———, *Acts: An Exegetical Commentary*. Grand Rapids, Michigan: Baker, 2014.

Koren, H. J., *To the Ends of the earth: A General History of the Congregation of the Holy Ghost*. Pittsburgh: Duquesne University Press, 1983.

Layden, L., "Early Work of the Irish Province", in Go Teach All Nations: A History of the Irish Province of the Congregation of the Holy Spirit. ed. E. Watters; Dublin: Paraclete Press, 2000.

Leo XII, *Encyclical Catholicae Ecclesiae* 3 (1890), 258.

Longenecker, R. N., *The Christology of the Early Christianity*. Grand Rapids: Baker, 1981.

Mbiti, J. S., *African Religions and Philosophy*. London: Heinemann, 1969.

Mbogu, N. I., *Jesus in Post-Missionary Africa: Issues and Questions in African Contextual Christology*. Enugu: San, 2012.

Metuh, E. I., *God and Man in African Religion* (London: G. Chapman, 1981)20-40

─────, *Comparative Studies of African Traditional Religion*. Onitsha: Trinitas, 1987.

Neill, S., *Crisis of Belief*. London: Hodder and Stoughton, 1984.

Onwubiko, O. A., *The Church in Mission: In the Light of Ecclesia in Africa* (Nairobi, Kenya: Pauline Publications Africa, 2001) 183-185.

Paris, P. J., *The Spirituality of African People: The Search for a Common Moral Discourse*. Minneapolis: Kindle, 1995.

Parrinder, E. G., *West African Religion*. London: Epworth Press, 1961.

Paul VI, *Lumen Gentium – The Dogmatic Constitution on the Church*, 16.

─────, *Gaudium et Spes – Pastoral Constitution on the Church in the Modern World*.

─────, *Ecclesiam suam – An Encyclical*.

─────, *Nostra Aetate – Declaration on the Relation of the Church to Non-Christian Religions*.

Pius XI, *Rerum Ecclesiae*, AAS 18. 1926.

Pius XII, *Evangelii Praecones (1961) – On Promoting Catholic Missions*.

Sikes, W. W., "the Anti-Semitism of the Fourth Gospel," *Journal of Religion*, 21 (1941).

Swidler, L – Cobb, J. et al., *Death or Dialogue: From the Age of Monologue to the Age of Dialogue*. London: SCM Press, 1990.

Vatican City, 09 November, 2019 (ACI Africa).

CHAPTER SIX

The Role of Religion in Africa's Twentieth Century Wars and Genocides: Lessons for African Churches

SimonMary Asese Aihiokhai

Introduction

The twentieth century was marked by conflicts and was shaped and sustained by religio-political and ethnic ideologies; brutal African dictatorships with no development-oriented agenda; and a perpetuation of the colonial heritage of divide and rule that was legitimized by the hyper-consciousness of tribal, religious, linguistic, and class identities. The question arises: How can Africa break away from these vicious cycles of exploitation and negative hyper-religiosity that define the contours of violence shaping the history of the continent?

In addressing this question, the greatest temptation Africans must resist is the urge to rush to embrace simplistic conclusions that fail to explain the complex issues that define the crises the continent faces. The narrative of blaming everything solely on the colonial heritage is, at best, stale. Africa's dilemma is shaped by both colonial and post-colonial realities. These realities will be critiqued in this chapter.

This chapter will do the following: Articulate the factors shaping these conflicts while also providing a critique of religious fundamentalism playing out in the continent of Africa. Finally, in this chapter, I seek to provide a new vision of religious harmony amongst the religiously and culturally diverse communities in Africa; one that takes seriously Africa's religious and cultural focus on the sacredness of life as well as the preservation of communal peace.

Understanding Africa's Religious Conflicts

The starting point for an analysis of the religious conflicts in Africa has to begin with the factors defining the human condition and how that condition is realised. For this, I turn to Hannah Arendt. In her work, *The Human Condition*, Arendt makes the following observation:

> The human condition comprehends more than the conditions under which life has been given to man. Men are conditioned beings because everything they come in contact with turns immediately into a condition of their existence. The world in which the *vita activa* spends itself consists of things produced by human activities; but the things that owe their existence exclusively to men nevertheless constantly condition their human makers. In addition to the conditions under which life is given to man on earth, and partly out of them, men constantly create their own, self-made conditions, which, their human origin and their variability notwithstanding, possess the same conditioning power as natural things. Whatever touches or enters into a sustained relationship with human life immediately assumes the character of a condition of human existence. This is why men, no matter what they do, are always conditioned beings...[193]

Arendt postulates that the human condition plays out within the framework of the concept of *vita activa*. *Vita activa* covers the following "human activities: labour, work, and action."[194] These three categories define human life in society. With these categories in mind, one has to ask the question: What are the enduring conditions defining life in Africa? For the pre-colonial era, I

---

[193] Hannah Arendt, *The Human Condition. Second Edition* (Chicago: The University of Chicago Press, 1998), 9.

[194] Ibid., 7.

turn to Chinua Achebe, whose novel, *Things Fall Apart*, offers a glimpes into that period in African history. The novel presents stories of pre-colonial life in a fictional town in Igboland; one that showcases notions of communalism, fraternity; matrilineal and patrilineal social and kindred structures; as well as a rich religiosity that highlight indigenous religious thoughts.[195]

Furthermore, for the colonial and post-colonial realities shaping Africans and their way of life, I turn to John Reader. In his work, *Africa: A Biography of the Continent,* Reader notes that the colonial venture in Africa by the European powers of the nineteenth century ignored the pre-colonial political and cultural realities in the continent by creating new nation-states with national and cultural boundaries that did not reflect the historical, cultural, and socio-political realities in the continent. The colonial agenda has led to a socio-political Africa that is defined by persistent conflicts among some ethnic groups in the continent.[196]

Again, Arendt's postulation must force one to think of the things that have and continue to define Africans and their societies since colonial times. Colonialism and its vestiges cannot be removed from the discourse. It is important to give a working definition of colonialism. "Colonialism is a practice of domination, which involves the subjugation of one people to another."[197] The range of such a practice of domination include politics, economics, culture, language, epistemology, hermeneutics, and religion; especially as they help define the identity of a people – the identity of the colonized people.

As noted by Achebe and Reader, vestiges of colonialism play a role in shaping contemporary African condition. Such vestiges

---

[195] See Chinua Achebe, *Things Fall Apart* (London: Penguin Books 1994).

[196] John Reader, *Africa: A Biography of the Continent* (New York: Vintage Books, 1997), 609 – 610.

[197] Margaret Kohn and Kavita Reddy, "Colonialism," in *The Stanford Encyclopedia of Philosophy, Fall 2017 edition,* ed. Edward n. Zalta, https://plato.stanford.edu/entries/colonialism/.

are addressed head-on by the insights of Jean-Paul Sartre; while reflecting on the effect of colonialism on the 'Third World,' Africa included. For him, the Third World "still contains subjected peoples, some of whom have acquired a false independence, others who are fighting to conquer their sovereignty, and yet others who have won their freedom, but who live under the constant threat of imperialist aggression. These differences are born out of colonial history, in other words, oppression."[198]

Violence, as an operative mechanism, is central to the colonial venture. Here, violence is to be broadly understood to include intellectual, linguistic, cultural, religious, political, economic, gender, racial, and so on. Colonialism operates with a sense of superiority of the coloniser over the colonized. Any form of resistance towards this perception is met with violence. To ensure that such resistance does not occur or is under control, the ideological praxis of divide and rule is introduced into all levels of encounter between the coloniser and the colonized.

Tribalism serves as the modus vivendi introduced by the coloniser to radically define the identity markers of the colonized; such as language, culture; religion; knowledge production; and so on. Reader captures the functioning dynamics of tribalism in colonial Africa when he writes: "Tribalism is the most pernicious of the traditions which the colonial period bequeathed to Africa....[It] has [a] distinctly dark and nasty African connotation: the Maasai and the Kikuyu in Kenya; the Zulu and the Xhosa in South Africa; the Yoruba, Hausa, and Igbo in Nigeria; the Hutu and Tutsi in Rwanda and Burundi.

These and other groups have at times seemed determined to eliminate each other simply because they claimed differences of birthright."[199] Furthering his analysis on the role of tribal iden-

---

[198] Jean-Paul Sartre, "Preface," in Franz Fanon, *The Wretched of the Earth*, trans. Richard Philcox (New York: Grove Press, 2004), xlvi.

[199] Reader, *Africa: A Biography of the Continent*, 614 – 615.

tities in shaping the trajectory of African nation-states, Reader makes the following relevant claims about Kenya and Nigeria:

> In Kenya, the conviction that the Kikuyu and Maasai were sworn enemies, which had motivated a good deal of colonial policy, was a fiction invented by the colonial administration for their own convenience.... In Nigeria, although broad cultural identities – pan-Igbo, pan-Hausa, and pan-Yoruba – had emerged before the missionaries and the British administration arrived to make their mark on the social landscape, they did not correspond to the colonial notion of static tribal identities. They were a reality, but they waxed and waned under changing conditions; they were units of inclusivity as often as of exclusivity, which embodied the notion of linguistic and cultural affinity rather than a rigid idea of shared descent.[200]

On another note, an enduring manifestation of the colonial heritage can be seen in the domain of the religious praxis of evangelisation. Within the context of colonialism, Christian evangelisation presented the religious heritage of Africans as fetishism that needed to be stamped out. This narrative was not always well received by Africans, especially when the political, economic, and religious agenda of the Europeans were seen by Africans as mean of subjugating them as a people. Sometimes, such a narrative led to religio-political conflicts.

An example of such conflicts is the Matabeleland Rebellion of 1896. In this struggle, the M'limo (spiritual leader of the Matabele people) used his spiritual authority to call for a rebellion against British imperialism in Matabeleland; an imperialism that threatened their socio-cultural and religious way of life.[201] Another example is the initial contacts between Portuguese

---

[200] Ibid., 615.

[201] See Terence Ranger, "The Role of The Ndebele and Shona Religious Authorities in The Rebellions of 1896 and 1897," in *The Zambesian Past: Studies in Central History*, eds. Eric Stokes and Richard Brown (Manchester: Manchester University Press, 1966), 94 – 136.

Christian explorers and African Muslims.

The colonial strategy of the Portuguese for consolidating their positions in Africa, especially in East Africa, was defended by the false narrative of fighting the "battle in the Christian war against Islam."[202] As noted by Reader, "On his second voyage to India ... Vasco da Gama encountered a ship laden with pilgrims going to Mecca. There were 380 men on board, besides many women and children. The ship was primed with gunpowder and then blown up, with the pilgrims on board."[203]

Furthermore, looking closely at Nigeria's post-colonial history, Olufemi Vaughan offers the following insights: "Social and political platform on which modern Nigeria was constructed after the imposition of colonial rule at the beginning of the twentieth century was shaped by the factors defining Christianity and Islam in the respective regions that were amalgamated to form Nigeria."[204] In the North, for example, tensions arose between the dominant Muslim Hausa-Fulani party, NPC (Northern Peoples Party) and the multi ethno-religious party, the United Middle Belt Congress, that represented the interests of the minority groups in the region. The NPC officials were accused of using state power to oppress the non-Hausa-Fulani population that happened to be comprised of indigenous religionists and Christians.[205] Iheanyi M. Enwerem also makes the following observations:

> Bello's specific target for the final unification of the North was to convert the 'pagan' enclaves in the region of Islam. He was determined to sway them away from the Christian missionaries. This move was understandable, principally because the enclaves were not only the major sources of Christian growth in the North,

---

[202] Reader, *Africa: A Biography of the Continent*, 361.

[203] Ibid., 361 – 362.

[204] Olufemi Vaughan, *Religion and the Making of Nigeria* (Durham and London: Duke University Press, 2016), 14.

[205] Ibid., 113.

but could also become the seedbed of a political threat to Islamic interest in the region if the trend were allowed to continue. Besides, Christian missionaries had erroneously resigned themselves to the belief that these 'pagan' enclaves were the reserved domain for their missionary enterprise. [206]

Similarly, Christianity has also been ethno-politicized in Nigeria's history. The Nigerian civil war cannot be understood in its complex nature without a critical study of the role of religio-ethnic identity markers that defined the conflict. As noted by Niels Kastfelt, "Religion was a decisive element in the social identity of the fighting parties, not the least of the predominantly Roman Catholic Igbos."[207] On another note, "a more nuanced framework for the analysis of religion in conflict and peacebuilding underscores the public nature of religion and the incoherence of the thesis of governmental neutrality – incoherence most pronounced in zones of conflict defined by ethnoreligious national claims and objectives."[208]

Reflecting on the factors shaping Africa's 20th century wars, Kastfelt argues the following: "Conflicts do, of course, have local reasons but we should avoid an African exceptionalism in at least two respects. We should, firstly, keep in mind that globally the twentieth century experienced more systematic killing and violence than any other century in history. So, while African wars are indeed African and have African roots, they take place in the most violent century in world history, in the 'age of massacre.' Secondly, we should be careful not to exoticise post-

---

[206] Iheanyi M. Enwerem, *A Dangerous Awakening: The Politicization of Religion in Nigeria* (Ibadan: Institut Français de Recherche en Afrique, 1995), 52.

[207] Niels Kastfelt, "Religion and African Civil Wars. Themes and Interpretations," *Religion and African Civil Wars*, ed. Niels Kastfelt (London: Hurst and Company, 2005), 3.

[208] Atalia Omer, "Conflict and Peacebuilding," in *Religion and Culture. Contemporary Practices and Perspectives*, eds. Richard D. Hecht and Vincent F. Biondo III (Minneapolis: Fortress Press, 2012), 4.

colonial violence in Africa and thereby, by implication, normalise colonial violence."²⁰⁹ To appreciate Kastfelt's point, one has to go back to the insight of Arendt on how the human condition plays out in society. Vestiges of colonialism continue to define African way of life.

Again, colonialism legitimizes violence as a tool for perpetuating its inherent agenda, the exploitation of its victims on multiple levels. One form of such exploitation is found in the strategic claim to the right by the League of Nations to hand over Rwanda and Burundi to the Belgians as 'a sacred trust of civilization.' "The Belgian response to 'civilization's sacred trust' concerning Ruanda-Urundi was to treat the territories as an extension of the Belgian Congo. The two countries became economically subservient to the greedy monster on their western flank. There was no mineral wealth to be exploited in either Ruanda or Urundi, but high population densities made them a valuable labour pool for the copper mine in Katanga. For example, more than 2 percent of the entire able-bodied male population of Ruanda-Urundi was working in the Congo, most of them in Katanga."²¹⁰

To conclude this section of this chapter, I make the following claim: Insofar as the vestiges of colonialism are still present in Africa. Such vestiges like political, economic, religious, cultural, and economic exploitations resurrect multiple types of conflicts like "liberation insurgencies; separatist insurgencies; reform insurgencies; and warlord insurgencies."²¹¹ An example of a separatist insurgency is the Sudanese civil war under its former ruler, Omar al-Bashir.²¹² After overthrowing the elected government in 1989,

---

209 Kastfelt, "Religion and African Civil Wars. Themes and Interpretations", 2.

210 Reader, *Africa: A Biography of the Continent*, 620

211 For a detailed explanation and with particular examples of how these insurgencies are playing out in post-colonial Africa see Christopher Clapham, "Introduction: Analysing African Insurgencies," in. *African Guerrillas*, ed. Christopher Clapham (Oxford: James Currey, 1998), 6 – 7.

212 See Kenneth Ingham, "Omar al-Bashir. President of Sudan," in *Encyclopedia*

he began the systematic Islamization of the country that clearly favoured the Arab-Sudanese population. By doing this, he alienated the southern part of the country that is made up of indigenous African Christians and indigenous religionists.

A Critique of Post-Colonial African Religious Fundamentalism

In his critique of global North epistemological hegemony, the sociologist Boaventura de Sousa Santos speaks of how "the epistemologies of the North are grounded in the idea of the rational subject, a subject that is epistemic rather than concrete or empirical."[213] Re-postulating this insight of Santos, the issue is about identity. For the global North, to speak of identity is to speak of cognitive postulations that do not always reflect the concrete historicity of the person, either as an individual or as a community of persons. This approach to identity construction defines the vestiges of colonialism one finds today among the colonized people of Africa.

Consequently, the epistemological heritage of the global North speaks in terms and concepts such as "self-proclaimed universal concepts of reason, rationality, human nature, and human mind, all that does not fit such a concept is irrationality, superstition, primitivism, mysticism, prelogical thinking, and emotivism."[214] How is one to understand human nature outside of the human condition? Better stated, what does it mean to be human outside of the social location and all the factors shaping

---

Britannica (Encyclopedia Britannica, Inc., 2019), https://www.britannica.com/biography/Omar-Hassan-Ahmad-al-Bashir.

[213] Boaventura de Sousa Santos, *The End of the Cognitive Empire. The Coming of Age of Epistemologies of the South* (Durham and London: Duke University Press, 2018), 87.

[214] Ibid., 38.

that context? What type of human nature comes to mind from the context of colonial heritage?

Contemporary African societies are victims of the European colonial agenda. Colonialism destroys all credibility that can be given to notions of identity used to define the coloniser in relation to the colonized because of the following: Colonialism operates with the understanding that the colonized is sub-human and lacks the ability to create and sustain a civilization. The colonized exists mainly as liminal beings in ways that they are to be considered dehumanized creatures.[215] Thus, concepts like rationality, that are used to define human nature in the epistemology of the North, do not have a universal element to them.[216] Human nature will always be understood to be fully manifested in European bodies and not in those of Africans. When applied to the religious context, those believed to be authentically human will definitely be considered to have the correct religion. This thought process is the main ingredient shaping religious fundamentalism.

Religious fundamentalism operates with the belief that one's religious affiliation represents God's truths fully and as such positions one in a superior state of being over others who do not share one's beliefs. Fundamentalism does not build community. While it attempts to build a community of likeminded individuals, in the long run, it ends up fragmenting the community that already exists because of its inability to preserve difference. In the words of R. Scott Appleby:

---

[215] For a detailed treatment on how this dehumanizing process functions in the operative discourse on identity in the hermeneutic tradition of the global North, see Nelson Maldonado-Torres, "On the Coloniality of Being: Contributions to the Development of A Concept," *Cultural Studies*, vol. 21, nos. 2-3 (2007): 242, 257.

[216] See Enrique Dussel, "Europe, Modernity and Eurocentrism," *Nepantla: Views from South* 1, no. 3 (2000): 465 – 478.

> Fundamentalists remain dualists at heart; they imagine the world divided into unambiguous realms of light and darkness peopled by the elect and reprobate, the pure and impure, the orthodox and infidel. Many if not all fundamentalists further dramatize this Manichaean worldview by setting it within an apocalyptic framework: the world is in spiritual crisis, perhaps near its end, when God will bring terrible judgement on the children of darkness. When the children of light are depicted in such millenarian imaginings as the agents of this divine wrath, violent intolerance toward outsiders appears justified on theological grounds.[217]

The history of the Sudanese Civil War sheds light on the insight of Appleby. Hassan al-Turabi's and al-Bashir's plan to have an Islamic state in Sudan led to a strategic infiltration of all levels of government and society while using violence as means to suppress any form of dissent. To be considered a good citizen, one had to be a Muslim as opposed to the indigenous religions and Christianity. Racial identity was closely linked to cultural superiority. Consequently, Sudanese of Arab descent considered themselves to be culturally and racially superior to the indigenous African Sudanese. Al-Turabi's National Islamist Front strategically merged these ideologies to create an Islamic fundamentalist society that had no room for persons who did not belong to the religio-cultural and political world they have created.[218]

Fundamentalism is closely linked to colonialism. Both lead to the obliteration of difference and a denial of robust national identities. In fact, Franz Fanon states this aptly in his discourse on colonialism: "The sweeping, levelling nature of colonial domination was quick to dislocate in spectacular fashion the

---

[217] R. Scott Appleby, *The Ambivalence of the Sacred. Religion, Violence, and Reconciliation* (Lanham: Rowman & Littlefield Publishers, Inc., 2000), 88.

[218] For a detailed study of the Sudanese Civil War, see Bill Berkeley, *The Graves Are not yet Full: Race, Tribe and Power in the Heart of Africa* (New York: Basic Books, 2001), 195 – 226.

cultural life of a conquered people. The denial of a national reality, the new legal system imposed by the occupying power, the marginalisation of the indigenous population and the systematic enslavement of men and women, all contributed to this cultural obliteration."[219]

Reflecting further on Fanon's insight, one notices that colonialism has the power to inhibit creative social imagination. Social imagination allows for a people to envision new horizons of being where new life-giving conditions are allowed to shape their world. In a colonized world, social imagination is truncated and traumatized in ways that it tends to reproduce fundamentalist conclusions on living in society that adhere to realities experienced in the era of colonialism. Social imagination becomes a type of collective aridity manifesting itself as a way of being for a traumatized people. Furthermore, the phenomenon of coloniality of imagination has been addressed by two prominent authors in their literary works; though not primarily labelling what I have called it – coloniality of imagination – Ayi Kwei Armah and Achebe.

In Armah's work, *The Beautiful Ones Are Not Yet Born*, the question is explored: Why is it that an independent Ghana is unable to imagine a new way of existence that does away with the vestiges of colonialism – oppressions; a class system; exploitation; corruption; and violence? Armah concludes that the beautiful ones, who can imagine a new way of existence have not yet arrived. Those who can creatively imagine how freedom is to be lived out in Ghana are not yet born.[220] Achebe addresses this phenomenon of coloniality of imagination in his work, *There Was A Country: A Personal History of Biafra*. He looks closely at the collapse of an independent Nigeria that was going to undo

---

[219] Franz Fanon, *The Wretched of the Earth*, trans. Richard Philcox (New York: Grove Press, 2004), 170.

[220] See Ayi Kwei Armah. *The Beautiful Ones Are Not Yet Born* (Portsmouth, New Hampshire: Heinemann, 1989).

all structures and vestiges of colonialism. Just like Armah, he was disappointed that the political leaders of independent Nigeria were incapable to imagine a new way of being a nation.[221]

Furthermore, fundamentalism manifests as a form of existential trauma of a colonized people. They are forced to become victims of anthropological poverty; a people whose memories of self and history are reduced to sporadic memories that only serve the intended agenda of the colonizing agents. Albert Memmi captures this phenomenon when he writes: "The most serious blow suffered by the colonized is being removed from history and from the community. Colonization usurps any free role in either war or peace, every decision contributing to his destiny and that of the world, and all cultural and social responsibility."[222]

Embracing Religious Differences: A New Way of Being for African Societies

Both Homi Bhabha and Emmanuel Katongole argue that a new way of imagining who Africans are, is possible. For Bhabha, "Postcolonial critical discourses require forms of dialectical thinking that do not disavow or sublate the otherness (alterity) that constitutes the symbolic domain of psychic and social identifications."[223] In light of Bhabha's insight, Katongole, reflecting on Chinua Achebe's *Things Fall Apart*, makes the following conclusion that the Catholic Church in Africa cannot ignore as it helps to usher in a new way of being:

---

[221] See Chinua Achebe, *There Was A Country: A Personal History of Biafra* (New York: The Penguin Press, 2012), 48 – 51.

[222] Albert Memmi, *The Colonizer and The Colonized*, expanded edition (Boston: Beacon Press, 1967), 91.

[223] Homi Bhabha, *The Location of Culture* (New York and London: Routledge, 1994), 249.

Achebe's depiction of Umuofia ... seems to confirm that modern nation-states – not only superpowers like the United States, but all nations – are built on a vision of power as domination and invincibility. It seems that the desire of all nations is to be "the greatest," "the most successful," or "the most advanced" nation, which means that even small nations like Uganda are born with the soul of an empire. If this is the case, then the challenge for Africa is not simply to achieve sovereignty in order to determine its own destiny, but rather to interrupt this vision of power as domination with a different account of power and thus a different vision of society and politics.[224]

In this venture of learning to imagine a new vision for Africa, the churches in Africa ought to begin with a prophetic introspection and be courageous enough to rescind their promotion of a Christianity that reflects the contours of power. The churches in Africa should work collaboratively with other African religious and secular institutions to undo the colonial heritage that has shaped the African human condition; a condition that is radically defined by a culture of corruption; political tyranny; and religious violence. An example of a country where such exploitative colonial heritage occurs in Africa is Nigeria.

According to a 2016 report on Nigeria by Price Water House Coopers Limited, "if corruption is not addressed in Nigeria, by 2030, it will cost 37% of the national GDP."[225] Boko Haram Islamic terrorist group continues to ravage some regions of the country. It is believed that over 27,000 civilians have been killed since the insurgency began in 2009.[226]

---

[224] Emmanuel Katongole, *The Sacrifice of Africa. A Political Theology for Africa* (Grand Rapids/Cambridge: William B. Eerdmans Publishing Company, 2011), 129.

[225] PWC, *Impact of Corruption on Nigeria's Economy* (Price Water House Coopers Limited, 2016), https://www.pwc.com/ng/en/assets/pdf/impact-of-corruption-on-nigerias-economy.pdf

[226] Human Rights Watch, "Nigeria: Events of 2019," *World Report 2020*, https://www.hrw.org/world-report/2020/country-chapters/nigeria-0

An embrace of religious differences in Africa must necessarily have at its core the sacredness of all life. Colonialism has stripped life of its sacredness and made its relevance tied to commerce. One is no longer valued for their existence as part of an intricate web of relationships. Colonialism, as the bedfellow of capitalism, sees African life as a tool to be used to enhance the wealth of the colonizing countries and their allies. Quoting Malidoma Somé's work, *Of Water and the Spirit*, Douglas E. Thomas calls attention to a forgotten African wisdom that states: "chaos will pursue those who insist on defying the cosmic and communal harmony that binds traditional African communities."[227] This new way of being ought to take seriously the project of recapturing the meaning of what life means in African religious thought.

Again, this new way of being that celebrates religious differences calls for new stories; ones that open up new horizons for imagining and celebrating all that we are as a people.[228] On the part of the Catholic Church in Africa, Jean-Marc Éla spells out what dangers the Church faces should it refuse to embrace this task reimagining a new way of being in the continent. In his words:

> Too many people in African churches feel a kind of betrayal or guilt. Their return to certain practices and beliefs, which had been repressed by the violence of mission Christianity, illustrates the failure and lack of meaning of imported lifestyles, doctrines, and institutions. In these societies in disarray from rapid change, the resurgence of former magico-religious practices, and the proliferation of sects in regions where the Christian presence appeared to be established, challenge the official churches. At this time in our history, we need to take up problems of the people – and this opens up a broad field for those concerned with the incarnation of the gospel in Africa....The church has to reevaluate

---

[227] Douglas E. Thomas, *African Traditional Religion in the Modern World* (Jefferson, North Carolina and London: McFarland & Company, Inc., Publishers, 2005), 9.

[228] Katongole, *The Sacrifice of Africa*, 131.

its practices, attitudes, and teaching on questions that were left unanswered during the first phase of evangelisation.[229]

The scars of colonialism can never be erased from the collective memories of Africans; however, what matters now is how Africans work towards holistic healing of the collective trauma they experience. For this to be achieved, attempts at embracing religious differences in the continent must necessarily give way to the prophetic voices in African societies. Religious institutions must now demand from African leaders' transparent governance. Godfatherism must be condemned wherever it exists. And Tribalism must be rejected. A deliberate effort must now me made through the establishment of transparent institutions, religious and secular, that have the task of creating structures that allow for the flourishing of all Africans, irrespective of their religious or political affiliations; ethnic identities; gender and sexual orientations.

The embrace of religious differences that ought to characterize a new way of being for Africans is grounded on the historical knowledge that Africans served God before the Abrahamic religions were introduced into the continent. Religions that sometimes reflect negative divisions via their denominations that compete for power. This new way of being for Africans ought to encourage interfaith and intrafaith encounters that allow for religious communities and denominations to embrace productive dialogue on multiple levels with the intent of fostering religious, cultural, political, and social harmony.

Furthermore, apologetics that present other faith traditions in negative light have been part of the factors causing religious violence in the continent. It is time for African theologians from the different faith traditions to begin to reimagine how God works in the continent. African interfaith theologies ought to

---

[229] Jean-Marc Èla, *My Faith As An African*, trans. John Pairman Brown and Susan Perry (Eugene, Oregon: Wipf and Stock Publishers, 2009), 140.

build bridges of friendship and solidarity among all stakeholders in the continent. Such theologies ought to call for a new orientation towards members of other faith traditions—one best described by the insight of Martin Buber: "THE THOU MEETS ME THROUGH GRACE – it is not found by seeking. The primary word I – Thou can be spoken only with the whole being. Concentration and fusion into the whole being can never take place through agency, nor can it ever take place without me. I become through my relation to the Thou; as I become I, I say Thou. All real living is meeting."[230]

Conclusion

Studying the Holy Spirit Movement of Alice Lakwena closely, one must ask the following question: Does Christian theology present God in a way that promotes violence? To say that persons like Lakwena are religious fanatics who do not understand the peaceful nature of Christianity may reflect a failure on the part of theologians to critically evaluate the worldview that is created by the language of theology.[231] The language of chivalry has radically defined the vision of the Christian God. Did the great reformer, Martin Luther, not compose the hymn *A Mighty Fortress is Our God*? What comes to mind when Christians sing this song?

Pope Francis has summoned the Catholic Church to embrace a new vision of evangelisation, one that grounds evangelisation in the promotion of peace and the flourishing of life. This evangelisation of peacebuilding, argues Francis, must necessarily

---

[230] Martin Buber, *I and Thou*, trans. Ronald Gregor Smith (New York: Charles Scribner's Sons, 1958), 11.

[231] For a detailed analysis of the Holy Spirit Movement, see Heike Behrend, "War in Northern Uganda. The Holy Spirit Movements of Alice Lakwena, Severino Lukoya and Joseph Kony (1986 – 97)," in *African Guerrillas*, ed. Christopher Clapham (Oxford: James Currey, 1998), 107 – 118.

be grounded in solidarity. What are the markers of this form of evangelizing solidarity? Francis writes: "Solidarity, in its deepest and most challenging sense, thus becomes a way of making history in a life setting where conflicts, tensions and oppositions can achieve a diversified and life-giving unity. This is not to opt for a kind of syncretism, or for the absorption of one into the other, but rather for a resolution which takes place on higher plane and preserves what is valid and useful on both sides."[232]

Again, if this new form of evangelisation called for by Francis is to be practiced by the churches in Africa, it means then that these churches must be prophetically involved in building a new future for Africa. Again, the new evangelisation of Pope Francis is one of dialogue. Dialogue cannot be understood as with those who share common grounds or understood as toleration of the other. In the words of Cardinal John Onaiyekan: "Toleration is not enough; it is necessary also to accept and respect the other. This is because there is at least an element of truth in every religion worthy of the name, and truth comes from God and must be respected as divine."[233]

Finally, for colonized people, knowing how their history has been crafted by multiple factors is the beginning of their journey towards liberation. This work has shed light on how religion plays a role in shaping conflicts playing out in Africa with the intent to call attention to a deeper consciousness and an embrace of a peaceful future.

---

[232] Francis, Apostolic Exhortation: *The Joy of the Gospel (Evangelii Gaudium)*, (Washington, D.C.: United States Conference of Catholic Bishops, 2013), 111.

[233] John O. Onaiyekan, *Seeking Common Grounds. Interreligious Dialogue in Africa* (Nairobi: Paulines Publications Africa, 2013), 173.

Bibliography

Achebe, Chinua. *There Was A Country: A Personal History of Biafra*. New York: The Penguin Press, 2012.

___. *Things Fall Apart*. London: Penguin Books 1994.

Appleby, R. Scott. *The Ambivalence of the Sacred. Religion, Violence, and Reconciliation*. Lanham: Rowman & Littlefield Publishers, Inc., 2000.

Arendt, Hannah. *The Human Condition. Second Edition*. Chicago: The University of Chicago Press, 1998.

Armah, Ayi Kwei. *The Beautiful Ones Are Not Yet Born*. Portsmouth, New Hampshire: Heinemann, 1989

Behrend, Heike. "War in Northern Uganda. The Holy Spirit Movements of Alice Lakwena, Severino Lukoya and Joseph Kony (1986 – 97)." In *African Guerrillas*. Edited by Christopher Clapham, 107 – 118. Oxford: James Currey, 1998.

Berkeley, Bill. *The Graves Are not yet Full: Race, Tribe and Power in the Heart of Africa*. New York: Basic Books, 2001.

Bhabha, Homi. *The Location of Culture*. New York and London: Routledge, 1994.

Buber, Martin. *I and Thou*. Translated by Ronald Gregor Smith. New York: Charles Scribner's Sons, 1958.

Clapham, Christopher. "Introduction: Analysing African Insurgencies." In *African Guerrillas*, edited by Christopher Clapham, 1 – 18. Oxford: James Currey, 1998.

Dussel, Enrique. "Europe, Modernity and Eurocentrism," *Nepantla: Views from South* 1, no. 3 (2000): 465 – 478.

Èla, Jean-Marc. *My Faith As An African*. Translated by John Pairman Brown and Susan Perry. Eugene, Oregon: WIPF and Stock Publishers, 2009.

Enwerem, Iheanyi M. *A Dangerous Awakening: The Politicization of Religion in Nigeria*. Ibadan: Institut Français de Recherché en Afrique, 1995.

Fanon, Franz. *The Wretched of the Earth*. Translated by Richard Philcox. New York: Grove Press, 2004.

Francis. Apostolic Exhortation: *The Joy of the Gospel (Evangelii Gaudium)*. Washington, D.C.: United States Conference of Catholic Bishops, 2013.

Human Rights Watch. "Nigeria: Events of 2019." *World Report 2020*. https://www.hrw.org/world-report/2020/country-chapters/nigeria-0.

Ingham, Kenneth. "Omar al-Bashir. President of Sudan." In *Encyclopedia Britannica*. Encyclopedia Britannica, 2019. https://www.britannica.com/biography/Omar-Hassan-Ahmad-al-Bashir.

Kastfelt, Niels. "Religion and African Civil Wars. Themes and Interpretations." In *Religion and African Civil Wars*, edited by Niels Kastfelt, 1 – 27. London: Hurst and Company, 2005.

Katongole, Emmanuel. *The Sacrifice of Africa. A Political Theology for Africa*. Grand Rapids/Cambridge: William B. Eerdmans Publishing Company, 2011.

Kohn, Margaret and Kavita Reddy. "Colonialism." In *The Stanford Encyclopedia of Philosophy. Fall 2017 Edition*. Edited by Edward n. Zalta. https://plato.stanford.edu/entries/colonialism/

Maldonado-Torres, Nelson. "On the Coloniality of Being: Contributions to the Development of a Concept." *Cultural Studies*. Vol. 21. Nos. 2-3 (2007): 240 – 270.

Memmi, Albert. *The Colonizer and The Colonized*. Expanded Edition. Boston: Beacon Press, 1967.

Omer, Atalia. "Conflict and Peacebuilding." In *Religion and Culture. Contemporary Practices and Perspectives*, edited by Richard D. Hecht and Vincent F. Biondo III, 3 – 28. Minneapolis: Fortress Press, 2012.

Onaiyekan, John O. *Seeking Common Grounds. Interreligious Dialogue in Africa*. Nairobi: Paulines Publications Africa, 2013.

PWC. *Impact of Corruption on Nigeria's Economy*. Price Water House Coopers Limited, 2016. https://www.pwc.com/ng/en/assets/pdf/impact-of-corruption-on-nigerias-economy.pdf

Ranger, Terrence. "The Role of The Ndebele and Shona Religious Authorities in The Rebellions of 1896 and 1897." In *The Zambesian Past: Studies in Central History*. Edited by Eric Stokes and Richard Brown, 94 – 136. Manchester: Manchester University Press, 1966.

Reader, John. *Africa: A Biography of the Continent*. New York: Vintage Books, 1997.

Santos, Boaventura de Sousa. *The End of the Cognitive Empire. The Coming of Age of Epistemologies of the South*. Durham and London: Duke University Press, 2018.

Sartre, Jean-Paul. "Preface." In Franz Fanon, *The Wretched of the Earth*. Translated by Richard Philcox, xliii – lxii. New York: Grove Press, 2004.

Thomas, Douglas E. *African Traditional Religion in the Modern World*. Jefferson, North Carolina and London: McFarland & Company, Inc., Publishers, 2005.

Vaughan, Olufemi. *Religion and the Making of Nigeria*. Durham and London: Duke University Press, 2016.

**Communicating the Truths of Faith:
Marriage, Family Life, Health and Wellbeing**

CHAPTER SEVEN

The Challenges of Poverty in African Families: Ecclesial Action Since African Synods I & II

Raymond Olusesan Aina, MSP

Introduction

This chapter critically examines ecclesial actions regarding poverty in African families. The chapter examines these ecclesial actions from the perspective of the church's original and enduring mission. According to Robert Calderisi, the enduring mission consists of "...spreading the Gospel and improving society through justice and charity."[234] Why is it important to pay attention to the Church's role in Africa concerning poverty reduction, which is somewhat a mundane activity?

We recall Pope Francis' reminder immediately: "If indeed 'the just ordering of society and of the state is a central responsibility of politics', the Church 'cannot and must not remain on the sidelines in the fight for justice.'"[235] Since the joys and hopes, sufferings and anxieties of the world are that of the Church too (cf. GS 1), the Church cannot be passive towards African families as they battle with multidimensional poverty and economic

---

[234] Robert Calderisi, *Earthly Mission: The Catholic Church and World Development* (New Haven; London: Yale University Press, 2013), 109.

[235] Francis, *Apostolic Exhortation Evangelii Gaudium to the Bishops, Clergy, Consecrated Persons and the Lay Faithful on the Proclamation of the Gospel in Today's World* (Vatican City: Vatican Press, November 24 2013), no. 183 citing *Deus Caritas Est*, no. 28.

stagnation. Beyond the proclamation of salvation and redemption from evils, what else is the Church in Africa doing to give hope to African families?

This chapter argues that the Church in Africa, as Family of God on mission (*African Synod I*) towards justice, peace, and reconciliation in the continent (*African Synod II*), needs more concerted actions to empower African families out of poverty. The chapter examines indications and inspirations from the African Synods I and II on how to meet the challenges of poverty to African families.

This contribution equally highlights ecclesial actions towards poverty eradication within the decade after African Synod II in particular. Concluding its argument, the chapter insists that for more effective ecclesial action with and for Africa's low-income families, the Church needs to be full of 'fire in the belly.' 'Fire in the belly', inspired by the traditional Catholic Social Movements, signifies commitment and readiness to move out of one's comfort zones to contribute towards human flourishing.

Multidimensional Poverty and Economic Stagnation: Challenging the African Family

In the last four decades, the world has created wealth more than it did for over a century.[236] However, more than 90% of the world's population is denied the benefits of this global economic growth. There is growing inequality between the haves and the have-nots, particularly in Africa, that is witnessing the so-called

---

[236] Deborah Hardoon, Sophia Ayele, and Ricardo Fuentes-Nieva, *An Economy for the 1%: How privilege and power in the economy drive extreme inequality and how this can be stopped*, Oxfam International (Cowley, Oxford: Oxfam GB, January 18, 2016), 8-9, https://www.oxfam.org/sites/www.oxfam.org/files/file_attachments/bp210-economy-one-percent-tax-havens-180116-en_0.pdf. Oxfam International (Cowley, Oxford: Oxfam GB, January 18, 2016).

'Billionaire boom.'[237] It is noted that "there are 16 billionaires in sub-Saharan Africa, alongside the 358 million people living in extreme poverty."[238] This scenario has led to the conclusion that Africa has the greatest challenge eradicating extreme poverty. In fact, it is predicted that 80% of the world's poor will live in Africa by 2030. If nothing radically happens in nations' growth across the continent, then the level of poverty in Africa will increase significantly by 2075.[239]

These grim statistics are not letting up. For instance, Brookings Institution's Report (2018) stated that Nigeria, with its 87m poor people, had become the capital of poor people in the world.[240] Some in Nigeria might remember that when the Brookings Report came out, several pro-government agencies and officials contested and disparaged Brookings Institution. Instructively, Nigeria's Minister of Humanitarian Affairs, Disaster Management and Social Development, Mrs. Sadiya Farouq, on October 28, 2019, declared that about 90 million Nigerians live in extreme poverty, with about 40 million Nigerians unemployed.[241] Paradoxically, the 90 million figure of Nigerians living in extreme poverty is higher than the 2018 Brookings Institution's Report the same government tried to discredit as a lie.

Extreme poverty refers to "'multiple deprivations at the household level in education, health and standard of living.'"[242]

---

[237] Emma Seery and Ana Caistor Arendar, *Even It Up: Time to End Extreme Inequality*, Oxfam International (Oxford: Oxfam GB, October 2014 October 2014), 32-34.

[238] Ibid., 32.

[239] Ibid., 38.

[240] "The Start of a New Poverty Narrative," Brookings Institution, June 19, 2018, accessed 05.07., 2018, https://www.brookings.edu/blog/future-development/2018/06/19/the-start-of-anew-poverty-narrative/.

[241] " ICYMI: 90 million Nigerians live in extreme poverty - FG," The Punch online, October 29, 2019, accessed 29.10., 2019, https://punchng.com/90-million-nigerians-live-in-extreme-poverty-fg/.

[242] Raymond Olusesan Aina, "Good Governance and Overcoming Insecurity in

Concretely, multidimensional poverty is identified when no one in a household has completed at least six years of basic schooling; a child of school-age is not in school; members of the household are malnourished based on body mass index measured by age for adults, and by height for toddlers; at least a child of five had died within the past five years; the household does not have access to electricity, and clean water; or its source of clean water is about thirty minutes from the homestead.

Other elements are lack of improved sanitation; cooking with 'dirty' fuel (dung, wood, charcoal); the home is paved with dirt or dung (not cemented); regarding assets, the members of the home do not have access to information (lack of radio, telephone, and television), and the household has no asset associated with mobility (bicycle, motorcycle, car, truck, animal cart, or motorboat); finally the family does not have asset related to livelihood (fridge, farmland, livestock).[243]

Poverty Reduction, the Church, and African Synods I and II

The topic this chapter addresses has a presupposition that African Synods I and II offered some indications regarding multidimensional poverty and its impacts on the African Continent. Accordingly, we shall refer briefly to the inspirations from African Synod I by returning to *Ecclesia in Africa*,[244] and a contemporaneous study that in part highlights the major responses on

---

Nigeria: An Agenda for Pastoral Leaders and Agents," *Journal of Inculturation Theology* 16, no. 2 (December 2019): 218-33, at 20-23.

[243] For details, see United Nations Development Programme (UNDP), "Human Development Reports: 2018 Statistical Update", 10, Human Development Report Office; http://hdr.undp.org/en/2018-update (accessed 31.10. 2019).

[244] "Post-Synodal Apostolic Exhortation *Ecclesia in Africa*," September 14, 1995, accessed 01.11., 2019, http://w2.vatican.va/content/john-paul-ii/en/apost_exhortations/documents/hf_jp-ii_exh_14091995_ecclesia-in-africa.pdf

the heels of that synod.²⁴⁵ Thereafter, we shall devote some time to the documents from African Synod II. In particular, we shall re-examine the Propositions, Message, and post-synodal Exhortation issued by Pope Benedict after African Synod II.

African Synod I: Positions and Inspirations

By the time African Synod I took place in 1994, there was a strong impetus that saw the work of evangelisation as closely connected to integral human development.²⁴⁶ According to Stan Ilo, few developments on the African continent caused this reawakening. First, there was the theological development of Catholic Social Teaching from the African perspective. Second, this theological development became part of the theological curriculum in African seminaries and other Catholic tertiary institutions.

Third, the debate on a proposed moratorium on foreign missionaries in the early 1970s led to African Catholic bishops taking a position at the 1974 Synod of Bishops on co-responsibility for mission, theologies, pastoral and social ministries. Fourth, the growing familiarity in Africa to ecclesial documents through the emergence of the *African Ecclesial Review* and the Paulines Publication Africa reinforced the importance and tone of Catholic Social Teaching as taught in the Church's tertiary institutions in Africa. All these factors led to an unsurprising development that priests and other pastoral agents abandoned their neutrality on Africa's social condition.²⁴⁷

Hence, African Synod I, attentive to Africa's social conditions, put forward that a true understanding of the doctrine of Incarnation reveals humans' inalienable dignity. Consequently,

---

[245] Stan Chu Ilo, "The Enduring Significance of *Populorum Progressio* for the Church in Africa," *Journal of Moral Theology* 6, no. 1 (January 2017): 57-79.

[246] John Paul II, "*Ecclesia in Africa*," no. 68.

[247] Ilo, "Enduring Significance," 64-67.

the proclamation of the Gospel and evangelisation must embrace "the struggle for the defence of personal dignity, for justice and social peace, for the promotion, liberation and integral human development of all people and of every individual" (EA, 69). Accordingly, the Church's mission in Africa must evolve structures of evangelisation that include administration of temporal goods "for the promotion of human dignity, justice and peace" (EA n° 101), ranging from schools, tertiary institutions to associations and movements that empower the poor to escape extreme poverty (EA, 101-104).

Given the impetus from African Synod I, the Church in Africa upped the ante of its social mission to the bleeding and hurting continent. Hence, between African Synods I and II, "the Catholic Church in Africa was regarded as the biggest NGO in Africa in terms of her social mission."[248] The statistics offered by Ilo are staggering. The impact of the Church's social mission is felt in most sectors of the society – from schools, and medical institutions to housing for social outcasts and self-help projects for the poor. All these are coordinated by "53 national chapters of Caritas, 34 national commissions of justice and peace, and 12 institutes and centers promoting the social doctrine of the Church"[249]

This historical and theological amplification helps us to understand, therefore, Calderisi's elucidation on what the Church has done in Africa,[250] thus leading to his apt conclusion:

> In Africa, where states continue to struggle to establish reliable networks of basic health and education, the Church remains a central actor in giving poor people the confidence, literacy, and physical strength to change their own lives. As public policy improves, markets are linked, and opportunities open up, Catholic schools and clinics will have given hundreds of thousands of

---

[248] Ibid., 67.

[249] Ibid.

[250] Calderisi, *Earthly Mission*, 95-118, 205-16.

people across the continent access to the modern economy they otherwise would not have had.[251]

African Synod II: Positions and Inspirations

We should remember that the synod was on how to turn Africa's fate around from being a bleeding continent to a just, loving, peaceful, and reconciled one. Immediately, one can say, what then does this synod have to do with poverty and families' freedom from economic stagnation? I remember the Africa-Europe Network for Justice and Peace that devoted its 2008 AGM in Rome on the possibility of the synod being a foundation for sustainable economic transformation.

I did argue at that AGM that the forthcoming synod then could not do justice to its theme without addressing the nexus between Africa's haemorrhaging state and economic issues with the resultant multidimensional poverty, especially in Africa. So, let's see what the synod said after all about this nexus so that we can see how the synod has inspired a plethora of actions across Africa in the last decade.

Propositions[252] and Message[253] of African Synod II

Propositio, no. 17 is most decisive for us. Aware of the need for eradication of poverty if there will be social justice in the world, the synod fathers offered seven suggestions: the Church

---

[251] Ibid., 244.

[252] All references from Synodus Episcoporum, "II Coetus Specialis Pro Africa: The Church in Africa in Service to Reconciliation, Justice and Peace – Elenchus Finalis Propositionum," http://www.vatican.va/roman_curia/synod/documents/rc_synod_doc_20091023_elenco-prop-finali_en.html (accessed 30.08.2019).

[253] All references from "Message to the People of God of the Second Special Assembly for Africa of the Synod of Bishops," http://www.vatican.va/roman_curia/synod/documents/rc_synod_doc_20091023_message-synod_en.html (accessed 30.08.2019).

offers to recommit itself to the service of the vulnerable in Africa, especially the poor, orphans and marginalised, as it was in the early Church. This recommitment surely will cost money.

Hence, inspired again by the early Church, the Church in Africa has the obligation of sourcing for funds internally; hence, the need for a continental fund to deal with emergencies. The third suggestion addressed to "leaders" challenges them to address infrastructural deficit if there would be poverty reduction and food security across the continent. I will argue later that the 'leaders' in this suggestion are not just civil authorities. Ecclesial authorities are included in the leadership since most grassroots leaders in Africa are religious figures.

The fifth suggestion in *Propositio*, no. 17 is very instructive, to which I shall return later. The fifth suggestion says the poor and vulnerable in Africa need to be empowered. Hence, the synod fathers proposed that the Church should establish microfinance and agrarian programmes. This proposal should be understood against the backdrop of the ecclesial incarnation of solidarity. The final suggestion of *Propositio*, no. 17 emphasises the importance of promoting "integral human development and authentic human values." Which institution is best to do this if not the Church? How has the Church fared across Africa in offering and teaching integral human development based on Catholic Social Teaching? We shall return to this question later.

In *Propositio*, no. 19, the synod fathers noted that there was spiritual poverty in Africa, especially among the youth, due to defective emphasis in their education. Hence, to overcome this spiritual poverty, the Church recommits itself to the school apostolate. A new category of 'poor' in Africa is 'Migrants and Refugees' (also IDPs - Internally Displaced Persons), and the synod fathers recognised this. Hence, in *Propositio*, no. 28, the Church committed itself to 'pastoral care for migrants and their families' because apart from material poverty, they face deeper forms of poverty due to their circumstance of forced or even voluntary dislocation. We shall see how far the Church has responded to this proposition.

Propositiones, nos. 29 and 30 express the paradox of a resource-rich continent and its impoverished people due to the unconscionable exploitation of Africa's natural resources. Hence, if Africa's people will escape economic stagnation and contrived insecurity, then the Church needs to up the ante of its advocacy for the appropriate extraction of natural resources and its people enjoying the fruit of their land, be it minerals, water, or land for farming.

The "Message" of African Synod II echoes some of the *propositiones*. First, the Message identifies some of the internal contradictions in Africa, notably "tragic situations of refugees, abject poverty, disease and hunger" (no. 4). Second, these tragic situations are caused more by human agency than natural disasters (no. 5). Considering the enormity of Africa's scepter of tragic contradictions, "all members of the Church, clergy, religious and lay faithful, must be mobilised to work together in the unity that brings strength" (no. 15). Concerning Africans' debilitating poverty, the Message offers a concrete proposal for the Church in Africa: "...suggestions for micro-finance schemes deserve careful attention" (no. 19).

Africae Munus[254] on Inspiration for Church's Interventions on Poverty

As a sign and instrument of Christ's illuminating and transforming love in the world (LG 1; AM 133), the Church makes the joys and hopes, sufferings and anxieties of the people its own

---

[254] Benedict XVI, *Post-Synodal Apostolic Exhortation Africae Munus (Africa's Commitment) on the Church in Africa in Service to Reconciliation, Justice and Peace* (Nairobi: Paulines Publications Africa, 2011).

(cf. GS 1). Accordingly, the Church cannot be silent or passive to God's children living precariously. This section wonders if *Africae Munus* offers inspirations for actions beyond the proclamation of salvation and redemption from evils. What else should the Church in Africa do to give hope to African families living in states of lack of peace and justice?

The Post-Synodal Exhortation, *Africae Munus*, urges the Church to speak out against unjust economic systems and world order that thwart Africans rights of "consolidating their economies" (AM 79). Specifically, in tackling multidimensional poverty in Africa, one of the effects of these unjust economic systems, and inspired by the preferential option for the poor, the Church on her part, will make her contribution based on "the teaching of the Beatitudes" (AM 27; 130). According to Pope Benedict XVI, the beatitudes are anchored on Christ's kenotic and revolutionary love (AM 26).

Nonetheless, it seems that *Africae Munus* blunts the programmatic *Propositio*, no. 17 which, as stated earlier, enumerates specific actionable interventions regarding poverty reduction in Africa. Though *Africae Munus* 27 refers to *Propositio*, no. 17, it does not incorporate any of these specific interventions. Instead, it replaces the Church's commitment with a commitment based on the Beatitudes – an expression that is quite nebulous. Perhaps, Benedict XVI is staying faithful to his claim in *Deus Caritas Est* that actions of justice and similar corporeal actions as outlined in *Propositio*, no. 17 are outside the competence of the Church (cf. DCE 28-30). If this is so, one can aver that there is an ideological or even theological disconnect between the *Propositiones* and *Africae Munus* regarding the poor and how to tackle poverty in Africa.

One can notice this tendency again in *Africae Munus'* section treating migration and the refugee problem in Africa. As pointed out earlier, *Propositio*, no. 28 expresses the Church's commitment to 'pastoral care for migrants and their families' because of their precarious state. Indeed, *Africae Munus* asserts that migrants as a class of the poor ought to "awaken everyone's compassion and generous solidarity" (AM 84). However, *Africae Munus* appears to blunt the commitment of the Synod fathers on the concrete pastoral care of migrants, refugees, and IDPs, with the following commitment: "The Church will continue to make her voice heard and to campaign for the defence of all people" (AM 85).

There is no explicit mention of the commitment to 'pastoral care for migrants and their families.' Furthermore, some aspects of the Church's apostolate, relevant to addressing Africa's tragic situations include education since this is a matter of justice for the African child and "the future of Africa depends on it" (AM 134). It is instructive that education in *Africae Munus* is linked more to virtue formation. *Africae Munus* does not or misses the ineluctable connection between education and escape from generational poverty. Perhaps if it saw this connection, there might have been a greater push for more affordable education apostolate.

Still, on *Africae Munus*' attention to material poverty, Pope Benedict XVI praises Catholic women in Africa for standing up to "defend human dignity, the family and the values of religion" whenever poverty threatens the family and the society (AM 58). All lay people, especially the professionals, are exhorted to cultivate daily spirituality of preferential love of the poor. By this, the People of God shall increase its sensitivity and ethical responsibility towards the poor and how to alleviate their poverty (AM 130).

Furthermore, Pope Benedict encourages the lay faithful "to form associations in order to continue shaping your Christian conscience and supporting one another in the struggle for justice and peace" (AM 131). Though the Pontiff has the Small Christian Communities (SCCs) and the new ecclesial communities within the Church in mind when referring to associations that can form the laity's Christian conscience, one may see this as an inspiration for associations and sodalities that seek out the poor and work towards alleviating their economic stagnation. I will return to this position later when offering some actionable goals going forward.

Ecclessial Action in Africa after African Synod II: Empowerment and Advocacy

The synod was on how to turn Africa's fate around from being a bleeding continent to a just, loving, peaceful, and reconciled one. How has this synod inspired actions across Africa in the last decade?

SECAM-Driven Initiatives

During the 16th Plenary Assembly of the Symposium of Episcopal Conferences of Africa and Madagascar (SECAM) (July 8-14, 2013), a paper presented by Cardinal Théodore Adrien Sarr[255] critically appraised SECAM-driven initiatives inspired by African Synods I and II presumably. Let us preface Cardinal Sarr's appraisal with his assertion that, as sacrament and sign of Christ's transforming love in the world (LG 1; AM 133), the Church plays "a preventive and curative role among the population particularly in rural areas, with regard to access by the needy to better living conditions (health, education, development initiatives, etc.)."

Its role is not just to proclaim God's love and salvation. Like a sentinel, the Church has the responsibility to prevent avoidable economic stagnation and poverty. It equally has the task of redressing, enhancing and empowering over the same debilitating obstacles to human flourishing and welfare.[256] Some of the

---

[255] Théodore Adrien Cardinal Sarr, "A Look at SECAM in the Light of *Africae Munus*: Strengths, Weaknesses, Prospects," (Acts of the 16th Plenary Assembly of SECAM (July 8-14, 2013) Accra, SECAM, July 07, 2016).

[256] Ibid., 99.

initiatives Cardinal Sarr highlighted,[257] indeed, predate *Africae Munus*. However, by Cardinal Sarr's narrative, it appears that these initiatives intensified after *Africae Munus*.

Nevertheless, the Church in Africa has not fully realised its potentials in caring for the poor through defects in the "socio-pastoral structures of the Church;"[258] these range from lack of impactful structures for advancing people's development, lack of financial autonomy, fiscal responsibility, and good governance within the Church; lack of adequate knowledge of Catholic Social Doctrine for impactful application in the larger society.[259] In the light of the pauperisation of the African family and people, it becomes crucial, Cardinal Sarr passionately appeals, to "strengthen the social works of the Church (schools, health centres, HIV/AIDS, refugee and migrant care services, etc.) and initiate, if necessary, new projects at local, national and continental levels in line with the needs of the community..."[260]

Local Churches' Interventions

To effectively contribute to reducing poverty among families, which is widespread in Africa, the Roman Catholic Church, in

---

[257] "Justice and Peace" Commissions; *Caritas Africa*, which is part of *Caritas Internationalis* and extends its network to regional Episcopal Conferences, National Dioceses and Parishes; Local church organisations or movements committed to receiving refugees and migrants and providing them with information and assistance; Catholic Postal and Private Health Centres; Care and support services for people infected or affected by HIV-AIDS; Formal and non-formal Catholic Schools (pre-school levels, elementary, middle, secondary, vocational, higher); Ecclesial structures involved in the process of democratisation, the organisation and monitoring of free and transparent elections; aid to stigmatized and marginalized persons (albinos, individuals accused of witchcraft...), support for people in moral danger (girls and women in urban centres, teenage-mothers, prostitutes, street children)...." Ibid., 95.

[258] Ibid., 96.

[259] Ibid.

[260] Ibid., 97.

particular, has an extensive network, even to the remotest areas of the continent. The twin strengths of the Church, i.e. extensive proclamation of the Gospel and commitment to society transformation society through justice and charity, make it one of the most trusted and credible institutions in Africa.[261] The analytical framework provided by Jensen and Pestana[262] is constructive. According to Jensen and Pestana, poverty reduction interventions have three interdependent components: emergency relief, development activities, and policy/advocacy policies.

The first component relates to "interventions aimed at alleviating immediate suffering caused by external events such as war or natural calamities."[263] The Church makes its interventions through three principal activities: "distribution of food, medicine, clothing and agricultural material"[264] through various JDPCs (Justice Development & Peace Commissions) or national Caritas organisations. In different Sub-Sahara African countries that are either failed or failing states, the Church becomes a 'surrogate state' filling in the gaps caused by governance deficit, especially regarding the provision of the necessities of life.[265] So the coordinated response to humanitarian crises caused by war, violence, or governance deficit has ensured that the Church "mitigated the suffering of the poorest and most war-affected

---

[261] Søren Kirk Jensen and Nelson Pestana, *The Role of the Churches in Poverty Reduction in Angola*, Chr. Michelsen Institute (Bergen: Chr. Michelsen Institute, 2010), 1.

[262] Ibid.

[263]

[264] Jensen and Pestana, *Role of the Churches*, 17.

[265] A 2001 report in *The Washington Post* clearly states in relation to Angola. "In Angola, Church Is Surrogate State," *The Washington Post*, March 22, 2001, accessed 29.10., 2019, https://www.washingtonpost.com/archive/politics/2001/03/22/in-angola-church-is-surrogate-state/21d9a33a-4bda-411a-bd31-15ed626c7693/.

citizens."²⁶⁶ What Jensen and Pestana say of the role of the Catholic Church in Angola widely applies to the Catholic Church around the continent.

The second component of ecclesial intervention regarding poverty reduction in development is used to describe "interventions that focus on improving the standards of living of poor people with limited or no access to basic services such as agriculture, water, sanitation, health and education amongst others, in the medium term."²⁶⁷ These are empowerment programmes and projects provided, promoted and sponsored by the Church targeting capacity building of the poor.

These include the provision of basic education, orphanages, potable water, sanitation facilities, rural and mobile healthcare services, and interventions for subsistent farming. The Church holds that empowerment programmes are critical issues of justice and peace, attentiveness to solidarity, as part of that revolutionary love based on the Beatitudes. Part of ecclesial empowerment programmes and projects are the provision of soft loans to farmers and micros/small entrepreneurs, rehabilitation of street children, distribution of home-grown agricultural products, provision of scholarship to needy students, women cooperative societies for pro-women empowerment schemes and skill acquisition training for women.²⁶⁸

The third component is 'policy and advocacy.' Activities that fall under this component include interventions addressing

---

[266] Jensen and Pestana, *Role of the Churches*, 18.

[267] Ibid., 3.

[268] Anthonia Bolanle Ojo, "Catholic Social Teaching and Poverty Alleviation: The Nigerian Perspective," *JORAS - Nigerian Journal of Religion and Society* 9 (2019): 51-67, at 62-63; N.G. Onah, L.N. Okwuosa, and F.C. Uroko, "The Church and Poverty Alleviation in Nigeria," *HTS Teologiese Studies/Theological Studies* 74, no. 1 (2018): 4834, https://doi.org/https://doi.org/10.4102/hts.v74i1.4834.

"structural causes for poverty such as social and economic inequalities, accountability, transparency, human rights, democracy and participation in decisions that affect peoples' lives."[269] These pro-active interventions target issues of peace and reconciliation, democracy and socio-economic justice principally.

The third component understands that we can only address some social ills substantially from the roots. Even if the Church is successful at the micro and meso levels; there are macro issues that are beyond the Church's competence. However, without the structural changes, the Church's activities at the emergency and development spheres will remain palliatives. In the immediate context of the impact of poverty on families, there is a nexus between multidimensional poverty and social exclusion.[270]

The Church in Africa must increase its attentiveness to the challenge posed by poverty vis-à-vis social exclusion. This attentiveness calls for a structural assessment of the society. Some of the Church's institutions have lived up to this expectation. The Catholic Church across the African continent has been active and prophetic in pushing for pro-people policies, especially the most vulnerable in society. For instance, the national and regional Episcopal bodies in Cameroon have been very active and vocal, speaking truth to power. The Catholic Bishops' Conference of Nigeria (CBCN) is another inspiring example. In May 2018, the CBCN issued a statement, "When will this Barbarism End?" which largely de-legitimised the ruling government.

Furthermore, the bishops' moral outrage inspired Catholics in Nigeria to pursue, at the bishops' lead spiritual warfare with the National Day of Prayer in May 2018. As the 2019 General Elections drew closer, the bishops, individually and collectively, drummed

---

[269] Jensen and Pestana, *Role of the Churches*, 3.

[270] On the nexus between poverty and social exclusion, see European Union, *Combating Poverty and Social Exclusion: A Statistical Portrait of the European Union 2010*, Eurostat Statistical books series, (Luxembourg: Publications Office of the European Union, 2010), 7.

it into us that contrary to pretensions in some quarters, the fundamentals of "When will this Barbarism End?" had not changed. Prophetically, the bishops staked their credibility for their people, not minding they could become a laughing stock if the government that their May 2018 Statement de-legitimised returned to power. They all remained unflinching in their prophetic stance at a time when 'the barbarian was at the gates of the city.'

To sum up, and seen from the prism of poverty reduction, one can agree that the greatest contribution of the Church has been in the areas of humanitarian interventions and advocacy, particularly in the field of education, formation of conscience, and prophetic accompaniment in the stuttering transition from prebendalism and dictatorship to sustainable democracy.[271] The Church's twin efforts in humanitarian interventions and development cost about $3b annually. The Church's humanitarian network, Caritas, is the second largest humanitarian network in the world, only surpassed by the Red Cross.[272]

Beyond Palliative Interventions: Some Proposals

Even if addressed specifically to permanent deacons, Pope Benedict XVI's exhortation in AM 116 is valid for all: "Let your charity be imaginative." This papal exhortation has inspired the following suggestions. The Church can do and be more for African families trapped in generational poverty. Moving beyond what the Church in Africa has done since African Synods I and II, perhaps it is time to get more imaginative. For instance, the Church may need to direct its investments and assets to some infrastructural alternatives, especially where the Church is, unfortunately, a 'surrogate state.' Even if one may counter that this is not the primary focus of the Church's mission and competence

---

[271] Calderisi, *Earthly Mission*, 118.
[272] Ibid., 207.

(cf. *Deus Caritas Est,* nos. 25-29), we cannot at the same time fail to remind ourselves that the second component of the ecclesial mission is "improving society through justice and charity."[273]

Parish-based 4S for the Poor

In this sub-section, we offer a practical ministry towards low-income families as part of ecclesial interventions and development projects. The following 4S: *sowing, sharing, storing,* and *selling* identify this practical ministry.[274]

Sowing

This ecclesial action prioritises engaging in agricultural projects. Food security "is a major theme in the Church's development ministry."[275] The ministry of 'sowing' should reduce unemployment and lack of spending power, especially in rural areas, or where the Church has arable lands. There is a nexus between food security and poverty reduction. The 'sowing' project employs people instead of just seeking employment for them from various patrons. This project is a sustainable and economically sensible way of empowering people, especially deprived 'breadwinners' of the families.[276] The 'sowing' project will also

---

[273] Ibid., 109.

[274] This is inspired by a previous study on practical care of poor families by a Pentecostal church in South Africa. See M.S. Kgatle, "A Practical Theological Approach to the Challenge of Poverty in Post-1994 South Africa: Apostolic Faith Mission as a Case Study," *HTS Teologiese Studies/ Theological Studies* 73, no. 3 (2017): 1-9, doi.org/10.4102/hts.v73i3.4549.

[275] Julius Oladipo, "The Role of the Church in Poverty Alleviation in Africa," in *Faith in Development: Partnership between the World Bank and the Churches of Africa,* ed. Deryke Beishaw, Robert Calderisi, and Chris Sugden (Oxford; Irvine, CA: Regnum Books International, 2001), 219-36, at 27.

[276] M.S. Kgatle, "A Practical Theological Approach to the Challenge of Poverty in Post-1994 South Africa: Apostolic Faith Mission as a Case Study," *HTS Teologiese Studies/ Theological Studies* 73, no. 3 (2017): 6, https://doi.org/https://doi.

guarantee ownership, which is crucial for sustainability. The project empowers people through this form of cooperative farming. Hence, they will have a higher level of commitment. They know that their livelihood at little or no cost, and without hassles from unscrupulous patrons, is tied to the project. They will do all they can to protect and keep it going.

Sharing

This practical ecclesial project aims at bridging the 'hunger gap'. Some several families and homes cannot feed themselves due to their grave poverty.[277] The Church strategically becomes a preserver of life by feeding people, not just as a sporadic activity during emergencies. Through Soup Kitchen projects, as an ordinary ministry in parishes, the Church feeds the hungry within parishes' neighbourhoods. Through the St Vincent de Paul Society, for instance, the Church can distribute food in designated areas for families that need at least one decent meal per day.[278]

Alternatively, there may be a functional Soup Kitchen where a decent meal is served at least once a day, with the help of volunteers. Parishioners can volunteer foodstuffs. However, to be sustainable and be more impactful, diocesan JDPC, for instance, can approach several retailers' supermarkets like Shoprite, and SPAR, for partnership in hunger relief. It is doable since Shoprite, for instance, offers 'fighting hunger' as part of its corporate social responsibility.

---

org/10.4102/hts.v73i3.4549.

[277] Ibid.

[278] I know of just a single church in Nigeria that does this as a functional church ministry. The church is called 'God Bless Nigeria Church (GBN).' According to this church, its Soup Kitchen project "provides food for GBN folks on a weekly basis." Ultimately, its goal is "to establish kitchens in various locations of Lagos where the less privileged would be assured of free meals on a daily basis." See God Bless Nigeria Church (GBN), "Ministry Expressions," http://www.godblessnigeriachurch.org/ministry-expressions/ (accessed 31.10.2019).

Through this partnership, these retailers' supermarkets can donate food items to the Church, which can be distributed, perhaps at deanery levels, especially in the townships. In addition to the Soup Kitchen, there can also be a social services building, where, with the help of volunteers, some household consumables can be packed as food bags to be handed out to pre-registered families once a week. The 'sharing' project will significantly over time help to bridge the nutritional gaps common among families caught in multidimensional poverty. When the Church does this, the community sees us as not just taking from them; it is equally one that gives to them.

Storing

During food scarcity at certain times of the year, some rapacious food merchants exploit the poor. Respective churches or parishes can have 'food banks' where food can be stored and used in times of grave need, to protect low-income families from such food merchants, during food scarcity. Several buildings in parishes are underused. Parishes can use these buildings as 'food banks.' During food scarcity, pre-registered low-income families within the neighbourhood can be offered these stored foods freely as done in standard food banks. Apart from being proactive by thinking and planning acting as 'food sentinel,' the Church might as well be forming its members to save food instead of wasting them.[279]

Selling

Inflation rates and lack of purchasing power combine to deprive millions of low-income families of purchasing much-needed food. Given this, the Church can have cooperative food

---

[279] Kgatle, "Practical Theological Approach," 6.

stores that sell foodstuffs and other consumables at highly subsidised rates. It might be possible to do this since most of the items stocked might have been acquired through the partnership formed with the retailers' supermarkets referred to earlier. Instead of spending the little profit on payment of salaries, members of respective parishes can be urged to act as volunteers. Hence, the Church can plough back the profit from the entrepreneurial activity into the practical ministry of caring for needy families.[280]

Cooperative and Thrift Societies

We noted earlier that *Africae Munus* exhorts the church in Africa to embrace the SCCs and new ecclesial communities in the churchto step down the call to work for justice and peace. In this sub-section, we shall see how this appeal can be an inspiration for associations and sodalities that work to tackle poverty among African families. *Propositio*, no. 17.5 of African Synod II states: "The poor and marginalised be empowered through initiatives such as micro-finance, agrarian and similar programmes as the Church's concrete sign of solidarity with the poor and marginalised." This *Propositio* recognises the high strength of the Church in coordinating "selfhelp(sic) groups and in enhancing their capacity for self-actualisation."[281]

As noted earlier, some dioceses across Africa have been providing soft loans as part of promoting self-realisation and empowerment, especially to poor women,[282] considering the deepening 'feminisation of poverty' in Africa. However, ecclesial "development ministry organs" should consist more of "coop-

---

[280] Ibid.
[281] Oladipo, "The Role of the Church in Poverty Alleviation in Africa," 228.
[282] Onah, Okwuosa, and Uroko, "Church and Poverty Alleviation," 5.

eratives and associations built around the objectives of marketing and input supply" beyond the sporadic ones.[283]

Education as Empowerment – Reassessing School Ministry

The opportunities the Church gave children from poor homes to formal education helped some of them out of social exclusion and intergenerational poverty.[284] Notwithstanding, the irony I wish to emphasise as the Church's moral burden is that the majority of the poor are excluded from enjoying the benefits of the educational institutions especially in urban settingsbecause their children cannot attend those institutions. Only the children of upper-middle-class and the elite can afford most of the Church's educational institutions today. The poor can only afford to send their children to poorly funded public schools or substandard private educational institutions.

Fundamentally, what is the nature of the Church's educational institutions – profit-oriented venture or an apostolate? If it is an apostolate, then it has to revisit the profit-oriented tuition. First, the Church can have a consortium of Catholic schools, with standard entrance exams. These schools are heavily subsidised, open to all irrespective of accidents of birth, but based on cut-off marks. Alternatively, second, it can operate a dual educational model. One set consists of the elite-focused and profit-driven schools without an exceptional scholarship for needy students. The other set includes schools established in educationally and economically disadvantaged zones, with the same model, infrastructural facilities, remuneration package for teachers, financed principally from the profits from the elite-focused schools.

---

[283] Oladipo, "The Role of the Church in Poverty Alleviation in Africa," 228.

[284] Cf. Calderisi, *Earthly Mission*, 244.

The two-tier tuition system is 'no robbing Peter to pay Paul' because 'Peter' is justly billed for services rendered; the provider of the services chooses to use the proceeds to take care of 'Paul.' This system echoes the action of the landowner and his dual-layered approach to the workers in his vineyard (Lk 20:1-16a). This approach will ensure offering the children of the poor the same quality of education that can help them escape the trap of generational poverty, without taking them out of their familiar cultural and social milieu.

This approach will decisively demonstrate that the Church indeed opts for the poor. It shows a Church that is ready to go the extra mile in showing the example of how to provoke and promote societal transformation. This approach is equally a parablethat will speak truth to power that no nation can develop and be at peace with an educational system that is so uneven and inherently unjust to the poor and their children's future.

Church on Housing Projects

Homelessness and lack of housing are the two most acute indications of poverty and social exclusion, not just in advanced economies like the European Union,[285] but also in Sub-Saharan Africa.[286] Traditionally, the public sector envisaged its role regarding housing as providing not-for-profit housing for all, especially for low-income citizens. However, in Nigeria, for instance, as in several parts of Sub-Saharan Africa, the reality is far from this ideal.[287]

---

[285] European Union, *Combating Poverty and Social Exclusion*, 64.

[286] I. A. Ademiluyi, "Public Housing Delivery Strategies in Nigeria: A Historical Perspective of Policies and Programmes," *Journal of Sustainable Development in Africa* 12, no. 6 (2010): 153-61.

[287] Olumide Afolarin Adenuga, "Factors Affecting Quality in the Delivery of Public Housing Projects in Lagos State, Nigeria," *International Journal of Engineering and Technology* 3, no. 3 (March 2013): 332-44, at 35.

Exorbitant housing is a severe problem, particularly for the urban poor, who settle in informal settlements like slums, leading to overcrowding, with its associated issues like poor sanitation, diseases, and criminality.[288] A Church that is not just for but with the poor must respond along bridging the housing deficit. Calderisi recounted an incident in Rwanda some years ago. The Paul Kagame government arrested a young priest because he openly denounced "government's burning of straw houses in his parish (intended to force the poor inhabitants to build more salubrious dwellings)."[289]

The young priest, who refused his bishop's prodding to apologise for his public comments, saw speaking truth to power as central to his priestly ministry. He was ready to remain in jail if that would be the cost of standing up for the poor.[290] The critical question is: beyond speaking truth to power, what else can the Church do for parishioners who are still inhabiting straw houses today and cannot afford the government's "more salubrious dwellings?"

Some churches are aware of this acute social problem of low-income families and developed an initiative about bridging housing deficit. The Catholic Church particularly, can take inspiration from the Methodist Church of Southern Africa (MCSA). The MCSA understood that the government alone could not provide or guarantee affordable housing, especially for the poor and homeless.[291]

---

[288] P. Verster, "A Church with the Poor: Lessons from Scripture and from Congregations in Informal Settlements," *Acta Theologica Suppl.* 16 (2012): 70-88, at 71-72, https://doi.org/http://dx.doi.org/10.4314/actat.v32i1S.5.

[289] Calderisi, *Earthly Mission*, 174.

[290] Ibid.

[291] Yeboa-Mensa Seree, "Reducing Poverty in Sub-Saharan Africa: Two Development Theories and the Role of the Church" (MA Master's thesis, Helsinki: University of

Taking inspiration from the MCSA, the Catholic Church in various parts of Africa, with its vastly acquired lands, ought to step in and fill the housing gap for the sake of the people. Some portions of lands in designated areas in the urban, semi-urban and rural areas can be set aside for use by the poor and homeless. They are then helped to as much as possible maximise this opportunity, either by providing soft and interest-free loans, or flexible payment plans, guaranteed by individuals or corporate bodies in the Church.

The point is to help the poor and homeless have a roof over their heads on safe lands. Some surplus lands may be sold at competitive value "to establish funds for assisting homeless communities in land and housing projects."[292] Such an initiative shall help bridge the housing deficit for low-income families. This voluntary divesting of its land and putting them or the proceeds at the service of homeless families is an imaginative expression of charity that Pope Benedict XVI exhorts in *Africae Munus* (AM 116), and a prophetic expression of how the Church in Africa is becoming a poor church and a church of the poor as Pope Francis desires.[293] So, it is not out of place for the Church in Africa to respond prophetically and proactively to the Pope's vision for the sake of our people.

Helsinki, May 2012), 72, https://helda.helsinki.fi/bitstream/handle/10138/229853/Master_Thesis_COPY.pdf?sequence=2&isAllowed=y.

[292] Ibid.

[293] "Pope Francis wants 'poor Church for the poor'," *BBC News* (March 16, 2013), https://www.bbc.com/news/world-europe-21812545 (accessed 24.10.2019).

Ecclesial Mission at the Service of Poor Families: Lessons Learnt

Countering Poverty in African Families: Appreciating Catholic Social Movements

A crucial lesson learnt during this discussion is that we need to appreciate the Catholic Social Movements in the Church, especially in Africa. Catholic Social Movements are decisive in pursuing social transformation inspired by the Church's Tradition articulated in 'option for the poor.' *Catholic Social Movements are associations of persons, inspired by a MORAL IMAGINATION for social transformation within Roman Catholic Tradition, Memory, and Spirituality.*

From experience as a missionary priest, these three (i.e. Tradition, Memory, Spirituality) are decisively explicit than any definite reference to 'canonical' CST/Doctrine. Catholic Social Movements range from associations of Roman Catholics, urged on by biblically-inspired spirituality of 'option for the poor' working against structural and entrenched disorders to those who emphasise works of charity without interest in social and critical analysis of poverty and marginalisation. Option for the poor demands "'the prophets and activists, thinkers and analysts'" wrestling "'with the meaning of Christian faith amid turbulent social times.'"[294]

We have our fair share of the Catholic Social Movements in Africa. To ensure a lasting and more effective 'option for the poor' in this part of the world, we must revisit the response to the radicality of 'option for the poor'[295] by the Catholic Social

---

[294] Marvin L. KrierMich, *Catholic Social Teaching and Movements* (Mystic, CN: Twenty-Third Publications, 2000), 1, cited in Verstraeten, "International expert seminar Catholic Social Thought," 3.

[295] It is the radicality that Donal Dorr suggests as the radicality of renouncing "any likelihood of political success in the conventional sense, but rather to radically redefine the very notion of success. It is a decision to find joy and fulfilment in ways

Movements in our land. It brings us to a fundamental point. We have not clarified the relationship between the hierarchy and the CSM in Africa/Nigeria.

In particular, what is the relationship between popular CSM and the Church's hierarchy in Africa? It seems, at least in Africa, that lots of the popular CSMs (like CAFOD, Missio, Misereor, and Catholic Relief Services[296]) have lots going for them in responding to the poverty challenge because local ordinaries are still in love with them. What happens to the projects of these movements if the local ordinaries lose interest or become antagonistic? Or what if these movements run afoul of the Vatican, as some other international CSMs have found themselves recently: will the religious authorities in African countries remain enthusiastic about these movements that are contributing significantly in lifting millions of African families out of poverty and social exclusion?

Between Charity and Justice

Preparing this chapter, we have wrestled with the radicality of '*eleeo*'[297] in the principle of 'preferential option for the poor' and

---

that are incomprehensible in conventional terms." Donal Dorr, "Option for the Poor Revisited," in *Catholic Social Thought: Twilight or Renaissance*, ed. J.S. Boswell, F.P. McHugh, and J. Verstraeten, *Bibliotheca Ephemeridum Theologicarum Lovaniensium* (Leuven: University Press, 2000), 249-62, at 51.

[296] It is a growing concern in Africa that most of the aid agencies are not African in origin. It appears that the Church in Africa waits on others' charity before it can offer charitable assistance to Africans. This is changing. As part of coming of age of the Church in Africa, the Catholic Bishops' Conference of Nigeria, for instance, has established the Catholic Caritas Foundation of Nigeria (CCFN) (aka Caritas Nigeria). Caritas Nigeria is the Catholic Church's project-driven Agency in Nigeria. According to its "Vision and Mission" Statement, the Agency "shares in the mission of the Catholic Church to serve the poor and to promote charity and justice throughout the world." (I am grateful for one of the anonymous reviewers for posing the question about home-grown aid agencies in Africa). Caritas Nigeria, "Who We Are: Mission & Vision," accessed March 31, 2020, https://caritasnigeria.org/who/.

[297] This refers to the loving (quality) and enduring (constancy) graciousness in help-

Pope Francis' emerging 'apostleship of the poor.' This wrestling has further confirmed quite forcefully a conviction that the apparent split between 'charity' and 'justice' as demonstrated in *Deus Caritas Est* (nos. 28-30) makes sense within stable Western democracies that are protégés of Western modernity.

The articulation of ecclesial mission and its ethical responsibility during modernity was largely Western, middle class, and clerical. It was informed to some extent by modernity's separation of 'Church and State.' Hence, Charity, more like humanitarian assistance clothed in an evangelical cloak, came to characterise ecclesial mission. Justice was for the state. If we contrast this somewhat Eurocentric discussion with life in the South, especially Sub-Saharan Africa, one wonders if this split contributes to the church's original and enduring mission referred to in the beginning.[298]

The People of God in many parts of the world, especially in the South, see the Church as a 'sacrament of salvation' – and this salvation must be embodied. This claim is not different from the promise of God's salvation in the Hebrew Bible. The promise of blessing for God's People implied material well-being. So the split does not make much sense (if any) to us. In some places in our context, the Church might be the only viable institution that can promote – even PURSUE – justice for the people.

Hence, the various classes of the poor place their hope in the Church to stand by and for them to get justice. They expect the Church to offer inspirations, imaginations, and alternatives to confront the culture of impunity that is making social transfor-

---

ing those in need simply because they are in need. Mercy traditionally is not just about judgment and the judicial system. Harold A. Buetow, *God Still Speaks: Listen (Homily Reflections for Sundays and Holy Days - Cycle C)* (Mumbai: St Pauls, 1994; repr., 2006), 264; Jules Cambier and Xavier Léon-Dufour, "Mercy," in *Dictionary of Biblical Theology*, ed. Xavier Léon-Duffour (London: Geoffrey Chapman, 1967; reprint, 1997), 351-54.

[298] *See above* footnote 297

mation so difficult to realise. A question raised some years ago is still pertinent today in the light of the topic we are considering: "When victims/citizens suffer due to the criminality of the 'faceless', how does the Church respond to the need for culpability, responsibility, and reparation?"[299]

Conclusion: The Exigency of 'Fire in the Belly'

This chapter has argued that beyond exhortation and proclamation, the Church should increase its attempt at least in Sub-Saharan Africa to close the GAP between 'charity' and 'justice', and between Track 1 (official diplomacy) and Track 2 (non-state intervention) thinking and action. We need to radically challenge poverty and rural education in our society in the light of the future promises of God.[300]

Christian advocacy with and for the poor and ethics will succeed in contexts like Nigeria if we teach and promote 'fire in the belly.' As stated elsewhere, 'fire in the belly' symbolically refers to passionate stirring in one's guts for 'improving society through justice and charity:' "'Fire in the belly' signifies commitment, ethical movedness, and readiness (with risk) to move out of one's comfort zones in order to contribute towards human flourishing of one's society.

Fire in the belly makes us ready to become 'collateral damage' for the underside of history."[301] The Catholic Social Move-

---

[299] Raymond Olusesan Aina, "Overcoming 'Toxic' Emotions and the Role of Restorative Justice: A Christian Ethical Reflection on Restorative Justice's Promises, Ambiguities and Inspirations towards Peacebuilding in Nigeria," (PhD diss., Leuven: Katholieke Universiteit, 2010), 407.

[300] Christo Thesnaar, "Rural Education: Reimagining the Role of the Church in Transforming Poverty-stricken South Africa," *HTS Teologiese Studies/ Theological Studies* 70, no. 1 (2014): 1-7, at 3, https://doi.org/dx.doi.org/10.4102/hts.v70i1.2629.

[301] Raymond Olusesan Aina, "The Option for the Poor as a Lasting Challenge towards Societal Transformation," in *International Conference on the Catholic Church and Pentecostalism: Challenges in the Nigerian Context (Proceedings, Presentations*

ments exemplify, as stated earlier, the 'fire in the belly' which like the love of Christ urges the members of the movements for involvement along with the tripartite interventions for overcoming poverty: humanitarian interventions, development projects, and advocacy for structural transformation. To effectively confront the challenges of poverty in African families, the Church has to intensify the proclamation and evangelisation with "passion and power."[302]

& *Final Report)*, ed. Ralph Madu, Marco Moerschbacher, and Augustine Asogwa (Abuja: Directorate of Social Communications, Catholic Secretariat of Nigeria, 2016), 130-53, at 52.

[302] Ibid., 153.

Bibliography

Ademiluyi, I. A. "Public Housing Delivery Strategies in Nigeria: A Historical Perspective of Policies and Programmes." *Journal of Sustainable Development in Africa* 12, no. 6 (2010): 153-161.

Adenuga, Olumide Afolarin. "Factors Affecting Quality in the Delivery of Public Housing Projects in Lagos State, Nigeria." *International Journal of Engineering and Technology* 3, no. 3 (March 2013): 332-344.

Aina, Raymond Olusesan. "Good Governance and Overcoming Insecurity in Nigeria: An Agenda for Pastoral Leaders and Agents." *Journal of Inculturation Theology* 16, no. 2 (December 2019): 218-33.

———. "The Option for the Poor as a Lasting Challenge towards Societal Transformation." In *The Catholic Church and Pentecostalism: Challenges in the Nigerian Context*, edited by Ralph Madu, Marco Moerschbacher and Augustine Asogwa, 130-53. Abuja: Catholic Secretariat of Nigeria, 2016.

———. "Overcoming 'Toxic' Emotions and the Role of Restorative Justice: A Christian Ethical Reflection on Restorative Justice's Promises, Ambiguities and Inspirations towards Peacebuilding in Nigeria." PhD diss., Leuven: Katholieke Universiteit, 2010.

Baiyewu, Leke. " ICYMI: 90 million Nigerians live in extreme poverty - FG." https://punchng.com/90-million-nigerians-live-in-extreme-poverty-fg/ (accessed 29.10. 2019).

Benedict XVI. *Post-Synodal Apostolic Exhortation Africae Munus (Africa's Commitment) on the Church in Africa in Service to Reconciliation, Justice and Peace*. Nairobi: Paulines Publications Africa, 2011.

Buetow, Harold A. *God Still Speaks: Listen (Homily Reflections for Sundays and Holy Days - Cycle C)*. Mumbai: St Pauls, 1994. Reprint, 2006.

Calderisi, Robert. *Earthly Mission: The Catholic Church and World Development*. New Haven; London: Yale University Press, 2013.

Cambier, Jules, and Xavier Léon-Dufour. "Mercy." In *Dictionary of Biblical Theology*, edited by Xavier Léon-Duffour, 351-354. London: Geoffrey Chapman, 1967. Reprint, 1997.

Cardinal Sarr, Théodore Adrien. "A Look at SECAM in the Light of *Africae Munus*: Strengths, Weaknesses, Prospects." In *Acts of the 16th Plenary Assembly of SECAM (July 8-14, 2013)* 88-123. Accra: SECAM, July 07, 2016.

Dorr, Donal. "Option for the Poor Revisited." In *Catholic Social Thought: Twilight or Renaissance*, edited by J.S. Boswell, F.P. McHugh and J. Verstraeten, 249-262. Leuven: University Press, 2000.

European Union. *Combating Poverty and Social Exclusion: A Statistical Portrait of the European Union 2010* Eurostat Statistical books series. Luxembourg: Publications Office of the European Union, 2010.

Francis. *Apostolic Exhortation Evangelii Gaudium to the Bishops, Clergy, Consecrated Persons and the Lay Faithful on the Proclamation of the Gospel in Today's World*. Vatican City: Vatican Press, November 24 2013.

Hardoon, Deborah, Sophia Ayele, and Ricardo Fuentes-Nieva. *An Economy for the 1%: How privilege and power in the economy drive extreme inequality and how this can be stopped*. Cowley, Oxford: Oxfam International, January 18, 2016.

Ilo, Stan Chu. "The Enduring Significance of *Populorum Progressio* for the Church in Africa." *Journal of Moral Theology* 6, no. 1 (January 2017): 57-79.

Jensen, Søren Kirk, and Nelson Pestana. *The Role of the Churches in Poverty Reduction in Angola*. Bergen: Chr. Michelsen Institute, 2010.

Jeter, Jon. "In Angola, Church Is Surrogate State." https://www.washingtonpost.com/archive/politics/2001/03/22/in-angola-church-is-surrogate-state/21d9a33a-4bda-411a-bd31-15ed626c7693/ (accessed 29.10. 2019).

John Paul II. "Post-Synodal Apostolic Exhortation *Ecclesia in Africa*". http://w2.vatican.va/content/john-paul-ii/en/apost_exhortations/documents/hf_jp-ii_exh_14091995_ecclesia-in-africa.pdf (accessed 01.11. 2019).

Kgatle, M.S. "A Practical Theological Approach to the Challenge of Poverty in Post-1994 South Africa: Apostolic Faith Mission as a Case Study." *HTS Teologiese Studies/ Theological Studies* 73, no. 3 (2017): a4549, doi.org/10.4102/hts.v73i3.4549.

Kharas, Homi, Kristofer Hamel, and Martin Hofer. "The Start of a New Poverty Narrative," Brookings Institution. https://www.brookings.edu/blog/future-development/2018/06/19/the-start-of-anew-poverty-narrative/ (accessed 05.07. 2018).

Mani, Rama. *Beyond Retribution: Seeking Justice in the Shadows of War* Cambridge: Polity, 2002.

Message to the People of God of the Second Special Assembly for Africa of the Synod of Bishops. Synod of Bishops (Vatican City: 23.10.2009). http://www.vatican.va/roman_curia/synod/documents/rc_synod_doc_20091023_message-synod_en.html.

Ojo, Anthonia Bolanle. "Catholic Social Teaching and Poverty Alleviation: The Nigerian Perspective." *JORAS - Nigerian Journal of Religion and Society* 9 (2019): 51-67.

Oladipo, Julius. "The Role of the Church in Poverty Alleviation in Africa." In *Faith in Development: Partnership between the World Bank and the Churches of Africa,* edited by Deryke Beishaw, Robert Calderisi and Chris Sugden, 219-236. Oxford; Irvine, CA: Regnum Books International, 2001.

———. "The Role of the Church in Poverty Alleviation in Africa." *Transformation: An International Journal of Holistic Mission Studies* 17, no. 4 (October 2000): 146-152.

Onah, N.G., L.N. Okwuosa, and F.C. Uroko. "The Church and Poverty Alleviation in Nigeria." *HTS Teologiese Studies/Theological Studies* 74, no. 1 (2018): 4834, doi.org/10.4102/hts.v74i1.4834.

Pontifical Council for Justice and Peace, ed. *Compendium of the Social Doctrine of the Church*. London; New York: Burns & Oates, 2004.

Seery, Emma, and Ana Caistor Arendar. *Even It Up: Time to End Extreme Inequality*. Oxford: Oxfam International, October 2014.

Seree, Yeboa-Mensa. "Reducing Poverty in Sub-Saharan Africa: Two Development Theories and the Role of the Church." Master's thesis, Helsinki: University of Helsinki, May 2012.

Synodus Episcoporum. *II Coetus Specialis Pro Africa: The Church in Africa in Service to Reconciliation, Justice and Peace – Elenchus Finalis Propositionum*. Syond of Bishops (Vatican City). http://www.vatican.va/roman_curia/synod/documents/rc_synod_doc_20091023_elenco-prop-finali_en.html.

Thesnaar, Christo. "Rural Education: Reimagining the Role of the Church in Transforming Poverty-stricken South Africa." *HTS Teologiese Studies/ Theological Studies* 70, no. 1 (2014): 1-7, doi.org/10.4102/hts.v70i1.2629.

Verster, P. "A Church with the Poor: Lessons from Scripture and from Congregations in Informal Settlements." *Acta Theologica Suppl.* 16 (2012): 70-88, doi/10.4314/actat.v32i1S.5.

CHAPTER EIGHT

Serving the Vulnerable Among us with Integrity: Best Practices of Accompaniment

Annah Nyadoma

Introduction

The global perspective of vulnerability is a complex phenomenon that is often influenced by social, economic, political, and cultural factors, thus making it an issue with multiple dimensions. Exposure to a variety of different risks gives way to vulnerability, and it is common among diverse groups of people irrespective of their economic status. Given this broad definition of vulnerability, it is clear that the world in which we live is inundated with vulnerable populations living amongst us— those exposed to the physical, social, economic, and environmental dimensions of vulnerability.

The presence of vulnerability has been acknowledged as a phenomenon being universal, constant, and inherent to the human condition[303]. Some of the elements that render people in these communities vulnerable include dominance, power, unemployment, personal incapacities, educational accomplishment, interactions with the environment, and limited access to health services. These factors are a result of the interaction between resources that are available to them and the challenges that are associated with them.

---

[303] Martha Albertson Fineman, "The Vulnerable Subject: Anchoring Equality in the Human Condition," *Yale Journal of Law & Feminism* 20, no. 1 (2008): 10.

Key Terms

Vulnerability is a primal human condition and the Church plays a crucial role in the care of those affected by ministering to them. As stated by Paul in his Epistle to the Romans: "We, then, that are strong ought to bear the infirmities of the weak" (15:1). This is in line with the vulnerability theory which advocates that the state and stakeholders must be there to share the burden of vulnerable persons.[304] Although the Church is already committed to assisting the vulnerable, there is still more work that needs to be done to help those in need. When serving the vulnerable, integrity should be at the center of any actions taken by the Church. This chapter focuses on five aspects of vulnerability: cultural, social, economic, political, and environmental

The term vulnerable refers to one or more people in need of special care, support, or protection due to their age, social status, disability, abuse, or neglect. A vulnerable person can be referred to as a person in an infirm state, of physical, or mental deficiency, or deprivation of personal freedom, that in fact, even occasionally, limits their capacity to intend, or to want, or in any way to resist the offense.[305] In general, vulnerability can be understood as characteristics determined by physical, social, economic, and environmental factors or processes, which increase the susceptibility of an individual, a community, assets, or systems to hopelessness, or the impacts of hazards. Vulnerable groups include the elderly, people with disabilities, men and women, boys and girls, and children under the age of eighteen.

The term integrity can be defined as the quality of being honest, upright, and having strong principles. *Integrity is the person-*

---

[304] Frank Ruddy Cooper, "Always Already Suspect: Revising Vulnerability Theory," *North Carolina Law Review* 93 (2015): 2.

[305] Ed Condon, "Analysis: Pope Francis Issues new definition of 'vulnerable' adult," Catholic News Agency, March 29, 2019, www.catholicnewsagency.com/news/analysis-pope-francis-issues-new-definition-of-vulnerable-adult-74015.

al choice to maintain an uncompromising and predictably consistent commitment to honour — moral, ethical, spiritual, and artistic values and principles.[306] Best practices of accompaniment are methods or techniques that are practical and can be used successfully to assist vulnerable populations. Hence, the topic urges Christians to work together to protect, help, and find solutions to the problems being faced by the helpless and the unguarded. The best task initiatives for protecting minors and vulnerable adults are advocated by the Pontifical Commission for the Protection of Minors (PCPM), empowered by the Pope.[307]

Factors that Make People Vulnerable and the Way Forward

Vulnerability is a multi-dimensional issue that can be distinguished through four dimensions which are cultural, social, economic and political.[308] The members of the Church are to play a significant role in serving the vulnerable.

Cultural Vulnerability

Various cultural practices have an impact on the social construction of vulnerability. For example, the prevalence of patriarchal systems in African countries results in women and girls

---

[306] Barbara Killinger, *Integrity: Doing the Right Thing for the Right Reason* (Montreal: McGill-Queen's University Press, 2010).

[307] Francis appointed Cardinal Seán O'Malley, OFM Cap., as President of the Pontifical Commission for the Protection of Minors [PCPM], and named sixteen members to this advisory body responsible for championing best practice initiatives for protecting minors and vulnerable adults. See Christopher Wells, "Pope Francis Appoints New Members to Commission for Protection of Minors," *Vatican News*, February 17, 2018, www.vaticannews.va/en/pope/news/2018-02/pope-francis-protection-of-minors-new-members.html.

308 D. Alexander, "Vulnerability," in *Encyclopedia of Crisis Management*, ed. K. Bradley Penuel, Matt Statler, and Ryan Hagen, vol. 2 (Thousand Oaks, CA: SAGE Publications, 2013), 980.

being made particularly vulnerable. Patriarchy is reflected in the people's strong preferences for male children over female children, which has led to the neglect of female children. For instance, in Zimbabwe, boys are socialized from a young age to view themselves as breadwinners and heads of households, while girls are taught to be obedient and submissive housekeepers. In this case, the socialization process differs for male and female children.

Males are viewed as being superior, while females are viewed as being dependent on males.[309] This implies that the socialisation processes in families transmit patriarchal ideas of male domination and female subordination and this result in the female entrepreneur feeling inferior in the presence of her male counterparts or even in the presence of any male figure around.[310] In most African cultures such as in the Zimbabwean context, girls are often considered as being on transit in the family as they will be married and leave the family.

Though being born within the family, the cultural assumption is that the girls would not have permanence in staying with the family since they would be married and be incorporated in the husband's family and even getting the husband's surname. This cultural and social trait might disadvantage the girl child in terms of inheritance especially inheritance of the deceased estate due to the fact that they are taken to be on transit (to leave the family for their marriage) often also not supported to attain good education.

In an effort to assist female children, there is a need for advocacy on gender equality and equity so that females can be given the same opportunities to contribute to society and the economy

---

[309] Linda McDowell and Rosemary Pringle, *Defining Women: Social Institutions and Gender Divisions* (Oxford: Polity Press, 1992).

[310] Pamela Abbott, Claire Wallace, and Melissa Tyler, *An Introduction to Sociology: Feminist Perspectives* (New York: Routledge, 2005), 60.

just like males. When gender equality is promoted, peace and development are also promoted. Paul writes in his Epistle to the Galatians: "there can be neither Jew nor Greek, there can be neither slave nor freeman, there can be neither male nor female- for you are all one in Christ Jesus" (3:28). This means that the Church can serve the vulnerable by promoting equality and equity between gender as in the book of Genesis (1:27): "So God created humankind in his image, in the image of God he created them; male and female he created them."

Social Vulnerability

Vulnerability can also be socially constructed. Thus social vulnerability refers to the inability of people to withstand the adverse impacts of certain hazards because of characteristics inherent in social interactions, institutions, and systems of cultural values. well-being of individuals, communities, and society as a whole. Social vulnerability is also viewed as a factor which includes abuse, social exclusion and natural hazards.[311] This implies that there are vulnerable people and groups among us who are socially excluded in some policy decision making processes. "Vulnerability" thus is believed to the concept that we are born unable to protect ourselves and our social institutions might work against us.[312] From this insight, the government, society, the Church being inclusive should strive to achieve a more substantive equality through being more responsive.

Calls have, therefore, been raised and declared by the international community through the United Nations advocating that everyone is entitled to all the rights and freedoms with-

---

[311] Diego Sánchez González and Egea Jiménez Carmen, "Social Vulnerability Approach to Investigate the Social and Environmental Disadvantages: Its application in the study of Elderly People," *Papeles de Población* 17, no. 69 (2011): 151–185.

[312] Martha Albertson Fineman, "Beyond Identities: The Limits of an Antidiscrimination Approach to Equality," *BUL REV* 1713 (2012): 718-19.

out distinction of any kind such as race, colour, sex, language, religion, political, or other opinion, national, or social origin, property, birth or other status.[313] These human rights empower individuals to fit in the society without any prejudice. There is need for Church members to ensure on the inclusion of these vulnerable church members. The upholding of the human rights of the vulnerable may be done through the use of the Human rights model.

Economic Vulnerability

Economic vulnerability, which is the exposure of an economy to exogenous shocks, also impacts people negatively. Typical examples are unemployment and hyperinflation trends resulting in many people being poor. Depriving people of educational opportunities makes them vulnerable. Some parents cannot afford to send their children to school because of unemployment. The people are being incapacitated. Also, some households are child-headed due to orphanhood or family disintegration. As a result, some children end up engaging in child labour for survival and to afford school fees.

The Church is encouraged to draw on the Christian understanding of the God-given dignity of the individual, rights to freedom, and the respect that each individual deserves, which also apply to children.[314] This view echoes in the words of John Paul II, "in the family, which is a community of persons, special attention must be devoted to the children by developing a profound esteem for their personal dignity, and a great concern for

---

[313] United Nations, "Universal Declaration of Human Rights," December 10, 1948, www.un.org/en/universal-declaration-human-rights/; "Article 2: The Universal Declaration of Human Sights" sets out fundamental human rights to be protected.

[314] Pontifical Council for Justice and Peace, *Compendium of the Social Doctrine of the Church* (Vatican City: Libreria Editrice Vaticana, 2004), no. 49.

Serving the Vulnerable Among us with Integrity

their rights."³¹⁵ In most cases, the vulnerable adults in society tend to be ignored and are forgotten. The ministry of visiting the sick can be accompanied by the administering of sacraments, which help to give hope to the sick, disabled, and terminally ill.

In this regard, children should not be subjected to any kind of abuses. Their rights should be respected, including the right to education. The Church ought to uphold social justice which has principles of caring and provision of basic needs to the vulnerable. For instance, work still needs to be done to deal with the people who have trauma from different forms of abuse. The Church need to be a voice for the voiceless and the vulnerable. This demands a holistic approach in helping vulnerable persons, especially in promoting equity and justice. According to Pope Benedict XVI, justice is the primary way of charity.³¹⁶ Thus, by upholding social justice, the vulnerable can be served.

Another best practice is to train more teachers to assist those with special educational needs such that every individual benefits from the education system. The People of God can also assist by investing in education so that the curriculum becomes inclusive of different skills to empower the vulnerable who can then apply for scholarships to fund their education. Child protection policies are also crucial in caring for the children. Children should not be exposed to any form of harm, and they should feel secure and cared for. Pope Benedict XVI affirms that: "children are a gift of God to humanity, and they must be the object of particular concern on the part of their families, the Church, society and governments, for they are a source of hope and re-

---

315 John Paul II, *Familiaris Consortio*, apostolic exhortation, November 22, 1981, www.vatican.va/content/john-paul-ii/en/apost_exhortations/documents/hf_jp-ii_exh_19811122_familiaris-consortio.html, no. 26.

316 In *Caritas in Veritate*, Pope Benedict XVI's explains that without truth, "charity degenerates into sentimentality," and "love becomes an empty shell you be filled in an arbitrary way." Benedict XVI, *Caritas in Veritate*, encyclical letter, June 29, 2009, www.vatican.va/content/benedict-xvi/en/encyclicals/documents/hf_ben-xvi_enc_20090629_caritas-in-veritate.html, no. 3.

newed life."³¹⁷ It means the well-being of children should be at the heart of the Church's mission in order to serve the disadvantaged children by establishing support groups to help children from abusive families.

Another factor that makes children more vulnerable is the practice of child marriages. Child marriage is the marriage of a girl or a boy, be it formal marriage, or informal union in which a child under the age of 18 lives with a partner as if married.[318] These marriages are usually a result of poverty, ignorance, religion and culture.[319] Child marriages hinder childhood development since children have to pass through certain stages of development before they reach adolescence. In this way, child marriages affect both boys and girls, with girls being the most impacted demographically. Girls face a double burden due to domestic violence as a result of poverty that makes them more vulnerable to not continuing education. This results in some girls being married at a tender age, thereby violating the children's rights to reach their full potential, and thus making them more vulnerable.[320]

In a bid to serve these vulnerable populations, the Church can mobilize families and communities, educating them on the adverse impact of child marriage, particularly on girls. Since

---

[317] Benedict XVI, *Africae Munus*, post-synodal apostolic exhortation, November 19, 2011, www.vatican.va/content/benedict-xvi/en/apost_exhortations/documents/hf_ben-xvi_exh_20111119_africae-munus.html, no. 65.

[318] UNICEF, *Child Marriage: Latest Trends and Future Prospects* (New York: UNICEF, 2018). The data from UNICEF show that 650 million girls and women alive today were married as children before the age of 19. This prevalence of child marriages is a violation of human rights.

[319] UNICEF, "Progress for Children: Achieving the MDGs with Equity," Number 9, September, 2010, www.unicef.org/protection/Progress_for_Children-No.9_EN_081710.pdf, 47.

[320] International Center for Research on Women (ICRW), "Child Marriage and Domestic Violence," 2006, www.icrw.org/files/images/Child-Marriage-Fact-Sheet-Domestic-Violence.pdf.

girls are victims of religious and socio-cultural practices, education and awareness by the Church will go a long way to save these vulnerable individuals in society. An estimated 25 million child marriages have already been prevented globally due to efforts by stakeholders to fight this fundamental violation of human rights.[321]

Sexual violence is also a pressing social problem with victims of sexual assault having to cope with physical and psychological consequences.[322] The perpetrators of sexual assault are rarely strangers, but people whom the victims know and trust.[323] Sexual violence commonly affects females and males in schools, in the community, at workplaces, and even within marriages. It has been noted that the sex offenders are more likely to target individuals with mental health problems since these individuals are made vulnerable by the way in which their psychological well-being interacts with their environment and they are more susceptible to harm.

However, the concept of "rape prevention" may be used—a concept which encourages everyone to take responsibility to prevent rape. The Church may take a central role promoting rape prevention and other prevention strategies for sexual violence perpetration.[324] For instance, the People of God can offer psycho-social support and counseling to the sexually assaulted which can help them to cope and become resilient in the face of

---

[321] See UNICEF, *Child Marriage*.

[322] Jan Welch and Fiona Mason, "Rape and Sexual Assault," *BMJ* 334 (2007): 1154–58.

[323] See Fiona Mason and Zoe Lodrick, "Psychological Consequences of Sexual Assault," *Best Practice & Research Clinical Obstetrics & Gynaecology* 27, no. 1 (February, 2013), 27–37.

[324] For various rape prevention strategies, see Sarah A. DeGue, Linda Anne Valle, Melissa Holt, and Greta Masseti, "A Systematic Review of Primary Prevention Strategies for Sexual Violence Perpetration," *Aggression and Violent Behaviour* 9, no. 14 (2014): 346–62.

traumatic experiences. Also, advocating for strict law and policies that act against the perpetrators can help protect vulnerable populations.

Disability which can be defined as an impairment that may be cognitive, developmental, intellectual, mental, physical, sensory, or some combination of these which limits or restricts activity participation, is a contributory factor to child vulnerability.[325] People with disabilities are often stereotyped and isolated because others do not believe that they possess the same capacities as the non-disabled. In this view, they are vulnerable since they are not given the chance to air out their views and share their giftedness. For instance, only a few schools accommodate people with disabilities and most of these schools are very expensive. Also, very few companies employ people with disabilities, limiting them to opportunities for self-actualization.

Best practices of assisting people with disabilities include promoting inclusive education at all educational levels. This can be done through the construction of disability-friendly structures in schools so that people with disabilities can have equal access to buildings. Also, people with special needs should be given opportunities to take part in every activity that leads to the nation's social, economic and political development. The Church can also take part in the conscientisation of the community on disabilities and on methods of help, assistance and support for people with disabilities. These are prerequisites for them in society. Pope John Paul II advocated that vulnerable persons deserve respect because human beings have the responsibility to respect the dignity and worth of every individual.[326]

---

[325] See *World Health Organization, "Disabilities," accessed July 31, 2020,* www.who.int/health-topics/disability.

[326] John Paul II, *Laborem Exercens*, papal encyclical, September 14, 1981, www.vatican.va/content/john-paul-ii/en/encyclicals/documents/hf_jp-ii_enc_14091981_laborem-exercens.html.

The service rendered by the Church must uphold integrity as its guiding principle. Since irresponsible and corrupt behaviour patterns and actions are prevalent, the Catholic Church must be seen to promote integrity, sincerity, and transparency of its services to the vulnerable.[327] For instance, allowing transparency in the fund-raising programmes shows high levels of integrity. The counsellor must be someone who is empathetic and sensitive, a good listener, trustworthy, able to affirm and build up confidence, and motivate the individual to cultivate self-esteem.

Political Vulnerability

Politics has always been a thorny issue and has placed people into vulnerable positions.[328] In some parts of the world, politics has led to genocide. On this note, the words of the prophet Isaiah is instructive: *"Learn to do right. See that justice is done – help those who are oppressed"* (1:17). Based on this biblical text, the Church needs to play a crucial role in serving vulnerable populations and ensuring social justice. For instance, the Catholic Church has been in the forefront in mediating political settlements in Zimbabwe's politics, perhaps stirred by Mother Theresa's famous quote: *"We do not need guns and bombs to bring peace, we need love and compassion."*

Politics is also seen as a factor which results in people being placed into political subjectivity. People are often threatened and killed on the basis of their political stance.[329] This violates

---

[327] New evidence shows that almost 40% of people are economically vulnerable. See Organisation for Economic Co-operation and Development, "Statistical Insights," accessed July 31, 2020, www.oecd.org/sdd/statistical-insights.htm.

[328] Estelle Ferrarese, "The Vulnerability and the Political: On the Seeming Impossibility of Thinking Vulnerability and the Political Together and Its Consequences," *Critical Horizons* 17, no. 2 (2016): 224–39.

[329] Adolfo Mascarenhas and Ben Wisner, "Politics, Power and Disaster," in *The Routledge Handbook of Hazards and Disasters Risk Reduction*, ed. Ben Wisner, J. C. Galland and Ilan Kelman (New York: Routledge, 2012) 28–60.

people's freedom of expression. Based on Isaiah 58: 5-7 affirmation of true worship a demanding work for justice and care for the poor and oppressed, the Church plays a crucial role in serving those exposed to political vulnerability. The role of the Church is to mediate for the poor and vulnerable in the political arena. However, for the best practice to be attained, there is need for the Church to rise above political patronage. For instance, in situations where the Church is used in political mediation, cognizance must be taken of the fact, that political dialogue may not be realised if the churches fail to rise above political patronage.[330] Rising above patronage would thus ensure integrity since it should be the virtue of compromise.[331]

Furthermore, access to health services remains a problem in most countries making people more vulnerable, especially the poor who do not have enough money for medication or medical aid covers. The low-income individuals are more likely to have chronic illnesses, and the impact of those illnesses is more severe. For example, hospitals and clinics in Zimbabwe require hospital user fees for one to be treated, and those who cannot afford can be helped with Assisted Medical Treatment Orders (AMTOs).[332]

The problem is that there is an excessive demand for medications, which makes it difficult for the responsible authorities to assist every individual without user fees. As a result, there is an increase in the morbidity and mortality rates, which undermines a nation's growth and development. In an attempt to

---

[330] Joram Tarusarira, "An Emergent Consciousness of the Role of Christianity on Zimbabwe's Political Field: A Case of Non-doctrinal Religio-political Actors," *Journal for the Study of Religion* 29, no. 2 (2016): 56–77.

[331] Ari Schwartz and Rob Knake, *Government's Role in Vulnerability Disclosure: Creating a Permanent and Accountable Vulnerability Equities Process* (Cambridge: Harvard Kennedy School, 2016).

[332] See Juan Carlos Villagran De Leon, *Vulnerability: A Conceptual and Methodological Review* (Bonn: UNU-EHS, 2006).

serve the vulnerable, health care systems should be rooted in values that respect human dignity, protect human life, and meet the needs of the poor and uninsured, especially born and unborn children, pregnant women, immigrants, and other vulnerable populations.

The Church can provide care for the sick that reflects Catholic morals. This is often done in church mission hospitals where most of the vulnerable seek health advice and medication, given the fact that most private clinics and hospitals are charging health fees way beyond the affordability of the vulnerable. The vulnerable also cannot afford to subscribe to medical aid societies. The RAW Justice model can be used as a tool to help develop the self-esteem of individuals who are made vulnerable through illness, unemployment, neglect, or isolation.[333] The process of the RAW model is to establish a relationship which was lost by using the Head (minds), Heart, and Hands: Minds that open up to welcome, Hearts that join to support, and Hands that work to provide food.

The three stages of the RAW model are a process whereby the person affected is helped to search for a new identity. This process starts by recognizing the problem, acknowledging that it exists, and welcoming the person. Then it grows to reciprocity whereby the sufferer is able to dialogue, is affirmed, and their well-being becomes the priority. After this, the supporting agent fosters a relationship to establish trust. The relationship grows and is made increasingly stronger to meet the needs which are being addressed, resulting in something which is mutually beneficial. The needy persons are helped to think for themselves; they are encouraged to participate and to decide the best ways that they can be helped.[334]

---

[333] Paul Voice, *Rawls Explained: From Fairness to Utopia* (Chicago: Open Court, 2011), 41–48.

[334] Thomas Pogge and Andreas Føllesdal, *Real World Justice Grounds, Principles, Human Rights, and Social Institutions* (Dordrecht: Springer, 2005), 88.

The best practices also include the seven P's: Prayer, Prevention, Protection, Promotion, Policy, Participation, Partnership, and Prosecution. These indicate areas where the church is to be involved through collaboration and working together as a family with the clergy, religious, lay experienced people, and professionals. Professionals are the people who can help to support in areas that require specific expertise. These instances might include dealing with political issues to help figure out the proper ways of breaking through in a non-violent way while also promoting the social teachings of the Church.

The sick need to be empowered through the sacraments of healing—penance and anointing the sick (Ez 18:21). In addition, the People of God can campaign against religious groups and hospitals that discriminate against the poor to save lives, thus serving the vulnerable. Another course of action that can be taken by the Church is that of social protection initiatives such as cash transfers to ensure that disadvantaged groups such as the terminally ill, HIV patients, people with disabilities, and the poor have access to basic services.

Furthermore, the tendency of the environment to respond negatively to changes in human behavior and climatic conditions also places people around the world into vulnerable positions. The earth's climate system is creating what many people are calling a "New Normal" which is defined by extreme weather events such as storms, droughts, and rising sea levels all around the world.[335]

Key factors that also influence environmental vulnerability are natural resource depletion and resource degradation.[336] This

---

[335] See Burrell E. Montz and Graham A. Tobin, "Vulnerability, Risks and Hazards," in *Oxford Bibliographies in Geography*, ed. Barney Warf (Oxford: Oxford University Press, 2016).

[336] Jörn Birkmann, "Measuring Vulnerability to Promote Disaster-Resilient Societies: Conceptual Frameworks and Definitions," in *Measuring Vulnerability to Natural Hazards: Towards Disaster Resilient Societies*, ed. Jörn Birkmann (Hong Kong:

can be seen through some people having dilapidated houses, no access to safe drinking water reflecting in the poor living and working in areas exposed to potential hazards, and they are less likely to have the resources to cope when disaster strikes. One example is the victims of Cyclone Idai in Zimbabwe, Mozambique and Malawi. Most people in Chimanimani who were affected by the cyclone Idai lacked proper housing, clothing, food, and other basic needs. This means that they are victims of environmental vulnerability, since their houses and other buildings were unable to withstand the cyclone.

The existence of populaces subjected to vulnerability through cyclones, droughts or other extreme weather events inspire Catholics to take action to fulfill the teachings of Paul in Galatians 6:2: "Carry each other's burdens, and in this way, you will fulfill the law of Christ." One way of serving these vulnerable populations would be for the People of God to help implement early warning systems that can detect possible hazards. Thus detailed sectoral strategies to address the risks of droughts and floods need to be undertaken through follow-up disaster risk management activities in vulnerable countries, like in Malawi and Mozambique.[337]

This can help people prepare for such disasters. In addition, provision of psycho-social support by the Church to those who have been affected by natural disasters can be helpful to the victims. Also, assistance through donations of clean water, sanitation, food, clothing, and building materials for the victims is a way of helping the vulnerable in such situations.

The Church should always recognise, acknowledge, welcome and integrate the vulnerable, using collective minds to re-

---

UNU Press, 2006), 9–54.

[337] Global Facility for Disaster Reduction and Recovery, International Food Policy Research Institute, RMSI, and World Bank, *Economic Vulnerability and Disaster Risk Assessment in Malawi and Mozambique: Measuring Economic Risks of Droughts and Floods*, 2009, www.preventionweb.net/publications/view/15520, 12.

spond to the needs of vulnerable people. The Church needs to be inclusive in its leadership roles and engage the faithful with different skills and talents to work as teams within their parishes and dioceses.

The best practices are always to be transparent and accountable, that is, showing maturity and responsibility for one's actions. To avoid manipulation, people should be included in decision-making processes. The church as family of God expects its members to remain vigilant, to observe professional boundaries, and to avoid any form of abuse that will cause harm to the Church. Those appointed to be finance officers should go through proper training to avoid blame or accusations of misusing public funds.

There is also a need for social protection, especially when dealing with disabled populations and children. The institutions responsible for these vulnerable people are to be registered so that they can receive outside support and work in partnership with the government. Social workers are to have police clearance and training for the job, which might include training in child safeguarding policy as required by the local church and Catholic expectations.

The Church as the Body of Christ unites to reach out to the vulnerable by joining hands, opening hearts, and walking an extra mile using their feet for the common good. People with disabilities also need to have the opportunity to explore their talents. It should not be presumed that they are unable to do work, especially when they are never given the opportunity. The care provided should be tailored to each person's specific level of ability and vulnerability. Thus, faith in action is translated to transform life; the person's well-being is developed, and continued affirmation helps to build better lives.

Since vulnerability exposes the individual to the possibility of being attacked or harmed, either physically or emotionally or spiritually vulnerable, there is need for the Church to empower vulnerable groups through Education, Employment and Training (EET). Providing education and creating employment opportunities as well as training of the vulnerable is a good strategy for empowering the vulnerable. This may elevate them from poverty and break the poverty cycle in their lives. The vulnerable may also be empowered through participation: Actively involving vulnerable groups to participate in decision-making is another mechanism for empowering the vulnerable which raises their hopes in being considered in key decision making on issues particularly involving them. Another strategy is life skills training for young people from vulnerable backgrounds. This empowers them through the new skills acquired making them self- reliant.

Technology companies and government have shown leadership in this fight and must continue to innovate in order to better protect children. The church caregivers are to benefit from in-service training and equip themselves with relevant knowledge and skills. The Church must also awaken families and communities around the world and children themselves to the reality of the internet's impact upon children. To some extent television programs can be designed to suit the level of the children. To reduce online crimes parents are to be trained to understand how anyone can become vulnerable to digital gadgets. The leaders of technology companies are also to commit to the development and implementation of new tools and technologies to attack the proliferation of any images on the Internet, and to interdict the redistribution of the images.

Above all, the Catholic Church may employ the best practices identified above through the use of appropriate models to ensure child safeguarding as a means to mitigate child vulnerability. The models which may be used may be *Ubuntuism/Hunhuism* (Afrocentric approach), Human Rights Approach, and Ecological Approach. *Ubuntuism/Hunhuism* is an African moral philosophy that promotes the African traditional culture in promoting humanity and oneness, correcting social injustices of the past and promoting unity and peace.[338] Thus the Church might use *Ubuntuism* as a best practice approach to safeguard the vulnerable in society.

Alternatively, the Church might use the Human Rights approach which evolves from the United Nations' Declaration of Human Rights that advocates for upholding rights such as the right to be heard, freedom from violence, abuse and neglect, freedom of thought, freedom from fear, freedom of choice and the right to make decisions and ownership over one's body. Pursuance of these rights by the schools allows children to grow up healthy and free.[339]

The Church might also opt to use the Ecological Approach which is a conceptual framework for resolving ecosystem issues. Since these might expose individuals to a state of vulnerability. The Ecological Approach raises a worldwide wake up call to help humanity understand the destruction that man is rendering to the environment and his fellow man. This has been supported by the Pope Francis' Encyclical *Laudato Si*, a document that addresses the adverse impact of human activities on the environment.

Conclusion

This chapter looked at how best Catholics may serve the vulnerable with integrity, particularly by promoting accountability and transparency. The concept of vulnerability was explored, and this helped to highlight that the vulnerable in today's society are impacted by different dimensions of the issue. Increases

---

[338] Dalene Swanson, "Frames of Ubuntu: (Re)framing an Ethical Education," in *Framing Peace: Thinking about and Enacting Curriculum as "Radical Hope,"* eds. Hans Smits and Rahat Naqvi (New York: Peter Lang, 2015), 49–63.

[339] Collete Chabbott, *UNICEF's Child-Friendly Schools Framework: A Desk Review* (New York: UNICEF, 2004), www.academia.edu/16523393/UNICEFs_Child_Friendly_Schools_A_Desk_Review.

in vulnerability can be triggered by socio-political, economic, environmental, and technological factors that affect the well-being of individuals.

It has been noted that to be vulnerable is part and parcel of human life, but its impact can be minimized if people work together towards achieving one goal. People are affected in all sectors of life, socially, economically, politically, and environmentally. Best practices which can be employed to serve the vulnerable include advocacy, lobbying, investing in human capital, promoting social justice, and promoting equality and equity. In this light, the People of God can prevent as well as reduce vulnerability among various populations through capacity building, respect, and motivation. Thus ccontemplating our shared vulnerability becomes apparent that human beings need each other, and that we must structure our institutions in response to this fundamental human reality.[340]

---

[340] Fineman, *The Vulnerable Subject*, 12.

Bibliography

Abbott, Pamela, Claire Wallace, and Melissa Tyler. *An Introduction to Sociology: Feminist Perspectives.* New York: Routledge, 2005.

Alexander, D. "Vulnerability." In *Encyclopedia of Crisis Management*, edited by K. Bradley Penuel, Matt Statler, and Ryan Hagen, vol. 2. Thousand Oaks, CA: SAGE Publications, 2013.

Benedict XVI. *Africae Munus.* Post-synodal apostolic exhortation, November 19, 2011. www.vatican.va/content/benedict-xvi/en/apost_exhortations/documents/hf_ben-xvi_exh_20111119_africae-munus.html.

— — —. *Caritas in Veritate.* Encyclical letter, June 29, 2009. www.vatican.va/content/benedict-xvi/en/encyclicals/documents/hf_ben-xvi_enc_20090629_caritas-in-veritate.html.

Birkmann, Jörn. "Measuring Vulnerability to Promote Disaster-Resilient Societies: Conceptual Frameworks and Definitions." In *Measuring Vulnerability to Natural Hazards: Towards Disaster Resilient Societies*, edited by Jörn Birkmann, 9–54. Hong Kong, New York: UNU Press, 2006.

Chabbott, Collete. *UNICEF's Child-Friendly Schools Framework: A Desk Review.* New York: UNICEF, 2004. www.academia.edu/16523393/UNICEFs_Child_Friendly_Schools_A_Desk_Review.

Condon, Ed. "Analysis: Pope Francis Issues new definition of 'vulnerable' adult." Catholic News Agency, March 29, 2019. www.catholicnewsagency.com/news/analysis-pope-francis-issues-new-definition-of-vulnerable-adult-74015.

Cooper, Frank Ruddy. "Always Already Suspect: Revising Vulnerability Theory." *North Carolina Law Review* 93 (2015): 1340-1379.

De Leon, Juan Carlos Villagran. *Vulnerability: A Conceptual and Methodological Review*. Bonn: UNU-EHS, 2006.

DeGue, Sarah A., Linda Anne Valle, Melissa Holt, and Greta Masseti. "A Systematic Review of Primary Prevention Strategies for Sexual Violence Perpetration." *Aggression and Violent Behaviour* 9, no. 14 (2014): 346–62.

Ferrarese, Estelle. "The Vulnerability and the Political: On the Seeming Impossibility of Thinking Vulnerability and the Political Together and Its Consequences." *Critical Horizons* 17, no. 2 (2016): 224–39.

Fineman, Martha Albertson. "The Vulnerable Subject: Anchoring Equality in the Human Condition." *Yale Journal of Law & Feminism* 20, no. 1 (2008): 8-40.

_____. "Beyond Identities: The Limits of an Antidiscrimination Approach to Equality." *BUL REV* 1713 (2012): 718-19.

Global Facility for Disaster Reduction and Recovery, International Food Policy Research Institute, RMSI, and World Bank. *Economic Vulnerability and Disaster Risk Assessment in Malawi and Mozambique: Measuring Economic Risks of Droughts and Floods*. 2009. www.preventionweb.net/publications/view/15520.

González, Diego Sánchez, and Egea Jiménez Carmen. "Social Vulnerability Approach to Investigate the Social and Environmental Disadvantages: Its application in the Study of Elderly People." *Papeles de Población* 17, no. 69 (2011): 151–185.

International Center for Research on Women (ICRW). "Child Marriage and Domestic Violence." 2006. www.icrw.org/files/images/Child-Marriage-Fact-Sheet-Domestic-Violence.pdf.

John Paul II. *Familiaris Consortio*. Apostolic exhortation, November 22, 1981. www.vatican.va/content/john-paul-ii/en/apost_exhortations/documents/hf_jp-ii_exh_19811122_familiaris-consortio.html.

———. *Laborem Exercens*. Papal encyclical, September 14, 1981. www.vatican.va/content/john-paul-ii/en/encyclicals/documents/hf_jp-ii_enc_14091981_laborem-exercens.html.

Killinger, Barbara. *Integrity: Doing the Right Thing for the Right Reason*. Montreal: McGill-Queen's University Press, 2010.

Mascarenhas, Adolfo, and Ben Wisner. "Politics, Power and Disaster." In *The Routledge Handbook of Hazards and Disasters Risk Reduction*, edited by Ben Wisner, J. C. Galland and Ilan Kelman, 28–60. New York: Routledge, 2012.

Mason, Fiona, and Zoe Lodrick. "Psychological Consequences of Sexual Assault." *Best Practice & Research Clinical Obstetrics & Gynaecology* 27, no. 1 (February, 2013), 27–37.

McDowell, Linda, and Rosemary Pringle. *Defining Women: Social Institutions and Gender Divisions*. Oxford: Polity Press, 1992.

Montz, Burrell E., and Graham A. Tobin. "Vulnerability, Risks and Hazards." In *Oxford Bibliographies in Geography*, edited by Barney Warf. Oxford: Oxford University Press, 2016.

Organisation for Economic Co-operation and Development. "Statistical Insights." Accessed July 31, 2020. www.oecd.org/sdd/statistical-insights.htm.

Pogge, Thomas, and Andreas Føllesdal. *Real World Justice Grounds, Principles, Human Rights, and Social Institutions*. Dordrecht: Springer, 2005.

Pontifical Council for Justice and Peace. *Compendium of the Social Doctrine of the Church*. Vatican City: Libreria Editrice Vaticana, 2004.

Schwartz, Ari, and Rob Knake. *Government's Role in Vulnerability Disclosure: Creating a Permanent and Accountable Vulnerability Equities Process*. Cambridge: Harvard Kennedy School, 2016.

Swanson, Dalene. "Frames of Ubuntu: (Re)framing an Ethical Education." In *Framing Peace: Thinking about and Enacting Curriculum as "Radical Hope,"* edited by Hans Smits and Rahat Naqvi, 49–63. New York: Peter Lang, 2015.

Tarusarira, Joram. "An Emergent Consciousness of the Role of Christianity on Zimbabwe's Political Field: A Case of Non-doctrinal Religio-political Actors." *Journal for the Study of Religion* 29, no. 2 (2016): 56–77.

UNICEF. "Progress for Children: Achieving the MDGs with Equity." Number 9, September, 2010. www.unicef.org/protection/Progress_for_Children-No.9_EN_081710.pdf.

———. *Child Marriage: Latest Trends and Future Prospects.* New York: UNICEF, 2018.

United Nations. "Universal Declaration of Human Rights." December 10, 1948. www.un.org/en/universal-declaration-human-rights/.

Voice, Paul. *Rawls Explained: From Fairness to Utopia.* Chicago: Open Court, 2011.

Welch, Jan, and Fiona Mason. "Rape and Sexual Assault." *BMJ* 334 (2007): 1154–58.

Wells, Christopher. "Pope Francis Appoints New Members to Commission for Protection of Minors." *Vatican News*, February 17, 2018. www.vaticannews.va/en/pope/news/2018-02/pope-francis-protection-of-minors-new-members.html.

World Health Organization. "Disabilities." Accessed July 31. 2020. www.who.int/health- topics/disability.

CHAPTER NINE

From Silos to System: Assessing Conditions for Integration of Faith-based Health Service Organisations

Barry C. Eneh and Theresa Abah

Introduction

Faith Based Organisations (FBOs) are generally considered as vital contributors to health care improvement in Africa. In many parts of the continent, both Islamic and Christian missionary hospitals provide up to 30% of the market share, caring for the sick, suffering, troubled, and disadvantaged persons and providing their services as private non-profit organisations.[341] The World Bank Group commend their distinctive resources, capabilities, assets and impact in delivering often structured developmental programs as frontline essential workers to communities in combatting poverty, illiteracy and useful medicines to mostly vulnerable populations.

There are few evaluations that provide understanding of how FBOs services are realigned to respond to the changing pattern of diseases, demographic transitions and the widening gaps between the wealthy and poor, amidst dwindling health funding within the African continent. In this review, we focus

---

[341] Omoboloji Ololade Olarinmoye, "Accountability in Faith-Based Organisations in Nigeria," *Transformation* 31, no. 1 (2014): 58, www.doi.org/10.1177/0265378813501733.

on the contributions of Christian FBOs which have experienced more research in the region.[342]

Despite their existence since the early nineteenth century, churches played a vital role in health system strengthening in low-and middle-income countries. These faith-based enterprises are motivated largely by Gospel values—a desire to heal the sick (Lk 10:1, 8-9), care for those who are ill (Mt 25:35-36), and announce the compassion of Jesus Christ towards those who suffer. Such enterprises thus act as strong advocates for equitable health care in society.[343]

The magnitude to which these FBOs supplement governmental health care delivery efforts provide meaningful access to quality, timely, equitable and affordable health care to citizens is constrained by a number of factors, as millions of Africans still lack quality care. One growing evidence suggest that policy makers and apex organisations fail to implement program agendas that foster partnerships, collaborations and networks among religious and faith-based groups in the decision-making process, which has the potential of providing people-centred and integrated care to improve quality of care, health outcomes, patient experience, and efficiency of health systems.

To succeed in today's highly intersectional ecosphere, a health service organisation must make specific choices regarding its essential functions such as: administrative, clinical, and patient-health outcomes by making investments that will empower

---

[342] Olakunle Odumosu, Rasheed Olaniyi, and Sunday Alonge, *Mapping the Activities of Faith-based Organisations in Development in Nigeria* (Birmingham, UK: University of Birmingham, 2009): 38, https://assets.publishing.service.gov.uk/media/57a08b6740f0b64974000b20/wp38.pdf.

[343] John Paul II, *Ecclesia in Oceania*, apostolic exhortation, January 11, 2020, www.vatican.va/content/john-paul-ii/en/apost_exhortations/documents/hf_jp-ii_exh_20011122_ecclesia-inoceania.html.

all patients as key participants in their own health, practice self-care, improve their lifestyle, eat healthily and exercise to prevent infection, injury, and complex health conditions.[344] In the same way, health care providers must provide support as key players in an increasingly market-based health care economy.

Through its medical outreach, Christian missions maintain the compelling imperative to uphold a fundamental commitment to Christ's Messianic mission of mercy, healing, forgiveness, and eternal salvation.[345] Over the years, these values have continued to inspire members to act with compassion towards the sick, suffering, forsaken, and dying. In this chapter, we examine the benefits and strategies for FBOs to transcend beyond the traditional methods of individualised care delivery model to embracing partnerships and successfully implement an integrated health care model to bolster operational efficiency.

These strategies for FBOs would strengthen organisational capacity, and improve access to affordable quality care for individual patients and diverse populations that address the changing health needs in the African continent. Our literature review identifies the significance of adopting a Complex Adaptive System (CAS) model in the design of FBOs projects as it provides guidance to implementing an integrated health care system that is nimble, adaptive, efficient, innovative, patient-centred, and cost-effective to patients and in the long run, the religious organisations when carefully implemented.[346]

---

[344] Lucinda Cash-Gibson and Magdalene Rosenmoller, "Project INTEGRATE - a common methodological approach to understand integrated health care in Europe," *International Journal of Integrated Care* 14 (Oct-Dec 2014): 8, www.ncbi.nlm.nih.gov/pmc/articles/PMC4276036/.

[345] John Paul II, *Ecclesia in Oceania*, no. 11.

[346] Lucinda Cash-Gibson et al., "Project Integrate: Developing a Framework to Guide Design, Implementation and Evaluation of People-centered Integrated Care Processes," *International Journal of Integrated Care* 19, no. 1 (2019): 3, www.ncbi.nlm.nih.gov/pmc/articles/PMC6396036/pdf/ijic-19-1-4178.pdf.

History of Research and Practice of FBOs

In high-income countries, it is well documented in the literature that religious organisations support the state by extending social support to communities in a well-structured manner. For example, in the United States and Britain, the contributions of FBOs are well recognised in their developmental efforts and form part of the Charitable Choice legislation of 1996. The legislation mandates the organs of government to extend state funding to FBOs, and other civil organisations to support their operations. These mandates are reinforced through executive orders to ensure that vulnerable populations and disadvantaged groups are well catered for by the engaged organisations to their communities. Further, the religious organisations demonstrate that both the spiritual and social lives of the people they serve are important.[347]

In the African continent, the activities of FBOs are not well defined. In fact, according to most evaluations, the funding support to these organisations are from international donors, with high level of religious affiliations to the region.[348] Moreover, donors are sceptical of the allocation of resources to fund development projects for fear of associating religion with developmental aid. Other challenges identified include the lack, or poor legislation by African states in understanding the scope of integration of religious organisations in development affairs devoid of political undertones and other external influences. In addition, several partnership initiatives achieved through interfaith collaborations among apex religious organisations yielded positive results in reducing the scourge of HIV/AIDS in sub-Saharan Africa, restored lands to indigent farmers in Uganda

---

[347] World Health Organization, "Integrated care models: an overview," 2016, www.euro.who.int/en/health-topics/Health-systems/health-services-delivery/publications/2016/integrated-care-models-an-overview-2016.

[348] Olarinmoye, "Accountability in Faith-Based Organization in Nigeria," 58.

(TerrAfrica partnership—a World Bank land restoration project), and provided numerous health infrastructures paralleled only by the states.[349]

The activities of FBOs in Nigeria for instance dates back to the post-colonial era (after 1861), Church Missionary Society (CMS)—a movement by a liberated slave who came back to Nigeria with missionaries to provide humanitarian services, partly for the purpose of converting the indigenes to their new religious movement. According to the U.S. Department of Housing and Urban Development Report, 2001, the need for social services as a means to alleviate the burdens of poverty, ignorance, weak governance and, in some cases, intense political crises, led to the intervention of two major religious organisations in the establishment of faith-based organisations outside usual political influence.[350] For the scope of this review, we provide a brief background of the composition for the Catholic FBOs by tracing their operations to the apex body to illustrate how health services is funded by this organisation in Nigeria.

Supported by the Catholic Relief Services, under the aegis of the National Office of the Justice Development and Peace Commission (JDPC), the JDPC operates 51 diocesan offices of the Catholic Church. The Christian Health Association of Nigeria (CHAN), founded in 1973 by the Catholic Bishops Conference of Nigeria has the primary goal of representing the visions of voluntary medical mission organisations to federal and state governments and providing health care services to approximately 40% of the population.[351]

---

[349] World Bank, "World Bank and HIV/AIDS: The Facts," August 27, 2013, www.worldbank.org/en/topic/ hivandaids/brief/world-bank-and-hivaids-the-facts.

[350] Avis C. Vidal, *Faith-Based Organisations in Community Development* (Washington DC: U.S. Department of Housing and Urban Development, 2001), www.huduser.gov/portal/publications/ faithbased.pdf.

[351] Olarinmoye, "Accountability in Faith-Based Organization in Nigeria," 59.

CHAN works through a network of 400-member institutions mostly situated in remote rural areas of Nigeria. CHAN heads some 140 hospitals and 187 clinics providing maternal and child health care services. In collaboration with 23 other churches, CHAN continues to provide health programs to rural populations through its 4000-plus outreach facilities and four leprosy clinics, reach people in remote communities, and provide them health care regardless of their religious status, gender, or ethnic origin.[352] The Complex Adaptive System (CAS) is founded on the principles of continuous learning, teamwork, customer service, quality improvement, and innovation. CAS's conceptual premise states that the complex nature of events; conditions; and individual human behaviors, actions, and interactions surrounding every episode of care and therapy, in addition to myriad other forces and factors, invariably shapes and influences a slew of processes that sway health outcomes.

Definitions and Models Specific to Integrated Health Networks

The WHO defines Integrated service delivery as: "the organisation and management of health services so that people get the care they need, when they need it, in ways that are user-friendly, achieve the desired results and provide value for money."[353] There are several models of care including—Individual Focused, Disease Focused, and Population Focused models. In this section, we limit our analysis to the population model of integrated care because of its amenability to formal or informal organisations, plus the availability of documented best practices to guide the design of an integrated health system.

---

352 Odumosu, "Religions and development research programme," 2009.
353 See World Health Organization, "Integrated care models."

While the individual and disease models of care delivery practiced by a vast majority of FBOs in Africa focus on the provision of structures, equipment, medicines and personnel, the people focused model has emerged over the years in most developed nations to include caring beyond the hospital system to the provision of a continuum of care to meet aspects of population needs.[354] Examples of population-based care models are evident with the following organisation: - the Cleveland Clinic, Kaiser Permanente (KP), Mayo Clinic, General Electric, Veterans Health Administration (VHA) and the Basque Country.[355]

These organisations operate a system approach through integration of care in either vertical or horizontal format. Vertical integration is where the resultant health care network supports multiple teams and services in acute care settings, such as: hospital units, primary care centres, ambulatory, rehabilitation, long term, and social services all within a unified network. Whereas, horizontal integration, refers to a network of care which manages multiple sites that provide similar services at two, or more independently owned hospitals and clinics, which may be adjoining, or located far from each other.[356]

Successful integration is rooted in three requisite principles: (1) a distinct culture and a commitment to a set of values; (2) dis-

---

[354] Jill Olivier et al., "Understanding the roles of faith-based health-care providers in Africa: review of the evidence with a focus on magnitude, reach, cost, and satisfaction," *The Lancet* 386, no. 10005 (2015): 1770, www.doi.org/10.1016/S0140-6736(15)60251-3.

[355] See Kenneth R. White and John R. Griffith, *The Well-Managed Healthcare Organization* (Chicago, IL: Health Administration Press, 2010).

[356] Pim Valentijn et al., "Understanding integrated care: a comprehensive conceptual framework based on the integrative functions of primary care," *International Journal of Integrated Care* 13 (March, 2013). https://pubmed.ncbi.nlm.nih.gov/23687482/. Nick Goodwin et al., "Providing integrated care for older people with complex needs: Lessons from seven international case studies," *The Kings Fund*, January, 2014, 2, www.kingsfund.org.uk/sites/default/files/field/field_publication_file/providing-integrated-care-for-older-people-with-complex-needs-kings-fund-jan14.pdf.

tinct operational goals that include the search for and development of opportunities that can potentially increase stakeholder values and the bottom-line; (3) strategic or long-term stakeholder interests that are closely monitored and promoted across the system through improved relationships, effective communication, better organisation, and the management of complex tasks and responsibilities of all parties and partners in the care network.[357]

By and large, a properly integrated care system has a better sense of when more issue-specification, process standardisation and/or the coordination of care are the most appropriate actions to take. It is worth noting that most integrated care systems follow at least four simple courses of action: (a) development of a common purpose; (b) identification of clear tasks and a vision; (c) identification of the internal motivation for integration and innovation, and an outline of a few ground rules that must guide both individual and team behaviours, plans, and action steps; and (d) a full description of how agreed upon plans or charter for a new network must function in order to achieve stated goals and objectives.[358]

All in all, an integrated health care system implies that all processes, procedures and performances as they pertain to the broad spectrum of health care delivery services—from physician visit, consultation, disease diagnosis, treatment, hospital stay, long-term care and rehabilitation constantly monitored, carefully coordinated, managed, and evaluated for best possible patient and provider outcomes.[359]

---

[357] Claire Leonie Ward et al., "Good collaborative practice: reforming capacity building governance of international health research partnerships," *Globalization and Health* 14 (2018), www.doi.org/10.12968/ijpn.2006.12.5.21177.

[358] Lars Edgren, "The meaning of integrated care: a systems approach," *International Journal of Integrated Care* 8, no. 4 (2008):3, www.doi.org/10.5334/ijic.256.

[359] Oliver Gröne and Mila Garcia-Barbero, "Integrated care: a position paper of the WHO European Office for Integrated Health Care Services," *International Journal of Integrated Care* 1, no. 1 (June, 2001): 3, www.ncbi.nlm.nih.gov/pmc/articles/PMC1525335/pdf/ijic2001-200121.pdf.

Pertinent Application of an Integrated System

The prevailing disease management and disease alleviation models operative at most hospitals today is a far cry from the health care wellness system that most people want and may be willing to pay to have. Getting past current episodic care practices requires new thought processes and, most of all, requires a paradigm shift from existing 'silos to systems' as well as the adoption of practices that resonate with what has called the critical dimensions of integrated care. Current fragmented care must be replaced with properly coordinated patient-centred, population focused services that put more emphasis on providing a continuum of quality and cost-effective care for patients.[360]

Complex Adaptive System (CAS)

As system improvement strategy, integrated care has been shown to improve health outcomes for target individuals, geographic regions and populations, by prioritising patients' needs over physician's demands succeed in providing a continuum of care coordinated to improve patient health outcomes.[361] This review shows that integrated care is better suited where the primary goal is_positive implications for policy changes, best practices, improved advocacy, and health services research, for health care leaders, providers, policy experts, researchers, and health advocates.

This work assessed the conditions for FBOs to implement an integrative network system or a complex adaptive system which requires health service organisations to provide high-quality care to patients in vulnerable communities to address a wide range of issues affecting people in Africa including Ebola,

---

360 Goodwin et al., "Providing integrated care," 6.
361 Cash-Gibson et al., "Project Integrate," 4.

Human Immunodeficiency Virus/Acquired Immune Deficiency Syndrome, HIV/AIDS, severe acute respiratory syndrome, SARS, Coronavirus, poverty, illiteracy and poor access to health care.[362] Integrated care will enable FBOs collect data related to their unique strengths, opportunities and expertise for growth and expansion of services within communities.

Understanding how this integrative system may ease hardships that result from disease epidemics, famines, droughts and other natural disasters, the review was guided by the following considerations: — understanding the integrated model currently in use by FBOs globally; how the model affects performance in healthcare delivery (the bottom line) and health outcomes for patients; what evidence has informed decisions and choice of strategy, and the key benefits anticipated from adopting the integrative care delivery model. These are issues we tried to address in this review of literature to examine how African FBOs can traverse from operating in silos to develop partnership systems that might leverage on existing opportunities in the various religious organisations.[363]

CAS has been used to examine the contributions of multiple stakeholders, interest groups, specialties, organisations, constituencies, and agencies (with varied and diverse vested interests, behaviours, and conflicting goals and expectations),[364] to understand the nature of the complexity that exists within organisations' proximate and remote environments, and to competently

---

[362] Olivier et al., "Understanding the roles of faith-based health-care providers in Africa," 1767.

[363] Olivier et al., "Understanding the roles of faith-based health-care providers in Africa," 1767; William B. Rouse, "Managing complexity: Disease Control as a Complex Adaptive System," Information-Knowledge-Systems Management 2, no. 2 (April, 2000): 143, https://dl.acm.org/doi/abs/10.5555/1234153.1234158.

[364] William B. Rouse, "Health care as a complex adaptive system: implications for design and management," The Bridge 38, no. 1 (Spring, 2008): 17, www.nae.edu/7704/HealthCareasaComplexAdaptiveSystemImplicationsforDesignandManagement.

transcend these complexities by learning, adapting, and growing. Examples of areas where CAS have been applied include, In other sectors such as the aerospace industry, retail, automotive, and the telecom industries.

A study of 1047 hospital networks with both single and multiple ownerships ownership was compared for ease of management of services within their networks. The findings revealed critical information on performance- while, the highly centralised management structures increased organisation's financial performance metrics, the poorly centralised networks decreased their earnings within the same time frame.[365] All in all, careful assessment, analysis, and alignment of agency capabilities was shown to elicit favourable conditions for both collaborative and competitive advantages that are likely to result in tremendous returns in access (better patient experience and satisfaction), quality (efficiency of care delivery), and cost savings (improved patient payment index) for all parties: patients, partners, and stakeholders.

As a result, to take full advantage of the benefits of integration, an organisation must carefully survey whether, how, and when an integrated system is right for it. For the most part, fact-based answers to all the key dimension making about health care integration is highly advisable. A key finding from most FBOs in Africa suggest that funding to execute operations is centralized, this makes it easier to adopt CAS model which does not require a decomposition of all management functions into component parts, but rather requires all actors, agents, stakeholders working within the system to coordinate their individual tasks and functions in a seamless manner to achieve the desired goal.[366] For example, functions such as pharmacy, medical equipment,

---

[365] Gloria J. Bazzoli et al., "The Financial Performance of Hospitals Belonging to Health Networks and Systems," *Inquiry* 37, no. 3 (Fall, 2000): 234.

[366] Olivier et al., "Understanding the roles of faith-based health-care providers in Africa," 1768.

health insurance and medicine supply can be streamlined or managed through similar process, while health workers, support staff and adhoc staff are coordinated under a separate management to ensure roles are allocated as appropriate.

Cultural, Legislative, and Professional Issues that Impact the Specific Integrated Faith-Based Organization Approaches

The success of health care organisations has been linked to patients' perception of the end value. In an age of patient-centric movement, the patient experience is a supreme measure of success. Therefore, in this environment, success is more likely for organisations that focus their efforts on increasing patient satisfaction and simultaneously holding down patients' experience of the system's complexity, where this can be managed. Needless to say, it is profitable when organisations can put more creative thought into the design of their complex system, effectively monitoring, influencing, and incentivising stakeholder behaviour, and raising individual team commitment and performance. It is noteworthy that CAS, unlike traditional hierarchical health care, operates rather hierarchically. This simply means that decision-making is largely delegated not forced; it is fostered through incentives and inhibitions.

In addition, given that the determinants of health status are often linked to non-health related issues and circumstances such as behaviours and actions of players, a proactive engagement with the broad array of multi-sector stakeholders such as public health partners and other stakeholders is strongly advised.[367] Hence, organisations are encouraged to hook into health and social services in the community to increase the chances of good

---

[367] Leiyu Shi and James A. Johnson, *Novick and Morrow's Public Health Administration: Principles for Population-Based Management* (Burlington, MA: Jones and Bartlett, 2013).

health and wellness for the populations that they serve. Granted that time-tested actors and factors such as the global market, politics, socioeconomics, culture, and ecology influence health outcomes, organisations that wish to improve health access, quality, and cost of care must invest in these sectors.

Take, for instance, better management of health care practice (diagnosis, safety, and the use of technology), policy (financial payments, health insurance, pharmacy, purchases and reimbursements, laws and regulations, and the social determinants of health), research (evidence-based health care research and practice), and advocacy for health disparities for vulnerable populations must thus be complemented. An integrated care will also see to it that care is comprehensive (i.e. care of the whole person—mental health, medical care, drug and addiction care, and social well-being) by employing a team-based approach, data-driven technology, and evidence-based methodologies to advance care as a continuum even with limited resources and funding.[368]

Levels of Integration

With growing demand for improved patient experience and better health outcomes for multi-morbid and long-term-care patients integrated care is better positioned to enhance quality of life, quality of care, customer satisfaction, and system efficiency. To assess its readiness for effective care integration, an organisation will gauge its readiness by analysing the three components of an integrated care system.

Administrative components include the contextual factors that help organisations achieve their goal: the external environment and the internal characteristics required to produce desired output. Clinical Services describes issues to be consid-

---

[368] Gröne and Garcia-Barbero, "Integrated care," 4.

ered prior to implementation of clinical treatment, for example, organisations' strategies; structural designs; programs that provide clear directions such as training of staff; the implementation of patient-centred care; and preventive, curative, spiritual, and community-based care that improve patients' health care experience.

Through partnerships, professional integration, and care evaluation, the key building blocks for integrated care practices suitable within a given health network can be designed using a CAS.[369] This requires the inclusion of patients themselves in the design and planning processes — Patient-centred care refers to the provision of appropriate care, patient inclusion in decision-making, setting of achievable targets, and effective communication between patient-physician in order to improve experiences during and after care, a key determinant of organisational performance.[370]

Barriers to Integration Systems Network

Caroline Auschra identified several barriers to integration of care influenced by institutional, professional, political, administrative, regulative, and funding factor. Others include, inter-organisational governance mechanisms, accountability, design and management of collaborative relationships, and intra-organisational factors such as teamwork.[371] Overall, the major criticism levelled against integrated care is the unavoidability of system inertia over time due to potential breakdown in human communication and potential lack of cooperation and coordination among participating teams and network partners. Because

---

[369] Edgren, "The meaning of integrated care," 2.

[370] Cash-Gibson et al., "Project Integrate," 6.

[371] Carolin Auschra, "Barriers to the Integration of Care in Inter-Organizational Settings: A Literature Review," *International Journal of Integrated Care* 18, no. 1 (2018): 5, www.doi.org/10.5334/ijic.3068.

of the complex nature of an adaptive system, it creates uncertainty due to the existence of elements of insecurity, increased responsibility, increased decision-making responsibilities, and higher risk management protocols spread across team members within participating organisations.[372] Nevertheless, system integration can be a win for organisations that have set out to maintain their autonomy while hoping to reap the benefits of an integrated network.

Benefits of System Integration

The compelling logic of integrated care stems from the quality of its operational strategy, and particularly as a patient-centric, people-focused, outcome-driven, and cost-cutting health system option.[373] Integration of services and providers in a coordinated system have been shown to be more efficient and better incentivises evidence-based practices and the use of up-do-date information to monitor operations' inefficiencies. As a driver of performance, integration offers managers, planners and decision-makers a powerful evidence-based information tool for timely policy changes and improved practices in real time.[374] Some scholars argue that strong investment in organisational values, culture, social capital, research, and system evaluation are reliable mechanisms for averting potential failures.[375]

---

[372] Ann Rowe and Annette Hogarth, "Use of complex adaptive systems metaphor to achieve professional and organisational change," *Journal of Advanced Nursing* 51, no. 4 (August, 2005): 399, www.doi.org/10.1111/j.1365-2648.2005.03510.x.

[373] Gerd Schienstock and Timo Hämäläinen, "Transformation of the Finnish innovation system: A network approach," *Sitra Reports* 7, (2001), https://media.sitra.fi/2017/02/28142146/raportti7.pdf.

[374] Leiyu Shi and Douglas A. Singh, *Delivering Health Care in America: A Systems Approach*, 4th ed. (Burlington, MA: Jones and Barnett Publishers, 2008), 64–66.

[375] Goodwin et al., "Providing Integrated Care," 20.

From Silos to System 263

Research Critical to Issues Discussed in the Chapter

Several models of care integration were identified and analysed — individual care plans, disease management, population or community focused approaches. For this study, we limited our analysis of models to those that had explicit population focus and greater potential for compelling the use of best practices, and those that were suited for faith-based health service organisations. Six organisations formed the basis of our analysis because of the great successes they achieved in their operation of integrated care targeting population groups: Cleveland Clinic, Kaiser Permanente (KP), Mayo Clinic, General Electric, Veterans Health Administration (VHA), United States and Spain's Basque Country health care innovation.

The mechanism adopted by each of these health service organisations was either vertical or horizontal integration. Both models have well documented successes in integrated care.[376] All successful integrations are supported by the existence of (1) a distinct culture and a commitment to a set of values, (2) distinct operational goals including the search for and development of opportunities that can increase stakeholder values and improve the bottom line, and (3) a strategic or long-term stakeholder interest that is closely monitored and promoted across the system for improved relationships, effective communication, and management of complex tasks and responsibilities of all parties and partners in the care network.[377]

In sum, a properly integrated health system is designed in a way that shows when more or less specification, standardisation and care coordination are timely and appropriate interventions. In addition, research shows that integrated systems follow simple courses of action: a common purpose, some ground rules,

---

[376] Cash-Gibson et al., "Project Integrate," 4.

[377] Edgren, "The meaning of integrated care," 2.

and a clear definition of a plan to follow until desired goals are met. Furthermore, an integrated system fulfils three key functions: administrative, clinical service delivery, and patient-centred care.[378] By and large, an integrated health care system means that all processes, procedures, and performances as they pertain to health care delivery services are closely monitored to deliver on the desired goals for patient, provider, and payer.

With the vast majority of Nigerian rural populations lacking access to health insurance, basic health amenities, and liveable income earnings, an integrated health care system may be their last hope should they fall ill, or get injured or infected. Hence, leveraging the strength of faith-based health service organisations to make needed investments in the health care sector is perhaps the best way to stem the rising cost of health tourism for the super-rich, and conversely, the no-choice option for the ultra-poor. An investment in care integration will additionally enable organisations to care for the whole-person: body-, mind-, and soul-focusing more fully on the person, not on profit or the bottom-line. To achieve this, an effective management of three key contingencies: administration, clinical care, and patient experience are imperative.

Faith-based health service organisations wishing to integrate must address the four clarifying questions about self-identity and self-determination. Moving an organisation from a silo to a system of care can come at a great cost: becoming less bureaucratic and non-hierarchical in decision-making and nonlinear, more dynamic and self-organising with no single control point system.[379] In addition, learning to adapt and to control the forces and factors external to health care appears to be more pragmatic and more promising. Available evidence supports the idea that

---

[378] Cash-Gibson et al., "Project Integrate," 4.

[379] Rouse, "Health care as a complex adaptive system," 20; Ward et al., "Good collaborative practice," 5.

attainment of better population health is more guaranteed via smart integration of care.

Hence it seems only rational to recommend that the Catholic Church, government, foundations, and funding agencies should invest in health service organisations that seek to transform themselves in this way. Analysis of extant literature supports the idea that organisational and functional strategy seldom translates into improved patient-centred care. In this chapter, we highlight the benefits African societies stand to benefit by garnering the individual efforts of FBOs in a coordinated and efficient manner to provide opportunities to communities at the grassroots with poor access to care.

Lastly, the governance structure must promote partnerships that will advance health literacy, disease prevention, healthy lifestyles, environmental concerns, and a living wage. Granted that hierarchical governance structure is traditional to faith-based organisations, some behaviour changes may be required in order to avert the faltering of integration. To reap the full benefits of an integrated health care network, provider alignment, strong clinical integration, and reimbursement plus engaged community involvement are the building blocks.

Conclusion

With the growing disease burden, dwindling health budgets and the growing demand for better-coordinated care from patients, providers, and communities, integrated care is becoming a common practice. The greater the severity of health care needs among populations, the greater their need for an integrated system network that would deliver on the promise of patient care experience, reduce co-morbid health conditions, and offer timely and quality health interventions at prices that patients can afford.

The goal of this review is to assess the conditions for successful integration of faith-based health service organisations in resource-strapped environments to adapt to the rapidly changing-complex environment of care, examples include, new and emerging diseases (COVID-19), Ebola, Lassa fever and Dengue fever.

In Western societies, organisations understand and solve complexity largely by reducing, dismantling, or minimising its impact (reduction strategy) on their input, product, and services. On the contrary, in Eastern societies, organisations first seek to understand complexity so they can design fitting alternative solutions around it. This sometimes involves solving complex health delivery service by building alliances and risk hedging mechanisms through absorption strategy. Solving today's complex health problems calls for the deployment of both reduction and absorption strategies, firstly FBOs have centralized funding source through their apex religious organisations.

As a result, they have a great advantage over state actors or public health institutions in building expertise in their area of greatest strength to provide coordinated care to prevent, treat, rehabilitate, identify and manage diseases within the communities where they operate. Secondly, adopting the CAS model to transform the simple-model to a system where they can form a network to improve operations will benefit the state, organisation and the population.

Bibliography

Auschra, Carolin. "Barriers to the Integration of Care in Inter-Organizational Settings: A Literature Review." *International Journal of Integrated Care* 18, no. 1 (2018). www.doi.org/10.5334/ijic.3068.

Bazzoli, Gloria J., Benjamin Chan, Stephen M. Shortell, and Thomas D'Aunno. "The Financial Performance of Hospitals Belonging to Health Networks and Systems." *Inquiry* 37, no. 3 (Fall, 2000): 234–52.

Bettcher, Douglas W., Stephen A. Sapirie, and Eric HT Goon. "Essential public health functions: results of the international Delphi study." *World Health Statistics Quarterly* 51, no. 1 (1997): 44–54.

Cash-Gibson, Lucinda, and Magdalene Rosenmoller. "Project INTEGRATE - a common methodological approach to understand integrated health care in Europe." *International Journal of Integrated Care* 14 (Oct-Dec, 2014). www.ncbi.nlm.nih.gov/pmc/articles/PMC4276036/.

———, Lucinda, Olena Tigova, Albert Alonso, George Binkley, and Magda Rosenmöller. "Project Integrate: Developing a Framework to Guide Design, Implementation and Evaluation of People-centered Integrated Care Processes." *International Journal of Integrated Care* 19, no. 1 (2019). www.ncbi.nlm.nih.gov/pmc/articles/PMC6396036/pdf/ijic-19-1-4178.pdf.

Edgren, Lars. "The meaning of integrated care: a systems approach." *International Journal of Integrated Care* 8, no. 4 (2008). www.doi.org/10.5334/ijic.256.

Goodwin, Nick, Anna Dixon, Geoff Anderson, and Walter Wodchis. "Providing integrated care for older people with complex needs: Lessons from seven international case studies." The Kings Fund , January, 2014. www.kingsfund.org.uk/sites/default/files/field/field_publication_file/providing-integrated-care-for-older-people-with-complex-needs-kingsfund-jan14.pdf.

Gröne, Oliver, and Mila Garcia-Barbero. "Integrated care: a position paper of the WHO European Office for Integrated Health Care Services." *International Journal of Integrated Care* 1, no. 1 (June, 2001). www.ncbi.nlm.nih.gov/pmc/articles/PMC1525335/pdf/ijic2001-200121.pdf.

John Paul II. *Ecclesia in Oceania*. Apostolic exhortation, January 11, 2020. www.vatican. va/content/john-paul-ii/en/apost_exhortations/documents/hf_jp-ii_exh_20011122_ecclesia-inoceania.html.

Odumosu, Olakunle, Rasheed Olaniyi, and Sunday Alonge. *Mapping the Activities of Faith-based Organisations in Development in Nigeria*. Birmingham, UK: University of Birmingham, 2009. https://assets.publishing.service.gov.uk/media/ 57a08b-6740f0b64974000b20/wp38.pdf.

Olarinmoye, Omoboloji Ololade. "Accountability in Faith-Based Organisations in Nigeria." *Transformation* 31, no. 1 (January, 2014): 47–61. www.doi.org/10.1177/0265378813501733.

Olivier, Jill, Clarence Tsimpo, Regina Gemignani, Mari Shojo, Harold Coulombe, Frank Dimmock, Minh Cong Nguyen et al. "Understanding the roles of faith-based health-care providers in Africa: review of the evidence with a focus on magnitude, reach, cost, and satisfaction." *The Lancet* 386, no. 10005 (2015): 1765–75. www.doi.org/10.1016/S0140-6736(15)60251-3.

Rouse, William B. "Health care as a complex adaptive system: implications for design and management." *The Bridge* 38, no. 1 (Spring, 2008): 17–25. www.nae.edu/7704/HealthCareasaComplexAdaptiveSystemImplicationsforDesignandManagement.

———. "Managing complexity: Disease Control as a Complex Adaptive System." *Information-Knowledge-Systems Man-*

agement 2, no. 2 (April, 2000): 143–65. https://dl.acm.org/doi/abs/10.5555/1234153.1234158.

Rowe, Ann, and Annette Hogarth. "Use of complex adaptive systems metaphor to achieve professional and organisational change." *Journal of Advanced Nursing* 51, no. 4 (August, 2005): 396–405. www.doi.org/10.1111/j.1365-2648.2005.03510.x.

Schienstock, Gerd, and Timo Hämäläinen. "Transformation of the Finnish innovation system: A network approach." *Sitra Reports* 7, (2001). https://media.sitra.fi/2017/02/28142146/raportti7.pdf.

Shi, Leiyu, and Douglas A. Singh. *Delivering Health Care in America: A Systems Approach*, 4th ed. Burlington, MA: Jones and Barnett Publishers, 2008.

———, and James A. Johnson. *Novick and Morrow's Public Health Administration: Principles for Population-Based Management*. Burlington, MA: Jones and Bartlett, 2013.

Valentijn, Pim, Sanneke M Schepman, Wilfrid Opheij, and Marc A Bruijnzeels. "Understanding integrated care: a comprehensive conceptual framework based on the integrative functions of primary care." *International Journal of Integrated Care* 13 (March, 2013). https://pubmed.ncbi.nlm.nih.gov/23687482/.

Vidal, Avis. *Faith-Based Organisations in Community Development*. Washington DC: U.S. Department of Housing and Urban Development, 2001. www.huduser.gov/portal/publications/faithbased.pdf.

Ward, Claire Leonie, David Shaw, Dominique Sprumont, Osman Sankoh, Marcel Tanner, and Bernice Elger. "Good collaborative practice: reforming capacity building governance of international health research partnerships." *Globalization and Health* 14 (2018). www.doi.org/10.12968/ijpn.2006.12.5.21177.

White, Kenneth R., and John R. Griffith. *The Well-Managed Healthcare Organization*. Chicago, IL: Health Administration Press, 2010.

World Bank. "World Bank and HIV/AIDS: The Facts." August 27, 2013. www.worldbank.org/en/topic/hivandaids/brief/world-bank-and-hivaids-the-facts.

World Health Organization. "Integrated care models: an overview." 2016. www.euro.who.int/en/health-topics/Health-systems/health-services-delivery/publications/2016/integrated-care-models-an-overview-2016.

CHAPTER TEN

The Role of International Catholic Charities in Promoting Global Health

Susan Nedza

Introduction

The Catholic Church has responded to Jesus' command to "Go and tell John what you hear and see, the blind regain their sight, the lame walk, the lepers are cleansed, the deaf hear, the dead raised, the poor have the Good News proclaimed to them" (Mt 11:5 RSV). The 2010 Symposium of Episcopal Conference of Africa and Madagascar (SECAM) noted that there were more Catholic hospitals in Africa than in North and Central America collectively.[380] In *Africae Munus*, Benedict XVI recognised the commitment of the Synod Fathers to be resolutely engaged in the fight against infirmities, disease and the great pandemics.[381] Engagement in improving the health of the family of God is an integral part in promoting human development.

The question now facing the Church is not what it should do, but how it should continue to do it and with whom as it faces an ever-greater need for services while facing challenges in funding the work. The promotion of global health requires adopting new partnership models between the local church community,

---

[380] "Amid Explosive Church Growth, African Bishops Meet," *Catholic Culture,* 8 July 2010, https://www.catholicculture.org/news/headlines/index.cfm?storyid=7022.

[381] Benedict XVI, *Africae Munus*, post-synodal apostolic exhortation, Vatican website, 19 November, 2011. http://w2.vatican.va/content/benedictxvi/en/apost_exhortations/documents/hf_ben-xvi_exh_20111119_africaemunus.html, sec.47.

religious communities, the laity and international Catholic organisations. This change requires a purposeful movement away from charity toward human development. It must include a conscious rejection of the intrinsic asymmetry of the current paternalistic model— a model that is a remnant of the colonial past in which the greater benefit is reaped by the donor than the potential beneficiaries.

It means a conscious paradigm shift from this paternalistic mindset, in which donors determine what is required, to one in which the community defines the desired state and together they determine how best to achieve better health outcomes. In response to the theme of the congress; "What can we do to perform the works of God?" (Jn 6:28). The Church and religious communities in Africa should denounce the current neo-colonial, asymmetric model of charity that does not address the root causes of inequity that lead to poor health and instead, build collaborative partnerships with International Catholic Non-Governmental Organisations (CNGOs) committed to a model of accompaniment for those they serve.

This essay focuses on the opportunity to re-define the relationship of the Church, and Catholic Non-Governmental Organisations (previously referred to as Catholic charities) from one of asymmetry to one of accompaniment. The focus is on the US-based Catholic groups that provide short-term medical missions (STMM). This is not to diminish the important role played by large international charitable organisations such as Caritas, Catholic Relief Services, and the Catholic Medical Mission Board, but to recognise the difference in structure, resources and scope of smaller organisations. Likewise, it does not address the role of the Catholic institutions of higher learning whose mission of teaching and research encompasses global health experiences for students.

The initial focus is an examination of the risk of dependence on parish donations in an era when the number of Catholics actively engaged in parish communities is decreasing and the simultaneous expansion of alternatives to traditional Catholic charities is occurring. The secondary focus is on the question of ethics and efficacy of volunteer medical mission trips. A brief overview of traditional short-term mission trips follows and a review of the literature regarding their lack of efficacy and efficiency will be used to support the argument for change.

A case report of a US-based Catholic Non-Governmental Organization (CNGO) operating in Honduras details the journey from the neo-colonial model to one of accompaniment. This case study illustrates how this CNGO has made the transition from sponsoring traditional STMMs that give volunteers an opportunity to provide intermittent, curative-focused services, to one of a partnership with the local diocese focused on building capacity in areas of need identified by the community. Special attention is paid to the need for theological and pastoral guidance during such a transition. The challenges faced during this transition, as well as the relevance of the case and implications of its experience in Africa, are discussed.

The chapter concludes with three recommendations for consideration: that the Church and religious communities in Africa should move away from participation in any asymmetric models of medical mission work, international Catholic non-governmental organisations (CNGOs) active in promoting global health should adopt models of accompaniment that are based upon sustainable collaborative partnerships with the Church in the communities they wish to serve. Finally, the Church should commit to sponsor and participate in rigorous data collection in these collaboratives. These data must be focused on health outcomes, financial analysis and be standardized, aggregated, shared, and used to inform all models for improving global health.

The Imperative for a Paradigm Shift

The challenges to traditional fundraising models and questions regarding the ethics and efficacy of STMM trips have converged and make the *status quo* both financially unsustainable and ethically questionable. The need to diversify funding sources and to develop new models for health care initiatives provides an opportunity for organisations to seek new partners and modify the way in which global health initiatives are undertaken.

Dependence on financial support from US Catholic parishes becomes a liability in an era when there is a decrease in Church membership and participation. A 2019 survey found that the percentage of Catholics in the United States has fallen from nearly 25% to 20%. It also reported that in the Hispanic community, the prime source of membership growth in the Church, only 47% of Hispanics self-identified as Catholic.[382]

In 2019, Gallup found that fewer than 40% of self-identified Catholics attended mass in any given week. For those between the ages of 21 and 29, the number dropped to 25%.[383] Further examination of this age group revealed that 55% seldom or never attended mass. Overall, being religious is no longer synonymous with belonging to a religious institution. Sixty-four percent of those self-identified as religious do not feel the need to be members of organized religious institutions.[384] These surveys illustrate the peril of depending on special Sunday collections to fund charitable organisations.

These changes confirm that the potential donor pool is shrinking and reaching those who identify as Catholic is now even more challenging. At a recent conference of the Catholic Volunteer Network, the leading membership organisation of Christian volunteer and mission programs, non-profit organi-

---

[382] "In U.S., decline in Christianity continues at a rapid pace," *Pew Research Center*, 17 October, 2019, as https://www.pewforum.org/2019/10/17/in-u-s-decline-of-christianity-continues-at-rapid-pace/ 3.

[383] "Catholic church attendance resumes downward slide," *Gallup*, 9 April, 2019, https://news.gallup.com/poll/232226/church-attendance-among-catholics-resumes-downward-slide.aspx.

[384] Ibid.

sations in attendance were told in no uncertain terms that if they were dependent on parish collections their long-term viability was unlikely.[385]

The desire of high-net worth individuals to have more direct control over their charitable donations also presents a challenge. This trend is illustrated by the growth of family foundations and issue-focused 501(c)(3) non-profit entities. These new entities often directly fund groups that address global health, thus bypassing traditional faith-based charities. In 2011, 40,456 out of 73,764 private (family, corporate, independent and operating) foundations were family foundations.[386]

Foundations and Donors interested in Catholic Activities (FADICA) is a network of private foundations and donors supporting Catholic programs and institutions. Its *Catholic Funding Guide* cites $6 billion in annual grants by private foundations and nearly 1,500 sources of funding for Catholic institutions and programs.[387] This shifting landscape in funding sources and the emergence of private family foundations is re-defining the very nature of international CNGOs. It is also causing large, traditional CNGOs with broad missions to compete for donations with an increasing number of small family foundations and issue-specific NGOs.

The efficacy, efficiency, and ethics of the current model of international medical missions is undergoing scrutiny. Donors are not only requiring proof that their funds and material donations are having a sustainable impact on the communities served, they are also reconsidering funding traditional interna-

---

[385] Busekras, Zack, "Reaching New Audiences and Increasing Diversity," Presentation, Catholic Volunteer Network, Cleveland, OH, 7 November, 2019.

[386] "Key Facts on Family Foundations," *Council on Foundations*, 21 January, 2011, https://doi.org/f28b5.

[387] The Catholic Funding Guide, *Foundations and Donors Interested in Catholic Activities*. January, 2020. http://www.catholicfundingguide.com/main/.

tional mission trips based upon a body of research outlining the limited impact of these trips and the potential harm that may result in a community.

For example, The Catholic Hospital Association of the United States (CHA) published the booklet entitled *Guiding Principles for Conducting International Health Activities* that illustrates concern for their members' involvement in such activities. It opens with the quote from Pope Francis, "It is not enough to give a sandwich if it isn't accompanied by the possibility of learning to stand on one's own feet. Charity that does not change the situation of the poor isn't enough."[388] CHA warns against the belief, "that it could take no more than passports and plane tickets to provide medical services, deliver surplus equipment or provide financial support to communities halfway around the world," and calls for "assessment and evaluation as important components of responding to identified needs." [389] Research continues to build that questions a specific segment of these initiatives- the short-term medical mission (STMMs).

Literature Review

Short-term medical service trips (SMST) are defined as a trip in which volunteer medical providers from high-income countries travel to low and middle-income countries to provide health care over periods of time ranging from one day to eight weeks.[390] Caldron *et al.* extended this definition by addressing

---

[388] Francis, *Address of the Holy Father Francis to the Jesuit Retreat Service in Rome*, speech, Vatican website, 10 September 2013, http://www.vatican.va/content/francesco/en/speeches/2013/september/documents/papa-francesco_20130910_centro-astalli.html.

[389] "Guiding Principles for International Health Activities," *Catholic Hospital Association of the U.S.A.*,. 2015, https://www.chausa.org/internationaloutreach/orientation-resources/guiding-principles, 3.

[390] Kevin Sykes, "Short-Term Medical Service Trips: A Systematic Review of the Evidence," *Am J Pub Health* 104, no. 7 (July): 1.

the planned nature of these excursions and the use of unpaid volunteer physicians and other healthcare professionals who undertake this work.[391] These teams may consist of academically affiliated or unaffiliated medical professionals recruited to perform certain surgeries or a collection of individuals with personal connections, a shared religious affiliation through a church or linked only by a desire to provide service. These definitions exclude services provided by organisations such as Doctors Without Borders, emergency disaster relief efforts and emergent responses to pandemics.

What benefits do these trips provide and to whom? A systematic review of peer-reviewed studies published between 1993 and 2013 found that out of 1,164 publications reviewed, only sixty-seven studies met the criteria for inclusion in a qualitative and quantitative analysis attempting to answer this question. Excluded studies were usually case reports that did not address the short or long-term value to the community. Of the trips analysed, 81% were surgical and those were predominantly procedures for cleft lips and palates.

Overall, the cost of these trips varied between $12,600-$84,000 dollars. Only three of the surgical studies performed a cost-effectiveness analysis. In their conclusion, the authors drew attention to the paucity of literature regarding the economic and health benefits of non-surgical STMT. Despite insufficient evidence of beneficial outcomes, the authors noted the continued growth in unregulated SMSTs. Ethical concerns raised included concern about the variability of credentials of providers, lack of supervision and the quality of services provided to vulnerable patient population.[392]

---

[391] Paul H Calderon et al, "A Systematic Review of Social, Economic and Diplomatic Aspects of Short-Term Medical Missions," *BMC Health Services Research.* 15 380 (2015) :2, http://dx.doi 10.1186/s12913-015-0980-3.

[392] Sykes," Short Term Medical Mission Trips,"e38-e48.

To whom does the benefit of these endeavors flow? In 1993, Laura Montgomery, a researcher with extensive experience in Latin America questioned this model.[393] In 2007, she returned to the topic and argued that "short-term medical missions as currently constituted are neither the most appropriate nor the most effective means of providing health care or improving health status, *regardless of the good intentions of those who plan, support or participate in them.*" She went on to argue that, "the encounter between those who go and those who receive must be mutually beneficial and collaborative."[394]

A subset of STMTs is facilitated by faith-based organisations commonly referred to as short-term medical missions (STMMs). In 2005, Robert Wuthnow of Princeton carried out a national survey of church members that found that 1.6 million American church members claimed to have gone abroad as members of such a trip during the previous year and 3.5% also took such trips as teenagers. STMTs averaged eight days in length and estimated a total cost of $2.4 billion.[395] In 2008, a web search by these same authors identified 543 independent faith-based trips and made the conservative estimate that these trips represented $250 million dollars in expenditures. These numbers are in all likelihood low, as they may not capture trips sponsored by individual church communities that are closed to outside volunteers.[396]

---

[393] LM Montgomery, "Short-Term Medical Missions: Enhancing or Eroding Health?" *Missiology: An Annual Review* 21, no. 3 (July): 338.

[394] LM Montgomery, "Reinventing short-term medical missions in Latin America," *J Lat Am Theology* 2, no. 2 (2007) : 85-6.

[395] Robert Wuthnow quoted in J. Maki et al., "Health Impact Assessment and Short-term Medical Missions: A Methods Study to Evaluate Quality of Care," *BMC Health Services Research* 8 no.121 (2012): 134, http://doi:10.1186/1472-6963-8-121.

[396] J. Maki et al., "Health Impact Assessment and Short-term Medical Missions: A Methods Study to Evaluate Quality of Care," *BMC Health Services Research* 8 no.121 (2012): 135, https://doi:10.1186/1472-6963-8-121.

Do these trips have a lasting effect? Van Beek et al discovered that these trips do not effect lasting change, and that most short-term mission-trippers quickly return to the same assumptions and behaviors they had prior to the trip. They concluded that these projects do not routinely empower those being served, improve the locals' quality of life, change the lives of participants nor increase financial support for long-term mission.[397]

What is the perspective of the recipient communities? Historically, STMMs have not always been mutually beneficial to participants or recipients of services. A survey of 334 STMM organizers and seventy-five interviews with host communities revealed misalignment in preferences and processes. Criticism included the often-hierarchical relationship between volunteers and communities and the self-serving nature of much of the volunteer work.[398]

The same authors identify areas of asymmetry, including minimal effort to understand the needs of the community, infrequent assessment or post-trip evaluation, limited length of mission, limited levels of applicant screening, variable preparation of volunteers and lack of collaboration in decision making and planning with hosts. The authors acknowledged that the focus on curative medicine and the direct provision of care instead of prevention was accompanied by little concern for the unexpected consequences that result within the community served.[399] Al-

---

[397] Kurt Van Beek, "The Impact of Short-term Missions: A Case study of House Construction in Honduras after Hurricane Mitch," *Missiology* 34, no.4 (2006): 4, https://doi.org/10.1177/009182960603400406.

[398] Michael D. Rozier, Judith N. Lasker, and Bruce Compton,, "Short-term Volunteer Health Trips: Aligning Host Community Preferences and Organizer Practices," *Global Health Action* 10 no. 1 (2017): 1-8, https://doi.org/10.1080/16549716.2017.1267957.

[399] Ibid.,3-5.

though limited in scope, this study confirms similar viewpoints expressed by host communities about the asymmetric nature of power of this model.

Is there quantitative proof of the efficacy and efficiency of these endeavors? Researchers continue to highlight the need for data collection and transparency regarding STM trips. As early as 1991, in the review *Pioneer Medical Missions in Colonial Africa,* Charles Good identified the lack of a systematic review of the impact of the services provided by Protestant and Roman Catholic missions on the geography of health and social change in colonial Africa.[400] He proposed a framework and detailed research agenda focused on these traditional providers to address this gap, unfortunately it has not been adopted.[401]

Authors have continued to cite the qualitative nature, bias and limited scope of investigations of the impact of global short-term volunteer health trips.[402] Yet, reports of the value of these endeavors continue to be published across disciplines in peer reviewed journals as well as the lay press. A bias toward publication that has led to so many positive STMM narratives may be due to the *a priori* assumption that because these missions are charitable and altruistic, they are valid in their own right. Thus, the requirement for data collection and objective analysis as a pre-requisite for publication has been overlooked by publishers of these accounts.

What is the current state of affairs? As recently as 2015, Calderon and colleagues were unable to identify a periodic congress related to issues and practices of STMMs or an academic

---

[400] Charles M. Good, "Pioneer Medical Missions in Colonial Africa," *Soc Sci Med* 32, no. 1 (1991): 1, https://doi.org/10.1016/0277-9536(91)90120-2.

[401] Ibid., 6.

[402] A. Martinkuk, et al., "Brain Gains: A Lterature Review of Medical Missions to Low and Middle-income Countries," *BMC Health Services Research* 12 (2012): 134.e.

journal dedicated to covering these services. Of even more concern, they found no international sanctioning organisation overseeing the quality of these services nor the credentials of service providers.[403] Clearly, *caveat emptor* applies in the case of STMMs, as the community assumes the risk that a product may fail, have defects or fails to meet expectations. The literature provides sufficient cause to support the abandonment of the asymmetric model of traditional STMMs.

The growing body of literature concerning STMMs has contributed to the imperative to explore models of accompaniment. These new models respond to Pope Francis' call for solidarity with the poor in *Evangelii Gaudium* when he reminds us, "Solidarity is something more than a few sporadic acts of generosity. It presumes the creation of a new mindset which thinks in terms of community and the priority of the life of all over the appropriation of good by a few."[404]

Case Study: The Olancho Aid Foundation

The Olancho Aid Foundation (OAF) is a CNGO that has served the community of the Honduran Department of Olancho since 1996. Honduras is the second poorest country in Central America and 65% of the population is poor. In 2018, the population was estimated as 9,182,766 with a net migration rate of 1.1/1,000 population.[405] The rate of migration is accelerating due to climate instability, violence linked to gang-related drug trafficking and lack of economic opportunities. In 2019, at least

---

[403] Calderon, "A Systematic Review," 6.

[404] Francis, *The Joy of the Gospel: Evangelii Gaudium*, apostolic exhortation, (Washington D.C: United States Conference of Catholic Bishops, 2013), 187.

[405] "Honduras," United States Central Intelligence Agency: The World Fact Book, accessed October 30, 2019, https://www.cia.gov/library/publications/the-world-factbook/geos/ho.html.

285,000 Hondurans were detained trying to reach the US, accounting for 47% of apprehensions in Mexico and 33% from the top four countries on the Southwest US border.[406]

The Foundation's service area is aligned with the Diocese of Juticalpa that covers an area of 9,233 square miles. It supports fifteen parishes staffed by twenty-eight priests from religious orders as well as visiting and diocesan priests. The religious community *Las Hermanas Franciscanas Cooperadores de la Asunción* operates a bakery, an orphanage, a retirement home and supports primary education in the local community.

Growth

OAF has experienced four periods in its history. The years 1996-2007 were foundational years that led to its incorporation as a 501(c)(3) with a stated mission of providing education. Incorporation formalized what was a loosely affiliated group of donors into a board responsible for raising funds and leading mission teams in support of the expanding educational projects established by its founder, a diocesan priest from Massachusetts. Between 2008-2014 the organisation grew rapidly to include the expansion of its school providing special education services, a college-prep secondary school and the opening of K-12 bilingual schools.

Strategy and mission were under the control of the founder of the organisation who also served as chair of the board. The membership of the board was initially drawn solely from participants in parish-related short-term mission trips and former volunteers. STMT volunteers from the US participated in the construction and rehabilitation of structures and traditional

---

[406] Jorge Valencia, "Why many people are migrating from Honduras-and why many people want them to stay," *Arizona Public Media*, Sept 11,2019, https://news.azpm.org/p/news-features/2019/9/11/157941-why-people-are-migrating-from-honduras-and-why-many-want-them-to-stay/.

medical mission work in the villages surrounding the city. When a donor and sponsor of STMMs noted the futility of providing treatment for intestinal infections caused by water-borne parasites, the organisation expanded its focus to providing potable water at the schools and in the local community. 2015-2017 was a time of transition and stabilization precipitated by the return of the founder to the United States. In 2018 the focus shifted to sustainability and reinvention.

Transition to Leadership by the Laity

The initial years after the transfer of leadership were spent stabilizing finances, hiring of the first US employee to focus on advancement and US operations and recruiting personnel to support the Honduran executive director. The board faced four challenges- gaining an understanding of the community and its context, meeting the need to actively participate in operations, the need to review all active projects, and to remedy the lack of a theological framework and pastoral guidance to support their work.

Board members did not fully understand the history of the community or recognise the complexity of US-Honduran relations as they had spent limited time in the country. Governance decisions and compliance with Honduran laws were complicated by a lack of fluency in Spanish Language. These limitations left gaps with regards to the complicated relationship between the Honduran government and the Church. For the most part, board members were only vaguely aware of the "difficult times" that resulted in the murder of Catholic priests and farmers and the subsequent expulsion of individual priests and religious communities in 1975.[407]

---

[407] Penny Lernoux, *Cry of the Poor: The Struggle for Human Rights in Latin America- The Catholic Church in Conflict with U.S. Policy,* (New York, NY: Penguin Books, 1982), 107-114.

During the transition, board members became actively involved in the operations of specific projects to resolve problems as well as providing guidance to Honduran staff. This stabilization phase required an evaluation of corporate governance and a focus on compliance with US and Honduran statutes that affected day-to-day operations.

A review of the scope and viability of projects followed. During this phase, it became apparent that donors' perceptions of needs and wishes were driving the strategy of the organisation, not the reverse. The board chose to put a moratorium on new water projects, investment in expanding schools and to halt STMMs until an analysis of their impact on the community and sustainability could be determined. The board struggled to move beyond the unwritten vision of the founder as it sought to create a strategic plan. There was agreement that the plan needed to be aligned with the pastoral goals of the Catholic Church and Catholic teachings on education and social justice. Unfortunately, they lacked a theological framework and a pastoral model to aid them in this process. This was not surprising as the group did not reside in the same communities, had varying reasons for participation in mission work, had no formal theological or pastoral training, and lacked ties to a single religious order or diocese.

This deficiency was remedied when the Bishop of Juticalpa was invited to join the board as an ex-officio member. The Bishop provides guidance to the executive director, meets regularly with the president of the board, and interacts with board members during their annual retreat. In spite of a shortage of clergy, the Bishop has designated a priest who is assigned to OAF and is integrated into its day to day activities. In 2017, OAF signed a cooperative agreement with the Diocese of Juticalpa to formalize this partnership. The agreement is to ensure mission continuity during times of transition in leadership and well into the future.

Adoption of a Sustainable and Equitable Medical Mission Model

In seeking to answer the question of "What must we do to perform God's work?" (Jn 6:28) the board leadership began by consulting *The Aparecida Document* which was drafted under the leadership of then Cardinal Jorge Bergoglio at the conclusion of the meeting of the Fifth General Conference of the Bishops of Latin America and the Caribbean in 2007.[408]

Austen Ivereigh in his recent book, *Wounded Shepherd: Pope Francis and Struggle to Convert the Catholic Church,* points out that *Aparecida* served as the basis for *Evangelii Gaudium*. "In Francis's first months, before the publication of *Evangelii Gaudium*, it was the Aparecida document that he handed to visiting heads of state so they could understand what he was up to. He told a delegation of Latin American bishops that as pope he would be "doing nothing else but apply Aparecida."[409] This document provided guidance in a number of areas including the commitment to Catholic education, the role of the laity, and understanding of the legacy of the Church in Latin America while provided a framework for redefining the mission of the foundation.

How did this knowledge impact decisions regarding the foundation's traditional one-week STMM experiences for North Americans? These experiences were not unusual and focused on vision screening, oral health, routine medical examinations, treatment of waterborne intestinal parasites in children and dispensing free medications for residents in the poverty-stricken rural communities surrounding the city of Juticalpa.

---

[408] "The Aparecida Document," Conference of the Bishops of Latin America and the Caribbean, accessed October 31, 2019, https://www.celam.org/aparecida/Ingles.pdf.

[409] Austin Ivereigh, *Wounded Shepherd: Pope Francis and the Struggle to Convert the Catholic Church* (New York,NY: Henry Holt and Company, 2019), 159.

Participants were not screened, and little thought was given as to the positive and negative impact of these activities on the community. Decisions regarding the scope of these efforts were often driven not by an empiric evaluation or consultation with the medical community but by the volunteer groups themselves. Teams would return annually and repeat the same cycle in the same village or new ones. It was time to be open to the exhortation to change.

Pope Francis often speaks of the Church as a field hospital after battle and reminds us that in such a setting, "It is useless to ask a seriously injured person if he has high cholesterol and about the level of his blood sugars! You have to heal his wounds. Then we can talk about everything else. Heal the wounds…you have to start from the ground up." [410] The Foundation realised that treating children for parasitic infections in communities without access to clean water was futile and that one month of medication for hypertension or diabetes would not improve health.

This realization accelerated the shift from traditional cure-driven medical missions to a focus on building capacity within the local public hospital and increasing its efforts to provide potable water. OAF embarked on a transition from a model of treating disease to one of supporting public health, building infrastructure, focusing on long-term collaborations, supporting local providers, buying services and supplies locally and developing model that recruiting volunteers to this call to become a field hospital.

This work accelerated after a meeting between a heritage Spanish-speaking physician advisor with experience in medical missions and hospital leadership. He quickly learned that the hospital did not have the ability to support traditional surgical

---

[410] Antonio Spardo, SJ., "A Big Heart Open to God: An Interview with Pope Francis," *America*. September 30, 2013, https://www.americamagazine.org/faith/2013/09/30/big-heart-open-god-interview-pope-francis.

and primary care mission trips. They had experimented with the model in the past, but a rollover bus accident involving volunteers had curtailed any efforts to utilize volunteers in rural areas and the model was abandoned.

It was agreed to begin a collaborative effort to improve the medical staff's ability to provide necessary services. OAF served as a facilitator and provided funds to arrange for an evaluation of a US-based NGO with expertise in procuring equipment. Next steps include defining appropriate volunteer service opportunities that have been identified by the hospital leadership and developing relationships with members of the medical staff.

This new emphasis on partnership proved invaluable during a recent outbreak of hemorrhagic dengue fever. The medical advisor served as an intermediary between the hospital and US donors and confirmed the need for requested supplies with international agencies. OAF donors funded the purchase of needed supplies in the capital city and local employees delivered the supplies to the hospital in the name of the Diocese of Juticalpa. As delays in treatment can be lethal, OAF will be helping to provide education about the disease to its staff, students and the local communities it serves in support of the hospital.

Discussion

The survey of STMM by Rozier found that only 54% of organisations sponsoring mission teams always have a regular in-country partner and 18% usually do so.[411] OAF continues to invest in strengthening the infrastructure in Honduras, developing relationships with local health care providers and acting as an intermediary with US NGOs. In the community, this effort is recognised as the long-term commitment of the Catholic Church to the community.

---

[411] Rozier, 5.

This transition has not been easy. It requires the continual education of donors who wish to undertake STMMs that provide medications and intermittent health screening by untrained volunteers who lacked fluency in the language. It also means turning away well-meaning physicians, nurses and other health professionals who make inquiries into the availability of traditional volunteer opportunities.

Redesigning the volunteer model has allowed OAF to focus on the call to a New Evangelization. Pope Francis has called us "to embark upon a new chapter of evangelisation" by providing an opportunity to those seeking "a renewed personal encounter with Jesus Christ, or at least an openness to letting him encounter them."[412] Since its inception, OAF has attracted youth who were seeking to deepen their faith through service of the poor. Recently, our applicants have increasingly included older Catholics who may have drifted from the Church and are searching for a way to reconnect and to re-engage through volunteer activities.

These volunteers include successful professionals such as accountants, physicians, scientists, lawyers, educators, master craftsmen and executives. Efforts to redesign programs to respond to this need are in evolution and are being created in recognition that "going out to others in order to reach the fringes of humanity does not mean rushing out aimlessly into the world. Often it is better simply to slow down, to put aside our eagerness in order to see and listen to others, to stop rushing from one thing to another and to remain with someone who has faltered along the way."[413]

An important component of these efforts is the recognition that "one cannot evangelize without closeness." In drawing

---

[412] Francis, *Evangelii Gaudium*, 1.
[413] Ibid., 46.

close to others as Jesus did, "We become instruments in God's hands, so that Jesus can act in the world through us."[414] This has led us to provide volunteers extended opportunities to live in a faith community with other volunteers, opportunities for prayer and a focus on working side-by-side with the Honduran team in the community.

The experience of OAF provides an example of the challenges facing international CNGO serving in the Global South. This circuitous journey may not have been efficient, but it has brought the organisation into an alignment with Partners in Health (PIH) whose international mission is "to provide a preferential option for the poor in health care."[415] This not surprising as PIH's founder, Dr. Paul Farmer has been profoundly affected by the writings, work, and friendship and collaboration with Fr. Gustavo Gutierrez of Peru. OAF is striving to mimic PIH's success by establishing long-term relationships with sister organisations based in settings of poverty while striving to achieve two overarching goals: to bring the benefits of modern medical science to those most in need of them and to serve as an antidote to despair."[416]

It should not be lost that this case study serves as an example of the necessary role the local Church and religious organisations must play in supporting the evolution of CNGOs from asymmetric relationships based upon charity to accompaniment models based upon justice.

---

[414] Francis, *Go Forth: Toward a Community of Missionary Disciples* (Maryknoll, NY: Obris Books, 2019), 27.

[415] "Our Mission at PIH," Partners in Health, accessed January 12, 2020, https://www.pih.org/pages/our-mission.

[416] Ibid.

Relevance and Implications for Africa

The case study illustrates the need to change the model for efforts to focused on improving global health. It illustrates the emerging model of a CNGO in Latin America that is led by the laity and is not dependent on traditional diocesan ties for fundraising. It was selected as it emphasizes the active role played by the local Church community in developing a collaborative model that responds to and recognises the unique needs of a laity-led NGO.

Why is this case study relevant to the work of the Church in Africa? As a superficial level, it is easy to see that Latin America and Africa share a common history of colonization by European countries and evangelisation by Catholic religious communities. On deeper examination, both the Latin American and African Church share the challenge of operating in very complex local environments that share certain characteristics. They share a common present in which they must grapple with conflicts between the Church and civil governments as they seek to ensure a commitment to human development by government and the private sector. They share a future in which there is acknowledgement that the successful creation of a just and equitable community is dependent on seeking justice for the poor, protection of the environment and embracing sustainable models of human development. The need to create sustainable communities where families can be safe, can be healthy and have an option to stay home is a burden shared by the Church, religious communities and international CNGOs across the Global South.

It is a fair criticism that the role of religious women has not been addressed in this case study. This omission should not be misconstrued as dismissal of the role of Catholic sisters in the Catholic missionary movement in healthcare in Africa and in Latin America. A discussion of the historical choices and events that may have contributed to the limited role of religious women in the community discussed in this case study is beyond the scope of this chapter.

In her comprehensive work, *Into Africa: A Transnational History of Catholic Medical Missions and Social Change,* Barbara Mann Wall argues that consideration of how these women have accomplished their work reveals that they have had different relationships with transnational actors; sometimes they competed, sometimes they collaborated and other times they integrated their resources.[417] She illustrates this perspective by pointing out that they have successfully worked ecumenically with Christian Medical Commission (CMC) and the secular World Health Organization (WHO) to greater coordinate services and integration with local healing systems.[418]

It is likely that emerging partnership models may more closely mirror those already in existence in Africa than the one that has been presented in this case study. Research is needed to identify how Catholic sisters in Africa are actively partnering with non-traditional CNGOs to providing services in the communities they serve as CNGOs fostering global health initiatives are active across the Global South, where the call to embrace a preferential option for the poor is heard. CNGOs active in Latin America should seek to understand how the religious women of the world have succeeded in becoming potent actors in local and global health. There is much to learn from the experience of their counterparts serving our African family.

The question "What should we do to perform the work of God?" is closely related to another question that has been asked by Fr Gustavo Gutiérrez, "How do we say and show persons living in the structure of violence, living in social injustice and seeming insignificance that 'God loves you?" His response to this challenge is that in order to do so, "We address the poor not only to make life better but to announce the gospel

---

[417] Barbara Mann Wall, *Into Africa: A Transnational History of Catholic Medical Missions and Social Change* (New Brunswick, NJ: Rutgers UP, 2015), Footnote 16.

[418] Ibid., 128.

to the world,"⁴¹⁹ In healthcare, this will require that CNGOs and Church embrace a model of accompaniment in our partnerships that address global health.

Conclusion

The role of independent international Catholic charities in global health must evolve toward a model of accompaniment in response to the great challenge facing God's people as we seek "to give compelling witness to the loving redemption of humanity by Jesus Christ."⁴²⁰ Improving global health requires embracing a pastoral model of service that moves beyond the western-European model that focuses on the treatment of disease and the relief of suffering for a few.

New models for collaboration with CNGOs provide an opportunity to re-evangelize participants in this work. In *Africae Munus*, Pope Benedict reminded the African Church "to be patient, stand firm and do not lose heart. While financial and material resources remain indispensable, seek also constantly to form and inform people, especially the young."⁴²¹ This exhortation directly calls on the Church to incorporate the "formation of the young" into these efforts. Catholics who are seeking to encounter God through the performance of his loving works should find a Church that welcomes them, and CNGOs should commit to making the experience that they provide one that deepens faith and provides an opportunity for conversion for the next generation.

---

[419] Michael Griffin and Jennie Weiss Block, eds. 2013. *In the Company of the Poor: Conversations with Dr. Paul Farmer and Fr. Gustavo Gutiérrez* (Maryknoll, NY: Orbis Books, 2013), 27.

[420] Francis, *Go Forth*, 7.

[421] Benedict XVI, *Africae Munus*, 140,193.

The challenge that lies before us is to recognise the need for the Church to accompany non-traditional international CNGOs such as the one discussed in this chapter. Without the influence and accompaniment of the local Church, these organisations will become like the pitiful NGOs Pope Francis, in his first homily after election as Pope, warned: "Without faith in Christ's sacrifice on the cross, the church is nothing more than a 'pitiful NGO,' focused on plans and projects,"[422] Three recommendations should be implemented if we are to avoid this future.

First, the Church and religious communities in Africa should move away from participation in current asymmetric, neo-colonial models of charity promulgated by charitable organisations that do not address the root causes of the inequity that leads to poor health. Simultaneously, international CNGOs active in promoting global health must adopt models of accompaniment that rest upon sustainable, collaborative partnerships with the Church in the communities they serve. Finally, expanding and sustaining this transformation requires a commitment by the Church to sponsor and participate in rigorous data collection that focuses on health outcomes; while ensuring that these data are aggregated, shared, and used to inform all models for improving global health. This data collection will be critical if international Catholic non-governmental organisations are to continue and expand their investment in Africa.

---

[422] Francis. X. Rocca, "Pope Francis: Without faith in Christ, church is just 'pitiful NGO,'" Catholic News Service, March 14, 2013, https://www.catholicnews.com/services/englishnews/2013/pope-francis-without-faith-in-christ-church-is-just-pitiful-ngo.cfm.

Bibliography

"Amid Explosive Church Growth, African Bishops Meet." *Catholic Culture.* July 8, 2010. https://www.catholicculture.org/news/headlines/index.cfm?storyid=7022.

"The Aparecida Document." *V. General Conference of the Bishops of Latin American and the Caribbean.* Accessed October 31, 2019, https://www.celam.org/aparecida/Ingles.pdf.

Benedict XVI, *Africae Munus,* Post-synodal Apostolic Exhortation, Vatican website. November 19, 2011, 47. http://w2.vatican.va/content/benedictxvi/en/apost_exhortations/documents/hf_ben-xvi_exh_20111119_africaemunus.html.

Calderon, Paul H, Ann Imperrs, Melena Pavlova, Wm Groot. A Systematic Review of Social, Economic and Diplomatic Aspects of Short-term Medical Missions. *BMC Health Services Research.* 15(2015): 380-385. https://doi 10.1186/s12913-015-0980-3.

"Catholic Church Attendance Resumes Downward Slide." *Gallup.* April 9, 2019. "https://news.gallup.com/poll/232226/church-attendance-among-catholics-resumes-downward-slide.aspx.

"The Catholic Funding Guide." *Foundations and Donors Interested in Catholic Activities.* January, 2020. http://www.catholic-fundingguide.com/main/.

Francis. *The Joy of the Gospel: Evangelii Gaudium.* Washington D.C: United States Conference of Catholic Bishops, 2013.

Francis. *Go Forth: Toward a Community of Missionary Disciples.* Maryknoll, NY: Orbis Books, 2019.

Good, Charles M. Pioneer Medical Missions in Colonial Africa. *Soc Sci Med,* 32, no. 1 (1991): 1-10.

Griffin, Michael and Jennie Weiss Block, eds. *In the Company of the Poor: Conversations with Dr. Paul Farmer and Fr. Gustavo Gutiérrez*. Mary Knoll, NY: Orbis Books, 2013.

"Guiding Principles for International Health Activities." *Catholic Hospital Association of the U.S.A.*, 2015. Accessed on April 24, 2020. https://www.chausa.org/internationaloutreach/orientation-resources/guiding-principles

"Honduras." *United States Central Intelligence Agency: The World Fact Book*, accessed October 30, 2019. https://www.cia.gov/library/publications/the-world-factbook/geos/ho.html.

"In U.S., Decline in Christianity continues at Rapid Pace." Pew Charitable Trust. accessed on January 10, 2020. https://www.pewforum.org/2019/10/17/in-u-s-decline-of-christianity-continues-at-rapid-pace/

Ivereigh, Austin. *Wounded Shepherd: Pope Francis and the Struggle to Convert the Catholic Church*. New York,NY: Henry Holt and Company, 2019.

"Key Facts on Family Foundations." *Council on Foundations*. 21 January, 2011. https://doi.org/f28b5.

Lernoux, Penny. *Cry of the Poor: The Struggle for Human Rights in Latin America- The Catholic Church in Conflict with U.S. Policy*. New York, NY: Penguin Books, 1982.

Maki, J., M Qualls, M., B. White, S. Kleefield, and R. Crown. "Health Impact Assessment and Short-term Medical Missions: A Methods Study to Evaluate Quality of Care." *BMC Health Serv Res*, 8, no. 121(2008). https://doi:10.1186/1472-6963-8-121.

Martinkuk, A., M. Manouchehrian, J.A. Negin, and A.B. Zwi. "Brain Gains: a Literature Review of Medical Missions to Low and Middle-income Countries. *BMC Health Services Research* 12, 134, 2012.

Montgomery LM. "Short-Term Medical Missions: Enhancing or Eroding Health? *Missiology: An Annual Review*. 21, no. 3 (July 1993) 333-341.

———. "Reinventing Short-term Medical Missions in Latin America." *J Lat Am Theology*. 2, no. 2 (2007): 84-103.

"Our Mission at PIH." Partners in Health, Accessed January 12, 2020, https://www.pih.org/pages/our-mission.

Rocca, Francis. X. "Pope Francis: Without faith in Christ, church is just 'pitiful NGO,'" *Catholic News Service*, March 14, 2013. Accessed on October 30, 2019. https://www.catholicnews.com/services/englishnews/2013/pope-francis-without-faith-in-christ-church-is-just-pitiful-ngo.cfm.

Rozier, Michael D., Judith N. Lasker, and Bruce Compton. "Short-term volunteer health trips: aligning host community preferences and organizer practices." *Global Health Action*. 10 no. 1 (2017): 1-8. https://doi.org/10.1080/16549716.2017.1267957.

Spardo, Antonio, SJ. "A Big Heart Open to God: An Interview with Pope Francis." *America*. September 30, 2013. Accessed on April 12, 2020.

https://www.americamagazine.org/faith/2013/09/30/big-heart-open-god-interview-pope-francis.

Sykes, Kevin J. 2014"Short-Term Medical Service Trips: A Systematic Review of the Evidence." *Am J Pub Health* 104, no. 7 (July): e38-e48.

Valencia, Jorge. "Why many people are migrating from Honduras-and why many people want them to stay." *Arizona Public Media*, Accessed on October 30, 2019, https://news.azpm.org/p/news-features/2019/9/11/157941-why-people-are-migrating-from-honduras-and-why-many-want-them-to-stay/.

Van Beek, Kurt. 2006. "The Impact of Short-term Missions: A Case Study of House Construction in Honduras after Hurricane Mitch." *Missiology* 34 no.4 (2006).

Wall, Barbara Mann. *Into Africa: A Transnational History of Catholic Medical Missions and Social Change*. New Brunswick, NJ. Rutgers UP, 2015.

Reflections on Doing the Works of God

CHAPTER ELEVEN

"Igniting Theologies from Below in Africa" Kairos Methodology as a resource:
a Case Study of Violence Against Women and Sexual Minorities

Nontando Hadebe

Introduction

> The Spirit of the Lord is upon me, because he has anointed me to bring good news to the poor. He has sent me to proclaim release to the captives and recovery of sight to the blind, to let the oppressed go free (Lk 4:18).

The starting point for theologies from below through Kairos methodology has its roots in both the ministry of Jesus and prophetic traditions in the Hebrew Bible. Liberation theologians in Latin America emerged through the base communities of the poor who questioned their oppression through the lens of their multiple interpretations and appropriation of the Word of God. Similarly, in the context of apartheid which was a system of racially based oppression, Christians applying contextual reading of the Bible began to interrogate the existing theologies that explicitly and implicitly supported apartheid. This interrogation and appropriation of the Gospel message led to the first step in producing a prophetic liberation theology as documented in *the Kairos Document*.

This prophetic theology produced from below empowered them to act in solidarity with liberation movements in the struggle against apartheid. This legacy of resistant theologies against oppression was critical in the emergence of African Theologies.

These theologies addressed oppressive systems operating at national levels as priority and in the process subsumed intragroup multiple oppressions that surfaced after independence such as gender inequality, ethnocentrism, classism and homophobia.

Women theologians through *The Circle of Concerned African Women Theologians* took the struggle for gender equality into the theological realm. In recent years, theologians in solidarity with sexual minorities have taken homophobia into theological spaces. These are examples of theologies from below which hold the key to the transformation of society so that the equal rights of all are respected and realised.

Thus, the continued relevance of the Catholic Church in Africa depends on these theologies from below. The challenge is to ignite these theologies from below driven by the oppressed. There are other resources that can be used and this chapter is proposing Kairos methodology through contextual bible studies as a resource. These themes will be discussed further in the rest of the chapter beginning with the theoretical framework of this paper which includes Bevans two theological methods, liberation theology, Kairos methodology and contextual bible studies.

Conceptual Framework

The conceptual framework sets the context for the rest of the chapter particularly Kairos Methodology which has its roots in contextual and liberation theologies. These will be discussed first and thereafter the emergence of African theologies as background to Kairos methodology and contextual bible studies.

Contextual theologies: Bevans' Two Methods in Theology

In his definition of contextual theologies Bevans differentiates between classical and contextual theologies. Classical theologies are characterized by an orientation towards the past based on the premise that there are two sources for doing theology that is scripture and tradition both of which are trans historical. Bevans defines classical theologies as follows:

> Classical theology conceived theology as a kind of objective science of faith. It was understood as a reflection in faith on the two *loci theologici* (theological sources) of scripture and tradition, the content of which has not and never will be changed, and is above culture and historically conditioned expression.[423]

Two examples of classical theologies according to Dunn are Biblicist and Doctrinalist theologies.[424] In both cases the task of theology is defined as the transmission of propositional truth and faith as an intellectual assent to these truths. For Biblicists all theology is biblical theology and the role of theology is to "explain, defend and disseminate what is in scripture."[425] One consequence of Biblicism is biblical fundamentalism that views the bible as the "sole legitimate source of theology" and is therefore interpreted "literally and inerrantly."[426] Similarly, Doctrinalists define the task of theology as to interpret, defend and disseminate the official teachings or doctrines of churches which leads to doctrinal fundamentalism. Both are orientated towards the past and focus on preservation of historical faith with little or no application to the present.

In contrast, contextual theologies recognise,

> another *locus theologicus*: recent human experience. Theology that is contextual realises that culture, history, contemporary thought

---

[423] Bevans, Stephen B. 1992. *Models of Contextual Theology.* P. 1-2 Maryknoll: Orbis Books

[424] Dunn, Edmond J 1998 *What is theology? Foundational and Moral.* New York: Twenty Third Publications page 22

[425] Ibid, page 22

[426] Ibid, page 23

forms, and so forth are to be considered, along with scripture and tradition, as valid sources for theological expression.[427]

Thus, contextual theologies integrate contemporary experiences and knowledge alongside scripture and tradition. Further these theologies conceive both scripture and tradition as contextual that is produced in particular historical contexts because as noted by DeCrane, "foundational documents emerge from particular contexts and historical moments and address particular realities using symbols, images, linguistic structures and language belonging to a particular time, place and people."[428] Therefore, the contextuality of scripture and tradition sets a precedence for theology to develop in response to particular contexts as is the case with liberation, African and Kairos theologies.

Liberation Theology/ies

As mentioned earlier, liberation theologies are contextual theologies rooted in the lived experiences of the oppression and injustice experienced by the poor in Latin America. In contrast with some western theologies that address the challenge of atheism, liberation theologies according to Gutierrez liberation theologies are responsive to the poor as described in this quotation,

> In Latin America and Caribbean, the challenge comes not in the first instance from the non-believer, but from the 'non persons', those who are recognised as people by the existing social order; the poor, the exploited, those systematically and legally deprived of their status as human beings, those who barely realise that it is

---

[427] Bevans, Stephen B. 1992. *Models of Contextual Theology.* P. 2 Maryknoll: Orbis Books

[428] DeCrane, Susanne M. 2004. *Aquinas, Feminism and the common Good.* Washington, D C: Georgetown University Press page 1

to be a human being. The 'non-person' questions not so much our religious universe but above all our economic, social, political and cultural order, calling for a transformation of the very foundations of a dehumanising society[429]

Liberation theologies are not only in solidarity with the poor but actively resist social systems that create and sustain poverty in their countries through the adoption of 'see, judge and act' methodology. Leonard Boff explains this method as "*seeing* analytically, *judging* theologically and *acting* pastorally or politically, three phases in one commitment in faith."[430]

This methodology has been adopted by oppressed groups across world transforming liberation theology into a global phenomenon as defined by Fiorenza:

> In a broad sense, the term *liberation theology* refers to any theological movement that criticizes a specific form of oppression and views liberation as integral to the theological task. Feminist theologies, African American theologies and certain Asian theologies are major types of liberation theology (:62).

Indeed both African and Kairos theologies emerged in contexts of oppression and in that sense qualify as both contextual and liberation theologies.

African Theologies

The focus of this section is not to attempt a comprehensive historical and contemporary analysis of African theologies but rather to focus on one aspect namely the emergence of two forms

---

[429] Gutierrez, G. (translated by Judith Condor) "The task and content of Liberation Theology," in Rowland, Christopher (ed.) 1999. *The Cambridge Companion to Liberation Theology*. Cambridge: Cambridge University Press, pp. 19-38.

[430] Boff, Leonardo "What are third world Theologians" p. 12 *Theologies of the Third World" Convergences and Differences (Concilium* 199 (5/1988) Edinburgh: T. and T. Clark

of African theologies in response to colonialism and apartheid. The rationale for this focus is to argue that the legacy of African theologies is resistance against oppression. Martney describes the first two streams of ecumenical African theologies as follows,

> The African search for authentic and prophetic theology has at once been a *rejection* of the dominant Western theological paradigms and an *acceptance* of African realities and worldview in theological hermeneutics. Consequently, in Black Africa, African theology and South African, Black theologies have come to represent two different schools of theological hermeneutics. They are therefore not synonymous. Expressed respectively in terms of "inculturation" (or "Africanization" or "indigenization") and "liberation," there has thus been a tension or polarity between these two theological traditions since the early 1970s.[431]

African theologies focused on culture and pre-Christian religious traditions and employed a hermeneutics of inculturation, while Black theology focused on political oppression and employed liberation hermeneutics in an African setting.[432] The

---

[431] Martey, Emmanuel. *African theology Inculturation and Liberation.* Maryknowll, New York; Orbis books page xi. Other sources for these two streams of African theologies include: Rosino Gibellini (ed) 1994. *Paths of African Theology.* Maryknoll, NY: Orbis Books, Parratt, John 2004. *Introduction to Third World Theologies.* Cambridge: Cambridge University Press and Bate, Stuart C. O.M.I. 1991 *Evangelisation in the South African Context.* Roma:Editrice Pontificia Universita Gregoriana

[432] The two streams of theology are not the only divisions within African theology but are the basis found in almost all divisions. For example Nyamiti describes three trends in African theology; speculative school with stress on philosophy; social and biblical school pragmatic and biblical approach and militant school with emphasis on liberation – South African Black theology and Mushet describes African theology as evolving in two stages; theology of adaptation and critical African theology. See Nyamiti, Charles 1978 "Approaches to African Theology," in Sergio Torres and Virginia Fabella (eds) *The Emergent Gospel: theology from the developing world.* Maryknoll, New York; Orbis books page 32 and Mushete, Ngindu 1979 "The History of Theology in Africa: from Polemics to Critical Irenics" in Appiah-Kubi, Kofi and Sergio Torres (eds) *African Theology En Route* Maryknoll, New York:

tension that has characterised relationships between the two theologies is counterproductive because according to Martney these theologies are complimentary as,

> ..in the African theological reality, the two foci are not contradictory but complement each other. In fact they represent two sides of the same process. Consequently, theological hermeneutics in Africa must necessarily have a unitary perception of inculturation and liberation."[433]

African theologies are both contextual and liberational. The next section on Kairos methodology as reflected in the Kairos Document produced in the context of apartheid reflects the connection with contextual and liberation theologies.

Kairos Methodology: Kairos Document

The *Kairos Document* is the source of the *Kairos Methodology* and will be discussed in support of the central thesis of this chapter namely that the Kairos methodology is a resource for oppressed groups in their struggle for liberation through an analysis of theological and social factors implicated in their oppression, construction of prophetic liberation theology and lastly action in solidarity with social movements fighting for the same rights leading to participation in their own liberation.

Before describing the *Kairos Document*, it is significant to note that it was not generated from academic discourses of theologians but from outside academia in communities of Christians in Soweto who gathered together to interrogate theologies that implicitly and explicitly supported apartheid and produce pro-

---

Orbis Books page 27 and Martey, Emmanuel. *African theology Inculturation and Liberation*. Maryknowll, New York; Orbis books page 69

[433] Martey, Emmanuel. *African theology Inculturation and Liberation*. Maryknowll, New York; Orbis books page xi

phetic theology that would empower them to engage in the struggle against apartheid in solidarity with liberation movements. After extensive consultation and research the *Kairos Document* was published on 25th September 1985 as a 'people's document.[434'] Below is the description and purpose of the *Kairos Document*,

> The KAIROS document is a Christian, biblical and theological comment on the political crisis in South Africa today. It is an attempt by concerned Christians in South Africa to reflect on the situation of death in our country. It is a critique of the current theological models that determine the type of activities the Church engages in to try to resolve the problems of the country. It is an attempt to develop, out of this perplexing situation, an alternative biblical and theological model that will in turn lead to forms of activity that will make a real difference to the future of our country.[435]

Based on the above description it is evident that the methodology of the *Kairos document* reflects that of liberation and contextual theologies. Liberation theologies as noted earlier confront "a specific form of oppression and views liberation as integral to the theological task" and apply 'see, judge and act' methodology which is "seeing analytically, judging theologically and acting pastorally or politically, three phases in one commitment in faith."

The context was the political crisis in South Africa under apartheid that created a situation of 'death' for majority of the population which were black Africans. The analysis adopted in the *Kairos Document* was primarily theological because of the central role that theologies played in legitimating the apartheid

---

[434] Kairos Document 1985 http://ujamaa.ukzn.ac.za/Libraries/manuals/The_Kairos_Documents.sflb.ashx

[435] Kairos Document 1985 http://ujamaa.ukzn.ac.za/Libraries/manuals/The_Kairos_Documents.sflb.ashx

state. So naming the existing theologies in relation to apartheid was a critical step in the process of formulation of prophetic liberation theologies. The analysis of the theological landscape is described as follows,

> The moment of truth has compelled us to analyze more carefully the different theologies in our Churches and to speak out more clearly and boldly about the real significance of these theologies. We have been able to isolate three theologies and we have chosen to call them 'State Theology,' 'Church Theology' and 'Prophetic Theology.' In our thoroughgoing criticism of the first and second theologies we do not wish to mince our words. The situation is too critical for that.

State theology was defined as "simply the theological justification of the status quo with its racism, capitalism and totalitarianism. It blesses injustice, canonises the will of the powerful and reduces the poor to passivity, obedience and apathy."[436] This was done through "misusing theological concepts and biblical texts for its own political purposes." An example of one of the texts used by state theology was Romans 13:1-7. The first verse for instance states that authorities are instituted by God and must be obeyed: "Let every persons be subject to the governing authorities, for there is no authority except from God, and those authorities that exist have been instituted by God" (NRSV).

This text was interpreted as setting out divine sanction for civic obedience to governments irrespective of whether there are oppressive or not: "assumes that in this text Paul is presenting us with the absolute and definitive Christian doctrine about the State, in other words an absolute and universal principle that is equally valid for all times and in all circumstances."[437]

---

[436] Kairos Document 1985 http://ujamaa.ukzn.ac.za/Libraries/manuals/The_Kairos_Documents.sflb.ashx

[437] Ibid

The other theology was 'Church theology,' which applied Christian principles such as reconciliation and forgiveness in a context of systemic injustice as described in this quotation,

> We have seen how 'Church Theology' tends to make use of absolute principles like reconciliation, negotiation non-violence and peaceful solutions and applies them indiscriminately and uncritically to all situations. Very little attempt is made to analyze what is actually happening it our society and why it is happening.

The theology advocated by *Kairos Document* was 'prophetic theology' that was action orientated and would transform all church activities to be aligned to the struggle against apartheid that was already being advocated by liberation movements. Some of the practical actions listed were civil disobedience; participating in the political struggle for justice; transforming all activities in churches to address issues of injustice and empower Christians to act for their liberation as a moral duty. One of the contributions to the theological process that empowered the laity to initiate the process that ultimately led to the production of the Kairos Document was contextual bible studies.

Contextual Bible Studies (CBS)

The six principles of contextual bible study will be taken from a document produced by Ujaama Centre in Pietermaritzburg entitled *Doing Contextual Bible Study: Resource Manuel*.[438] These principles align with those developed by the Institute for Contextual Theology which was one of the founding organisations involved in the production of the Kairos Document and has since closed its operations. These six principles are,

---

[438] Ujaama Centre. 2015 Doing Contextual Bible Study: A Resource Manual http://ujamaa.ukzn.ac.za/Libraries/manuals/Ujaama_CBS_Manual_part_1_3.sflb.ashx

i. Community: "Community is the beginning and goal of CBS" and refers to "organized poor, working class and other marginalized groups."[439] CBS are not individual based or solely academic classroom type of bible studies because they draw their themes from the experiences of oppression defined by the group. As noted earlier, the process that led to the formulation of the Kairos Document was initiated by grassroot Christians who met regularly together to reflect on the political crisis and context of oppression from apartheid. The goal is liberation of communities that is 'the formation of redemptive communities." Individualism and isolation from community are practices that are inconsistent with the ethos and values of CBS.

ii. Criticality: "critical reading of life and bible' through 'range of structured and systematic questions.'[440] Critical reading includes freedom to ask questions and interrogate both life and the bible as part of the search for liberating prophetic theologies. The communal nature of CBS means that there is engagement within the group and development of critical thinking that is fearless and honest. The structured and systematic questions come from socially engaged scholars who bring deeper social and biblical analysis that opens up deeper critical thinking by the group. The group or community is always in the forefront and not subjected to scholars. The experience of oppression qualifies the community to speak with authority on issues and questions that affects them. There is no hierarchy of knowledge that places community knowledge below that of scholars.

iii. Collaboration: As mentioned in the previous points CBS are collaboration between communities and socially engaged scholars who serve as resource persons not lecturers or au-

---

[439] Ibid, p. 7
[440] Ibid, p. 7

thority figures. The interlocutors are the community who define and articulate their experiences as the starting point of their theological and social analysis/

iv. Contextual: 'CBS begins with the reality of local community's' experiences which include analysis of the 'economic, cultural, political and religious dimensions'[441] of the context so that the issues raised by the community are understood from a much wider social contexts particularly the intersecting social systems that sustain and drive inequality and oppression.

v. Change: The ultimate goal of CBS is change that is to "work towards transformation of self, society including the church" through "structural and systemic change.[442]" The oppressed become their own liberators through taking action in both society and church.

vi. Contestation: "Struggle as key socio-theological concept" and "characteristic of reality." For example with reference to the bible there are texts used against oppressed groups as seen in state theology's justification of apartheid that require 'wrestling' with in order to discover liberative aspects. So the bible for oppressed groups is contested texts because of the way it has been used by those in power to legitimate and perpetuate oppression.

These principles fit into the 'see, judge and act' methodology of liberation and contextual theologies described earlier and reflected in the Kairos Document. The next two sections will be case studies on violence against women and sexual minorities as providing examples of development of liberating theologies through use of liberation and Kairos methodology.

---

441 Ibid, p. 7
442 Ibid, p. 7

Case Studies: Violence against Women and Sexual Minorities

Violence against women and sexual minorities stem largely from intragroup inequalities similar to racially based oppression of apartheid that have social, economic and theological support and legitimation. In applying the Kairos methodology to these two forms of oppression the starting point is an understanding of the context of violence followed by an analysis of existing theologies that justify inequality and lastly to produce liberating prophetic theologies that will empower both women and sexual minorities to be agents of their own liberation.

Violence against Women

The World Health Organization (WHO) declared violence against women a "global health problem of epidemic proportions" with over a third of women experiencing "intimate partner or non-partner violence" with intimate partner violence accounting for most cases of violence against women[443]. The African Union through *The Protocol to the African Charter on Human and Peoples' Rights on the Rights of Women in Africa (the Maputo Protocol)*, which is "a legal legal instrument for the protection of the rights of women and girls in Africa" committed to the eradication of all forms of violence against women and girls in Africa. In Article 1 violence against women and girls is defined as

> all acts perpetrated against women which cause or could cause them physical, sexual, psychological, and economic harm, including the threat to take such acts; or to undertake the imposition of arbitrary restrictions on or deprivation of fundamental freedoms

---

[443] World Health Organization https://www.who.int/mediacentre/news/releases/2013/violence_against_women_20130620/en/

in private or public life in peacetime and during situations of armed conflicts or of war.[444]

Article 4 sets out the practical commitments to eradicate all forms of violence against women and girls and below are a few examples from this section,

1. Every woman shall be entitled to respect for her life and the integrity and security of her person. All forms of exploitation, cruel, inhuman or degrading punishment and treatment shall be prohibited.
2. States Parties shall take appropriate and effective measures to:

    a) Enact and enforce laws to prohibit all forms of violence against women including unwanted or forced sex whether the violence takes place in private or public;

    b) Adopt such other legislative, administrative, social and economic measures as may be necessary to ensure the prevention, punishment and eradication of all forms of violence against women;

    c) Identify the causes and consequences of violence against women and take appropriate measures to prevent and eliminate such violence;

    d) Actively promote peace education through curricula and social communication in order to eradicate elements in traditional and cultural beliefs, practices and stereotypes which legitimise and exacerbate the persistence and tolerance of violence against women;

---

[444] The Protocol to the African Charter on Human and Peoples' Rights on the Rights of Women in Africa https://www.un.org/en/africa/osaa/pdf/au/protocol_rights_women_africa_2003.pdf

e) Punish the perpetrators of violence against women and implement programmes for the rehabilitation of women victims;

f) Establish mechanisms and accessible services for effective information, rehabilitation and reparation for victims of violence against women[445];

These measures were not taken in a vacuum but through the tireless activism and advocacy of women's groups across the continent. The next section will describe violence against sexual minorities.

Violence against Sexual Minorities

'Sexual minorities' is an umbrella term used for diverse group of sexualities. Before discussing these three related concepts, I will define what I mean by sex, gender and sexual orientation. Sex refers to biological differences that categorize a person as either female, intersex or male; in contrast gender is the "distinctive roles and behaviours of men and women in a given culture dictated by that culture's gender norms and values"[446] and sexual orientation is about who one is spiritually, physically, sexually and emotionally attracted to and the diversity of attractions are used to categorize sexual minorities as lesbians (woman attracted to other women), gay (man attracted to other men), bi-sexual (attraction to both sexes), transgender (where a person's sex identity does not correspond with their identity) and queer as a term that refers to all these categories and more hence the acronym LGBTIQ.

---

[445] https://www.un.org/en/africa/osaa/pdf/au/protocol_rights_women_africa_2003.pdf

[446] World Health Organization. *Gender, Women and Health "Why gender and health?"* http://www.who.int/gender/genderandhealth.

According to Amnesty International (2014) report entitled *Speaking Out. Advocacy Experiences and tools of LGBTI Activists in Sub-Saharan Africa* multiple forms of violence in public and private spaces are the normal daily experiences of LGBTI queer persons as described below:

> The last decade has seen an unprecedented rise in the levels of discrimination and violence directed towards lesbian, gay, bisexual, transgender and intersex (LGBTI) people in sub-Saharan Africa. LGBTI people have faced harassment, persecution, and vilification. They have been subject to: forcible eviction from their homes because of who they are; being kicked out of churches and schools; laws that have been introduced to introduce or increase sanctions for consensual same-sex sexual activity; arbitrary arrest by police; imprisonment for actual or suspected consensual same-sex conduct (or for their identities); torture and other ill treatment whilst in detention; judicially-ordered forced anal examinations; murder; rape; beatings; stabbings; being branded paedophiles; accused of "recruiting" children into homosexuality"; accused of sorcery; disowned by their own families; public denigration by politicians and political parties; and blame by religious leaders for societies' economic and social ills. This is not an exhaustive list.[447]

These findings correlate with research done by the *Other Foundation* entitled *Canaries in the Coal Mines. An analysis of activism of spaces for LGBTI activism in Southern Africa*. One aspect of the research that will highlighted is the six dominant narratives on LGBTI in this region with a brief description on social exclusion narrative. The six narratives were: legal narrative- 'it is against the law (2016:15); moral narrative-'it is against God,' (:19); political narrative-'it is 'unAfrican" (:19); public health

---

[447] Amnesty International 2014 ttps://www.amnesty.org/en/documents/afr01/001/2014/en/

narrative- 'it is an illness' (:20); media narrative- 'it is scandalous' and social exclusion narrative- 'they don't belong' (2:25). The social exclusion narrative is,

> fed by all five of the above, is the most pernicious, for two reasons. As is evidenced by the Social Inclusion Benchmarking Index developed by this project, it is the basis for actual exclusionary discriminatory practice. And, as harmfully, it has become internalised by LGBTI people themselves, who understand themselves to be social outcasts (24).

Experiences of exclusion in public and private spaces that include educational institutions, employment, church and home. The home was described as the greatest exclusionary factor, and the area of greatest pain." (27)

However, unlike the continental support for women's rights and opposition to violence, there are no similar continental legal frameworks for sexual minorities. Currently 36 African countries criminalise sodomy, a legacy from colonial penal codes. Nineteen African nations, however, have never had sodomy laws or have decriminalised homosexuality.[448] Similar to the contexts of apartheid, colonialism the struggle for women's and LGBTIQ rights is being waged by civil society activists apart from churches because of the presence of theologies that are used to legitimate oppression. The *Kairos Methodology* which was forged in the midst of oppression by oppressed groups provides a critical resource for women and LGBTIQ persons to be agents together with socially engaged academics of their own prophetic theologies of liberation.

---

[448] Countries that do not criminalise homosexual acts are Benin, Burkina Faso, Cape Verde, Central African Republic, Congo, Chad, Côte d'Ivoire, Democratic Republic of Congo, Djibouti, Equatorial Guinea, Gabon, Guinea-Bissau, Lesotho, Madagascar, Mali, Mozambique, Niger, Rwanda and South Africa.

Application of Kairos Methodology for liberation of women and LGBTIQ persons

The *Kairos Methodology* provides a method and process for women and LGBTIQ persons to follow as a guide to the ultimate goal of prophetic theology of liberation and concrete action for justice. Critical to this methodology is to identify, interrogate, name and confront theologies in churches that legitimate oppression of women and LGBTIQ and prevent public expressions of solidarity with activists in civil society protesting against violence and advocating for equal rights. Women theologians in Africa through *The Circle of Concerned African Women Theologians* have taken the struggle for gender equality into the theological and cultural realms. Phiri defines African women's theologies as follows,

> African women's theologies are a critical, academic study of the causes of women oppression; particularly a struggle against societal, cultural and religious patriarchy. They are committed to the eradication of all forms of oppression against women through a critique of the social and religious dimensions both in African culture and Christianity. African women's theologies take women's experiences as its starting point, focusing on the oppressive areas of life caused by injustices such as patriarchy, colonialism, neo-colonialism, racism, capitalism, globalisation and sexist. It sees a need to include the voices of all women, not just theologians, because it acknowledges that the majority of African women are engaging in oral theology.[449]

The theologies of *The Circle* as described in the above quotation start from women's experiences of oppression appropriate

---

[449] Phiri, Isabel. A 2004. "Southern Africa," in Parratt, John 2004. *Introduction to Third World Theologies*. Cambridge: Cambridge University Press, pp. 137-162, page 156.

these as the lens to interrogate, expose and name theologies that perpetuate and justify the oppression of women. Through their research theologians of *The Circle* have advocated for women's rights through prophetic liberation theologies based on women's experiences in multiple sites of oppression such as HIV and AIDS, gender-based violence and child-marriages.

In this regard they reflect the of starting with experiences of oppressed groups as defined by them, then moving on to interrogate the theological justification for their oppression and finally producing a prophetic liberation theology that empowers them for action and solidarity with civil society groups advocating for women's equality and protection from violence. *The Circle Kairos* theologians are socially engaged scholars who collaborate with grassroot women in interrogating existing theologies. The challenge faced by theologians of *The Circle* is the academic nature of their research which make it accessible to the women that they are collaborating with. It would seem that one of the ways forward is to engage in a process that will produce a document co-authored with grassroot women similar to the *Kairos Document*.

With regards to LGBTIQ in Africa most of the writings are by socially engaged scholars in solidarity with them but *Kairos Methodology* requires them to be the ones at the center of the theological process. In their paper entitled *When Faith Does Violence: Reimaging Engagement Between Churches And LGBTI Groups On Homophobia In Africa*, Gerald West, Kapya Koama and Charlene van der Walt argue LGBTI queer persons must be given the 'epistemological privilege' in the construction of their liberation theologies,

> ..doing theology on sexuality requires that we grant an epistemological privilege to the lived reality of LGBTIQ Christians. We cannot do theology on sexuality without these realities. Putting it differently, rather than calling for the development of

a new theology of sexuality/ties (– an object to be produced), the call is for the development of a sexual theology appropriating as its starting point the embodied lived experiences of minority sexualities (– a theological process).[450]

Both women and LGBTIQ persons need to engage with scripture and church teachings on gender and homosexuality. In the Catholic Church the issues of gender, feminism and LGBTIQ are so highly contested and polarising that it is extremely challenging to address these issues openly. Given this restrictive context, can the *Kairos Methodology* be a resource for the Catholic Church in Africa particularly for the laity? Although there are no definitive answers either way there are signs that are moving towards a greater role of laity and women as well as explicit condemnation of violence against women and LGBTIQ. There is still a long way to go before there is the kind of freedom envisaged in CBS. Some of these signs include the following three:

a. Pope Francis' acknowledgement of the value of certain aspects of feminist theologies in *Joy of Love*: "If certain forms of feminism have arisen which we must consider inadequate, we must nonetheless see in the women's movement the working of the Spirit for a clearer recognition of the dignity and rights of women (43).[451]"

b. Synodality: "The term is generally understood to represent a process of discernment, with the aid of the Holy Spirit, involving bishops, priests, religious, and lay Catholics, each according to the gifts and charisms of their vocation.[452]" This opens up opportunities for laity to par-

---

[450]

[451] https://w2.vatican.va/content/dam/francesco/pdf/apost_exhortations/documents/papa-francesco_esortazione-ap_20160319_amoris-laetitia_en.pdf.

[452] https://www.catholicnewsagency.com/news/pope-francis-announces-a-2022-synod-on-synodality-21476.

ticipate fully "based on the fact that all the faithful are qualified and called to serve each other through the gifts they have all received from the Holy Spirit.[453]"

c. Condemnation of violence against women and sexual minorities by Pope Frances: "violence against them [women] is akin to profaning God and calling for [women] to be increasingly involved in making major decisions.[454]"

d. With respect to violence against LGBTI the Pope made this comment in *Joy of Love*,

> We would like before all else to reaffirm that every person, regardless of sexual orientation, ought to be respected in his or her dignity and treated with consideration, while 'every sign of unjust discrimination' is to be carefully avoided, particularly any form of aggression and violence (250).

These signs are among many others that promise an open door for critical engagement with scripture and tradition in ways that allow the experiences of oppressed groups to determine the trajectory of theological analysis that contribute to transformation and liberation. As long as there are persons in societies that face discrimination there will be need for liberation theologies and the Kairos Methodology is a resource that can play a critical role.

Conclusion

This chapter set out as its goal to explore Kairos methodology based on contextual and liberation theologies as a resource for igniting liberation theologies from oppressed groups in Africa.

---

[453] https://www.ncronline.org/news/quick-reads/pope-chooses-synodality-theme-2022-synod.

[454] https://abcnews.go.com/International/wireStory/pope-francis-equates-violence-women-profaning-god-68016422.

The emergence of African theologies was in response in part to colonial and apartheid oppression and could be done by theologians as they were part of the oppressed groups. However in the post-independence era other multiple sites of oppression have been identified including women, LGBTI, albinism, ethnicity, disability and much more.

Although the Kairos methodology was used to address national oppression, it can also be a resource for intragroup oppressions because it appropriates the legacy of liberation theologies that start with the experiences of oppressed who become the interlocutors of their own liberation. The method presents many challenges for the Catholic Church but develops primarily synodality provide possibilities for a new era of active participation of all the baptised.

Afterword

Celebrating and Assessing the Blessings of the Church in Africa: *Allocutio*

Bonaventure Ikenna Ugwu, CSSp

Africa has featured very prominently in the history of Christianity, beginning with the story of Jesus Christ and his immediate biological family's flight to Egypt for safety, through the baptism of the Ethiopian Eunuch (Acts 8: 26-36), to the contributions of our ancestors in faith such as St Augustine, Tertullian and St Athanasius of Alexandria to the formulation of Christian doctrines at the earliest stage of the Church. Down the ages, the continent of Africa has not only continued to contribute to the growth and spread of Christian faith but has also been a beneficiary of innumerable favours from the table of the Church.

Within the last fifty years, the Church in Africa has experienced some remarkable blessing in different dimensions which call for celebration, reflection and further thinking of how best their impact could be maximised. These blessings can be concretely named in the establishment of the Symposium of Episcopal Conferences of Africa and Madagascar (SECAM), the Special Assembly for Africa of the Synod of Bishops which gave birth to the Post-Synodal Apostolic Exhortation, *Ecclesia in Africa*, and the second Special Assembly for Africa of the Synod of Bishops which gave rise to the Post-Synodal Apostolic Exhortation, *Africae Munus*.

These important step-ladders in the history of the Church in Africa call for a moment set apart to celebrate them, to reflect on them and to assess the extent to which they have impacted and are impacting on the theology and practical life of and people in the Continent. This Congress provides this context for celebration, reflection, thinking, rethinking and charting new paths for the Church which is in Africa. Gathered as a people bound by faith in Christ and who share a common history as Africans or their associates, the participants in the Congress are called to celebrate the marvels which the Lord has done for Africans down the ages. In the context of this celebration, and the reflections and the thinking that go with them, the fundamental question that would continue to be asked is: "What must we do to perform the works of God?" (Jn 6:28).

It is important to recognise and appreciate most profoundly the role of the Second Vatican Council (1962–1965) in the making of the histories of the events which this Congress celebrates, namely: SECAM, the two Special Assemblies for Africa of the Synods of Bishops and the Post-Synodal Apostolic Exhortations that were born from them: *Ecclesia in Africa* and *Africae Munus*. These events are the fruits of the Second Vatican Council, such that without the Council, they would not have come to existence.

The connection between the Second Vatican Council and these events was clearly highlighted by John Paul II in the introduction to Post-Synodal Apostolic Exhortation, *Ecclesia in Africa*. He began the Exhortation by lauding the Council and he described it as a great event and the cornerstone of the twentieth century. Then, he went further to remark that "In the context of that great event, the Church of God in Africa experienced true moments of grace. Indeed, the idea of some form of meeting of the African Bishops to discuss the evangelisation of the Continent dates back to the time of the Council"[455]

---

[455] John Paul II, *Ecclesia in Africa, Post-Synodal Apostolic Exhortation on the Church*

The collegiality and communion among the bishops that were expressed and experienced in the Council and subsequently in SECAM coupled with contemporary challenges in the Continent ultimately gave rise to the synods of Bishops of Africa.

Beyond its contributory role in the formation SECAM, the Second Vatican Council paved way for other major growths in the Church in Africa. First, the Council acknowledged the presence of truth expressed in doctrines, moral precepts and sacred rites in other religions, and affirmed that the Catholic Church does not reject what is true and holy in these religions. It went further to urge Christians to enter into discussions and collaboration with members of other religions.[456] Though the African Traditional Religion was not explicitly mentioned in this document, the affirmation of the Council opened the way for the study of African religions and cultures as part of the programme of formation and training of Christians and theologians in Africa. This became a strong driving force for Inculturation in Africa.

Churches in Africa started to experiment on how to make the Christian faith authentically African. In the list of the experiments, "One may refer to the Ndzon-Melen Mass of Yaounde, the Zairian rite, the eucharistic liturgies in East Africa, and the Mossi initiation rite in Burkina Faso".[457] African theology also gained momentum with special interest in the theology of Inculturation. This was done with the belief that the pluralism of

---

in Africa and Its Evangelization Mission Towards the Year 2000, no. 2.

[456] Second Vatican Council, *Nostra Aetate, Declaration on the Relation of the Church to non-Christian Religions*, Vatican web site, October 28, 1965, www.vatican.va/archive/hist_councils/ii_vatican_council/documents/vat-ii_decl_19651028_nostra-aetate_en.html, sec. 2.

[457] Elochukwu, E. Uzukwu, *A Listening Church: Autonomy and Communion in African Churches,* Maryknoll, New York: Orbis Books, 1996, p. 62.

contexts necessarily give room for contextual theologies. The approval of the use of the vernacular in the celebration of the Mass, the administration of the sacraments, and in other parts of the liturgy by the Second Vatican Council strengthened the process of inculturation.[458]

Among other things, it brought about greater participation of the people in the celebration of the mysteries of faith, which also brought about better understanding of the mysteries. These positive remarks, notwithstanding, serious questions are still be raised about the inculturation project in the Church in Africa. Marc Ela expressed worries that inculturation is organized narrowly around the past, the cultural and the values of tradition without adequately addressing the contemporary problems of the African Church and people. A Continent beset by severe economic challenges, political misrule, insecurity and unemployment cannot keep acting as if everything depends on addressing cultural and anthropological problems.

So, he asks: "why should we orient theological research around rites and beliefs alone, while modernity causes the masses to be aware of another set of problems."[459] The point is that there is need to see that inculturation is viewed and practiced from a wider perspective. The importance of regaining our cultural identity as Africans is of primary importance, but this should be done without neglecting other major challenges facing the Church and people in Africa.

One other major landmark of the Second Vatican Council which has far-reaching effects on the Church in Africa is its recognition and affirmation of the presence and operation of the Holy Spirit in creation.[460] This recognition created room for

---

[458] Second Vatican Council, *Sacrosanctum Concilium, The Constitution on the Sacred Liturgy*, Vatican web site, December 4, 1963, no. 36.

[459] Jean-Marc Ela, *My Faith as an African*, New York: Orbis Books, 1988, p. 171.

[460] Cf. Second Vatican Council, *Gaudium et Spes, Pastoral Constitution on the Church*

researches and theological works on the Spirit in the symbols, cultures, traditions and existential situations of African people and society.[461] Traditionally, Africans believe that the world is made up of the visible and invisible realities which co-penetrate each other. Everything which the human beings can grasp with their senses fall with the visible world while the invisible realm of creation is the world of the spirits. Moreover, "the invisible sphere dictates the pace, regulates and influences what happens at the visible sphere. It is, therefore, a spirit filled world at the visible reality; a world where all activities are interpreted in terms of the intricate interactions of these realities."[462]

Elochukwu E. Uzukwu strongly supports the view that the African experience of the divine, of life and wholeness is through the spirit. The spirit is the ground for the interactions between humanity and divinity. In fact, he describes West Africa as "a constituency that lays high premium on spirit."[463] Furthermore, he observes that "the procedure for living in God or living in holiness among West African Christians and its Trinitarian dimensions"[464] is through the Holy Spirit. This means that "Life in God is through the Holy Spirit: God is Spirit, is (breath of) Life."[465]

It is evident, therefore, that the door which the Second Vatican Council opened which kick-started the study of spirits in

---

in the Modern World, December 7, 1965, no. 11.1 and no. 26. See also Second Vatican Council, *Presbyterorum Ordinis, Decree on the Ministry and Life of Priests*, December 7, 1965, no. 22.

[461] Cf. Bona. I. Ugwu, "Discovering the Holy Spirit in African Traditional/Religious Symbols and Institutions", in *African Journal of Contextual Theology*, 1, 2009, pp. 49-62.

[462] Anthony N. O. Ekwunife, *Christianity and the Challenges of Witchcraft in Contemporary Africa*, Enugu: SNAAP Press, 2011, p. 25.

[463] Elochukwu E. Uzukwu, God, Spirit, and Human Wholeness: Appropriating Faith and Culture in West African Style, Eugene, Oregon: PICKWICK Publications, 2012, p. 214.

[464] Uzukwu, *God, Spirit and Human Wholeness*, p. 158.

[465] Uzukwu, *God, Spirit and Human Wholeness*, p. 158.

Africa was of great significance to the Church in Africa. In the meantime, from the extent of available published work or experts in the area of Pneumatology, it seems that so much still needs to be done. This Congress would help to assess the extent of the work which Africans have so far done towards the development of indigenous Pneumatology with the Continent.

The Post-Synodal Apostolic Exhortation, Ecclesia in Africa (1994) adopted the idea of the Church as the Family of God as Africa's preferred model of being a Church. This understanding is expected to guide the building and growth of the people of God in Africa. On its part, *Africae Munus* called on the Church in Africa to the service of reconciliation, justice and peace particularly within the Continent. Years have passed since these noble calls were made and this Congress shall leave no stone unturned in evaluating critically how far the expectations of the Holy Father and the Synod Fathers expressed in the Exhortations (*Ecclesia in Africa* and *Africae Munus*) have been realised.

It is providential that the Congress takes place within the period of Advent; a period which places stress on the future and on hope as key realities in the message of Christian faith and the salvation it offers. Advent tells us that the future is greater, and that it holds more than we have seen or are seeing. Thus, there could have been no better season for the meeting of the family of God in Africa than now. In the spirit of this season, the participants at the Congress are expected to examine, question, and highlight the events of the past and present, all with a view to the future of the Church and people of Africa.

Sometimes, Africans get stuck in the problems of the past and present that they do not pay sufficient attention to the future. In the meantime, Christianity is a religion built on hope. The God of Abraham, of Moses, of the prophets and of Jesus is one who delights in making promises that create hope of their fulfilment in the future. In fact, "the future is the key for understanding the actions of the God of Jesus Christ in the past and now."[466]

The Church in Africa shares in the hope given by the Lord about his coming in glory at the fullness of time. It also lives in hope that despite all the challenges of dependency, poverty, misery, corruption, diseases, and bad leadership, it will gradually rediscover itself as a major player in the world Church. This hope will not be fulfilled without the committed cooperation of men and women from Africa and beyond. Should we fold our hands and expect already-made solutions and answers, the desires of the future may not be realised. Hope provides the ground on which the reflections, celebrations, sharing, discussions and proposals of this Congress will take place.

The Church in Africa today does not only have hope, it is in itself a beacon of hope for the future of the universal Church. As the Church and the witness of faith in the West dwindles, the situation in Africa is on the contrary. The number of Christians and of vocations to the priestly and consecrated life is continuously on the increase. Thus, looking at Africa, the Church universal is strengthened to believe that she is not dying but fully alive. Therefore, on the strength of the hope which the African Church has and is, one can be critical of the past and the present without falling into the temptation of despair or discouragement.

Finally, we should not forget that love is the measure of the authenticity of all Christian claims, theologizing and talks. The love of the Father and the Son and the Holy Spirit is the blood

---

[466] Bona. I. Ugwu, "My Hope as an African" in *Spiritan Horizons, A Journal of the Congregation of the Holy Spirit*, Issue 13, Fall 2018, p. 104.

that flows through the veins of all God's children. The world has its eyes widely open at all times and place to see the love which those who profess Christ, who talk about him, and teach others to believe in him, have for one another. We mean love built on justice, peace, reconciliation and the joy of the gospel. It is in this love that our faith and hope as Christians find fulfilment. Thus, we pray that this Congress contribute significantly in increasing the love which people have one another in the Church, in the world and in the Continent of Africa.

Long live the Church of Christ in Africa! Long live the Church in Nigeria! Long live all the Congress participants! Long live the Conveners and organizers of the Congress! Moved by the Holy Spirit, and backed by human cooperation, great are the expectations from this Congress and I believe they will be met beyond measure.

Bibliography

Ekwunife, Anthony O.N., *Christianity and the Challenges of Witchcraft in Contemporary Africa*, Enugu: Snaap Press, 2011.

Benedict XVI, Pope, *Africae Munus, Post-Synodal Apostolic Exhortation on the Church in Africa in Service to Reconciliation, Justice and Peace*, 2011.

Ela, Jean-Marc, *My Faith as an African*, New York: Orbis Books, 1988.

John Paul II, Pope, *Ecclesia in Africa, Post-Synodal Apostolic Exhortation, On the Church in Africa and Its Evangelization Mission Towards the Year 2000*.

Second Vatican Council. *Gaudium et Spes, Pastoral Constitution on the Church in the Modern World*. Vatican web site December 7, 1965. www.vatican.va/archive/hist_councils/ii_vatican_council/documents/vat-ii_cons_19651207_gaudium-et-spes_en.html.

––––. *Nostra Aetate, Declaration on the Relation of the Church to non-Christian Religions*. Vatican web site, October 28, 1965. www.vatican.va/archive/hist_councils/ii_vatican_council/documents/vat-ii_decl_19651028_nostra-aetate_en.html.

––––. *Presbyterorum Ordinis, Decree on the Ministry and Life of Priests*. Vatican web site, December 7, 1965. www.vatican.va/archive/hist_councils/ii_vatican_council/documents/vat-ii_decree_19651207_presbyterorum-ordinis_en.html.

––––. *Sacrosanctum Concilium, The Constitution on the Sacred Liturgy*. Vatican web site, December 4, 1963. www.vatican.va/archive/hist_councils/ii_vatican_council/documents/vat-ii_const_19631204_sacrosanctum-concilium_en.html.

Ugwu, Bona. I., "Discovering the Holy Spirit in African Traditional/Religious Symbols and Institutions, *African Journal of Contextual Theology*, Vol. I, 2009, pp. 49-62.

_____, "My Hope as an African" *Spiritan Horizons, A Journal of the Congregation of the Holy Spirit*, Issue 13, Fall 2018, pp. 99-109.

Uzukwu, E. Elochukwu, *A Listening Church: Autonomy and Communion in African Churches*, Maryknoll, New York: Orbis Books, 1996.

_____, *God, Spirit, and Human Wholeness: Appropriating Faith and Culture in West African Style*, Eugene, Oregon: PICKWICK Publications, 2012.

Contributors

Anna Theresa Nyadoma a Carmelite Sister of the Handmaids of Our Lady of Mount Carmel, Zimbabwe, is the coordinator of education and safeguarding for Catholic institutions for the Zimbabwe Catholic Bishops' Conference. She is also the coordinator of Talitha Kum Network in Zimbabwe. She is the author of *A Holistic Pastoral Approach to HIV and AIDS sufferers: Reduction of Stigmatisation in Zimbabwe* (Lambert, 2012), among other publications.

Barry Chukwugekwu Ene is a priest of Enugu Diocese, Nigeria. He is Chief of Chaplain Service at VA Salem Medical Center and, Director, APNO-USA Medical Services. His research focuses on eliminating health disparities among underserved and vulnerable populations; creating policies that improve services and strengthens systems of care delivery to support maternal, child and community health.

Bonaventure Ikenna Ugwu, CSSp is a Spiritan, and the Rector of Spiritan International School of Theology, Attakwu, Enugu, Nigeria. He specializes in Pneumatology, and in Religion and Society. He is the author of *The Holy Spirit as Present and Active in Cosmic Turmoil and Human Suffering: A Dialogue between Pierre Teilhard de Chardin and Jürgen Moltmann* (Rome, 2004), among other publications.

Charles Ebelebe, CSSp is a Spiritan priest of the Province of Nigeria South-East. He is a Senior Lecturer and the Academic Dean at the Spiritan International School of Theology, Enugu. He is the author of *Africa and the New Face of Mission: A Critical Assessment of the Legacy of the Irish Spiritans among the Igbo of Southeastern Nigeria* (UPA, 2009), among other publications.

Cosmas C. Uzowulu a priest of the Capuchin Friars Minor, is a Lecturer at the Spiritan International School of Theology Attakwu, Enugu and Bigard Memorial Seminary Enugu, Nigeria. He is the author of *Ambition and Rivalry Among the Chosen: An Exegetico-Theological Study of Mark 10,35-45 and Its Centrality in the Gospel of Mark* (De-Adroit Inovation, 2009), among other publications.

Ikenna Okafor a priest of the Catholic Diocese of Nnewi, Nigeria, is an adjunct professor of Intercultural Theology at the University of Vienna. He is the author of *Toward an African Theology of Fraternal Solidarity: UBE NWANNE* (Pickwick Publications, 2014) and other essay publications.

Justin Clemency Nabushawo a sister of the Sisters of Mary of Kakamega-Kenya, is a Lecturer of Communication and Media Studies, at the School of Information Sciences-Moi University, Eldoret. She is the author of *Dialogue for Leadership Performance* (Scholars Press, 2014), among other Publications.

Lawrence Nchekube Nwankwo a priest of the Catholic Diocese of Ekwulobia, is a lecturer at the Department of Religion and Human Relations, Nnamdi Azikiwe University Awka, Nigeria. He has numerous articles on African Christianity.

Nontando Hadebe is a senior lecturer at St Augustine College of South Africa. She has published numerous essay including "The Cry of the earth is the cry of women: Ecofeminisms in critical dialogue with *Laudato Si'*, Grace and Truth 42,2:50-65."

Raymond Olusesan Aina, MSP is Senior Lecturer at the National Missionary Seminary of St Paul, Abuja Nigeria, and the Vice-Rector of the institution; and also the past president of the Catholic Theological Association of Nigeria. Aina, a moral theologian, has research interests in restorative peacebuilding, African thought, sexual ethics, and contemporary issues in ethics.

SimonMary Asese Aihiokhai is an Assistant Professor of Systematic Theology at the University of Portland in the United States of America. He is the author of *Fostering Interreligious En-*

counters in Pluralist Societies: Hospitality and Friendship (Palgrave Macmillan, 2019).

Susan Nedza is an emergency physician, and researcher on models to transform international medical mission collaboratives. She is the president of the Olancho Aid Foundation, a Catholic, 501(c)(3). She served as an Adjunct Assistant Professor at the Feinberg School of Medicine of Northwestern University, guest lecturer at the Kellogg Graduate School of Business of Northwestern University.

Theresa Abah is an assistant professor at the California State University, Sacramento, with extensive healthcare management and geriatrics expertise. She has a track record of work experience in health promotion and education, vaccine security, disease surveillance, and health systems strengthening. Her research is centered on health policy development, for health systems strengthening applying interdisciplinary approaches.

Also Available in the Series

FAITH IN ACTION
Vol III

Reimagining the Mission of the Church in Education, Politics, and Servant Leadership in Africa

Stan Chu Ilo
Nora K. Nonterah
Ikenna U. Okafor
Justin C. Nabushawo
Idara Otu, MSP (Eds.)

Foreword by
Bishop Matthew Hassan Kukah

Paulines

www.ingramcontent.com/pod-product-compliance
Lightning Source LLC
Chambersburg PA
CBHW052146300426
44115CB00011B/1547